Learning Analytics

Learning Analytics

What, Why and How – A Study

Deepti Yadav

₹495; US$ 16.50
ISBN: 978-93-91978-83-9

2025
First Published in India

Learning Analytics
What, Why and How – A Study

Published by:
SHIPRA PUBLICATIONS
LG 18-19, Pankaj Central Market
I.P. Ext., Patparganj, Delhi 110092, India
91 11 2223 5152; 98105 22367
info@shiprapublication.com
www.shiprapublication.com

The Analogical Foreground

Learning Analytics (LA) drew attention among academicians in the 2000s and since then, it has gained popularity among researchers and academicians alike. The field has been explored, theorised, and experimented with for different possible dimensions. No one knows how far learning and education can go with Artificial Intelligence (AI) coming into the arena to discover the possibilities. But to reach end-users and reap benefits, a lot of research, planning and implementation must be done.

The present work was carried out in India which is still at the brink of the infusing stage of technology and thriving towards transforming education. Dated around 500 BCE, the *Tittha Sutta, Udāna 6.4, Khuddaka Nikaya*, a Buddhist text, contains a parable of five blind men and an elephant. These five blind men have never come across an elephant earlier and they imagine and conceptualise what an elephant is like by touching its different body parts. Now each blind man gets to feel a different body part of the elephant and they go on describing their limited experience. According to one, it's like a long pipe having experienced the trunk and tusk, the next one describes it to be like a wall having experienced the back and body, another describes it to be like a big leaf having experienced the ears, the next one describes it to be like a tree trunk having experienced the legs, whereas according to the last blind man, it's only like a broom having experienced the tail of the elephant. Each one's elephant is different from the other. But in reality, all are not entirely right, yet not entirely wrong. The conclusion of the parable is that subjective experience of the field leads to a one sided inclination and understanding.

Learning Analytics (LA) has risen through many advances, technological and theoretical, along with logical empiricism and logical positivism debate. The scientific knowledge has contributed tremendously to the field with growth of AI. A gap among the LA researchers, tech-providers and end users has been the sensitive spot to overcome. The work explores the prospects of taking the opportunity to the Indian classroom set-up where possibilities of Analytics-based Feedback were explored to improve the learning outcomes of English as Second Language (ESL).

Acknowledgements

I express my sincere gratitude to Prof. N.C. Ojha, Regional Institute of Education, NCERT, Bhopal, the former Director of NCERT, Prof. Hrushikesh Senapaty and former Principal of the Institute, Prof. Nityananda Pradhan, as well as the faculties of Regional Institute of Education, NCERT, Bhopal, including Prof. B. Ramesh Babu, Prof. Ratnamala Arya, Asso. Prof. Dr. Sanjay Pandagale, and Asst. Prof. Dr. Suresh Makwana., and Retd. Prof. D.N. Sansanwal, DAVV, Indore, and Retd. Prof. Anil Kumar, NITTTR, Bhopal, for their valuable time, guidance, support, sharing innovative ideas and immense discussions during the research work. In a special mention, I would like to appreciate then Studio Staff of RIE, Bhopal, who have been a great help and aid for preparing the E-course, My Learning Class.

This book could not have been shaped without the efforts of Shipra Publications and their editorial and production staff; I am thankful to them as well.

I offer my gratefulness to the *One Almighty* and regards to all who have been with me in all respect during the completion of this book. Lastly, but of great significance, I avail myself of this opportunity to express an unfathomable sense of gratitude and love to my ever-motivating and caring husband–Sanjay, inspiring daughter, my beloved parents and my family members, for their constant mental support, strength and comfort throughout. I dedicate this book to my daughter, Sharanya, who is my entire world.

Contents

The Analogical Foreground v
Acknowledgements vii

1. Learning Analytics: *Concept and importance* **1**

Analytics / 2; Learning Analytics — Concept and Definition / 3; Brief History of Analytics and Learning Analytics / 3; Importance / 6; Components / 7; Learning Analytics for School / 9; Learning Analytics and Analytics-Based Feedback / 9; Analytics-Based Feedback (AbF) / 10; Summary and Suggestions / 11

2. Language Teaching-Learning and Learning Analytics **12**

Learning Analytics for English Language-Learning / 12; Language-Learning / 13; English Language Teaching in India / 21; Conceptual Framework / 24; Stakeholders of the Study / 27; Other Components / 28; Summary and Conclusion / 32

3. Rationale with Literature Review: *Learning Analytics* **33**

Learning Analytics / 33; Feedback with Learning Analytics / 49; Learning Analytics in School / 56

4. Learning Analytics, Language and Other Components: *Literature Review* **65**

Learning Analytics and Language / 65; Learning Analytics and Motivation / 71; Language and Other Variables / 75

5. Learning Analytics Scenario — India vis-a-vis World: *Rationale with Literature Review* **98**

Global Research Developments related to AbF since Covid-19 / 98; Research Developments in India related to Learning Analytics / 100; Rationale of the Study / 102; Summary and Conclusion / 108

6. The Study Essentials **109**

Statement of the Problem / 109; Research Questions / 109; Objectives / 110; Hypotheses / 111; Delimitations / 111

7. Methodology and Approach **112**

Methodology / 112; Tools Used / 115; Procedure of Data Collection / 123; Statistical Techniques Used for Data Analysis / 124

8. Data Analysis, Results and Findings **126**

Effectiveness of Analytics-Based Feedback in Terms of Descriptive Analysis / 126; Trend of Effect of the Treatment on BICS Component of Achievement in English Language / 129; Trend of Effect of the Treatment on CALP Component of Achievement / 131; Trend of Effect of the Treatment on Overall Achievement / 133; Relationship between BICS Component of Achievement in English Language Progression and the Treatment, Gender, Socio-economic Status and Learning Style / 135; Relationship between CALP Component of Achievement in English Language Progression and the Treatment / 137; Relationship between Overall Achievement in English Language Progression and the Treatment / 139; Effect of Treatment and Interactive Effect of the Treatment and Gender on Study Habits by Taking the Pre-Test Scores of Study Habit as a Covariate / 140; Effect of Treatment and Interactive Effect of Treatment and Gender on the Attitude / 143; Effect of Treatment and Interactive Effect of Treatment and Gender on the Motivation Level of Students When Measured with MSLQ / 145; Effectiveness of Analytics-based Feedback in Terms of Qualitative Aspect / 147; Issues and Challenges Related to Conducting Learning Analytics Study in India / 151

9. Research Discussions, Implications and Suggestions **155**

Objective-wise Major Findings / 155; Interpretation of Results and Discussion / 157; Implications of the Study / 171; Suggestions for Further Studies / 174

Bibliography 177

1

Learning Analytics

Concept and importance

To ask larger questions is to risk getting things wrong.
Not to ask them at all is to constrain the life of understanding.

– George Steiner

Technology has revolutionised every aspect of life in the pursuit of a better tomorrow. Its contribution is infinite towards simplified solutions and facilitations. With the 21st century advancement, it has become essential for survival and indispensable for human life. As learning is a product of continuous interaction with environment, the field of education has also been reformed and modernised in its progress with technology. Every subject area has specialised technology to serve, focusing on the pedagogical component of learning. Several technological breakthroughs have also revolutionized language learning. The language-learning process can be facilitated more effectively with technological assistance. Therefore, it would be fascinating to observe languagelearning aided by technology. The work here presents the use of sophisticated tools of Learning Analytics to observe English languagelearning progression. The book defines Analytics-based feedback in an educational context to establish its essence in the field.

Information and communication technology (ICT) in the field of education for pedagogical usage advances in the four stages of emerging, application, infusion, and transformation. These stages in pedagogy represent the competency to use ICT; emerging is using productivity tools, applying is enhancing traditional teaching, infusing is facilitating blended learning with tools of ICT, whereas, transforming is creating interactive e-learning environments for digitalisation of learning. These stages differ according to the technological advances, development, and growth of a country. In India, ICT is undergoing a transformational change from stage three to stage four with a surge in its online courses and modules. Therefore, the study attempted to look for possible empirical evidences of technological advancement in language learning.

As advanced technology is reforming higher education and school education globally, modern pedagogical methods have equipped teachers to promote life skills among students such as problem-solving, creativity, critical thinking, and others. These pedagogical methods are clubbed together with modern technological tools which are used in the other walks of life to understand human behaviour. One such tool widely used and explored in education today is analytics. Analytics is applied worldwide in all fields for discovery, interpretation, and communication of significant patterns in information collected. Further, these derived patterns are used and applied for effective decision making. Analytics in education is extensively used for improving learning, feedback, student-retention, administrative purposes, and related decisionmaking.

Analytics

Along with analytics, two rapidly growing concepts in education are Academic Analytics and Learning Analytics (LA). They draw from the umbrella term Educational Data Mining (EDM), and are closely tied to several other fields of study, including business intelligence, web analytics, and action analytics. Thus, EDM is the umbrella term for Learning Analytics as well as Academic Analytics. The difference between the two subsets of EDM, academic analytics and learning analytics is important to distinguish and understand. Academic analytics *'combines select institutional data, statistical analysis, and predictive modelling to create intelligence upon which learners, instructors, or administrators can change academic behaviour'*, as provided by Baepler and Murdoch (2010). If Academic Analytics is useful for the administration of educational institutions by applying tools and strategies of Business Intelligence (BI) for better decision-making, Learning Analytics (LA) not only optimises learning but is used for several other purposes as well. Though the concept of LA is closely associated with Artificial Intelligence (AI) and Educational Data Mining (EDM), the term has been popularised recently along with Academic Analytics.

The prospects of analytics allow the evaluation of past actions and to estimate and plan accordingly the potential of future actions. This facilitates better decisions and the adoption of more effective strategies by organisations or individuals for improved outcomes. Today, there are several dynamics of analytics to encourage greater use of analytics. Though the use of Information and Communication Technology (ICT) has reached throughout almost all facets of our lives providing us with data at every moment but data alone is not sufficient to realise the benefits we may gain from analytics. It requires the effective exploitation of data through rich skills and techniques for data analysis with many tools and expertise. Let us understand Analytics – how it has been defined by its practitioners and expositors. This will be followed by a brief history of the concept and an understanding of the emergence and rise of LA.

Learning Analytics – Concept and Definition

The origin of the word 'Analytic' dates back to the late sixteenth century when this word was first used in the context of analysis. Thus, analytics pertains to or is preceded by some form of analysis. Since analysis has been an integral aspect of data and technology, with the growth of these fields, the term was popularised and contextualised accordingly. Practitioners and researchers in different fields have used the term extensively as per their needs. The field of education has also explored modern technology and data science for its growth. Consequently, analytics has gradually popularised and gained momentum in its usage for different purposes.

A widely used definition of the term has been provided, which defines LA as *'the measurement, collection, analysis and reporting of data about learners and their contexts, for purposes of understanding and optimising learning and the environments in which it occurs',* (Lang et al. SOLAR 2011, p. 4). The definition serves a functional as well as a conceptual purpose for this theoretical task. Some other writers have also attempted to define the term based on their experience and understanding.

A paper in the EDUCAUSE Learning Initiative by Van Barneveld et al. (2012) provides conceptual and functional definitions of not only analytics but every other of the various types of analytics. The paper defines analytics as 'an overarching concept that is defined as data-driven decision making.' Here, according to the definition, it seems that analytics is mainly about decision-making driven by data, which can be reconsidered for exploring, insights and problems identifying with the information provided by it. In another paper by Cooper (2012), it has been described by emphasising analytics as something that people do, providing a somewhat broader view. Analytics is described as the process in which actionable insights are developed through defining a problem and applying a statistical model to further analyse against simulated and/or existing future data.

Understanding the various defining contributions to the field, one may relate analytics to learning as a great utility-driven tool that can facilitate several academic and administrative purposes in education. Learning Analytics and Academic Analytics are two subsets of Analytics used in education. The book follows LA with the definition provided by SOLAR, where optimising learning with the help of feedback based on the data of previous performance was the objective and learning progression was measured, analysed, and reported.

Brief History of Analytics and Learning Analytics

The history of analytics may date back before the computer age. The field has witnessed tremendous growth over the last two decades in the academic context. With the Society for Learning Analytics presenting Learning Analytics

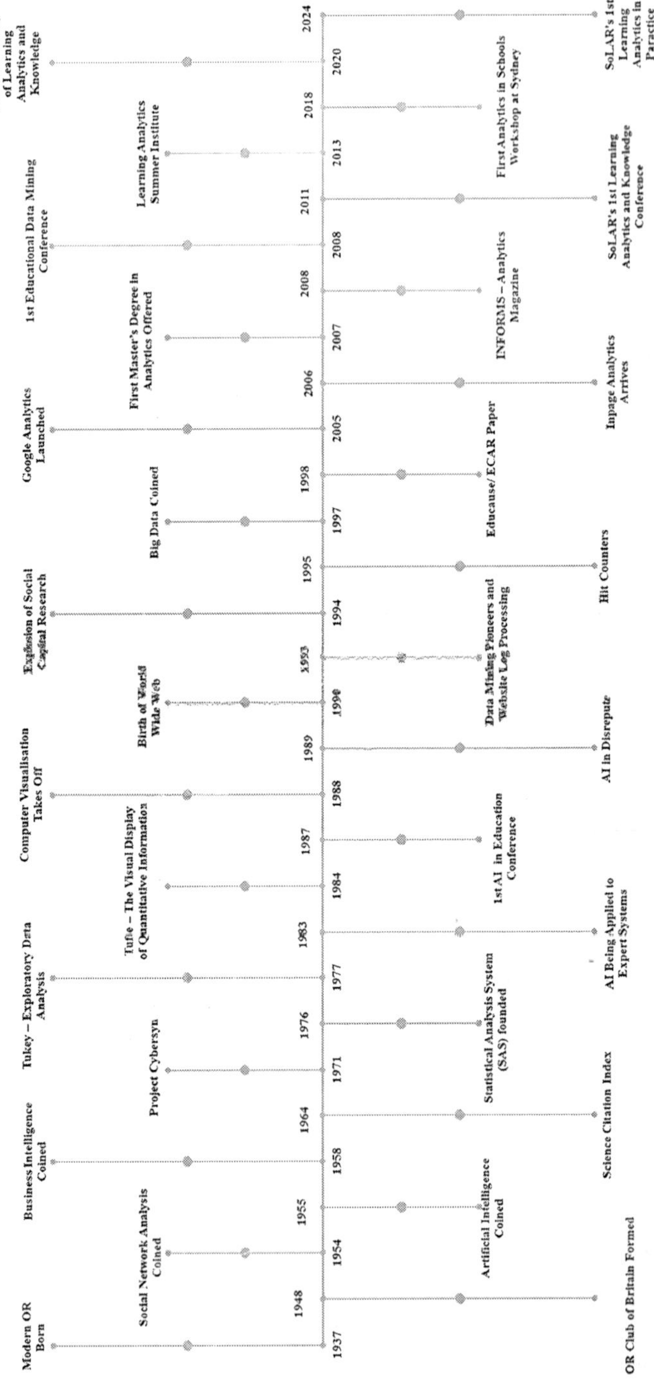

Figure 1: Timeline of Emergence of Learning Analytics with Growth of Technology, Data Mining and Artificial Intelligence since 1930s

in Practice recently in 2024, it has completed its first decade of Learning Analytics and Knowledge in 2020 as shown in Figure 1, and is now proceeding to the second decade. The current section presents the history of analytics since the inception of computer technology and how over a period of one century, it has grown with the ups and downs of the field. Figure 1 presents the timeline of the emergence of LA with the growth of technology, data mining and AI since the 1930s. Pioneered by Walter Shewhart in the early 1920's, the earliest attempts were made to understand how the components of a process contributed to product quality. It was in 1937-1938 when Operational Research (OR) for the Royal Air Force integrated radar and ground observations into its warning and control system based heavily on both mathematical models and statistical methods. After the World Wars, OR was applied to various industries throughout the 1950s and 1960s.

Coined by John McCarthy in 1956, the term 'artificial intelligence' was first applied to expert systems' in the early 1980's. Though AI is often associated with sci-fi, its research field has provided practical methods allowing machines to learn and facilitate learning. After the beginning of usage of AI in various expert systems in 1983, the first AI conference in education was held in 1987. Despite facing disrepute in 1989, AI continued to grow with the birth of the World Wide Web (WWW) in 1990 and data mining in 1993. Databases have been used to detect patterns with so-called 'machine learning algorithms' giving birth to data mining. Thus, a branch of AI, data mining was first used as a business tool in the early 1990's for retail basket analysis. Since then, it has found purposeful utility in different walks of life. It is usually concerned with patterns, the history of events, final outcomes, predictions, and clusters. The field of education has also explored the possibility of gaining benefits from its usage.

As mentioned earlier, educational applications of AI were experimented and explored across the world in the conferences on AI in Education. Since 2007, the conference on Educational Data Mining is conducted by the International Educational Data Mining Society. The field is chiefly concerned with Intelligent Tutoring Systems where this stream is constantly experimented and explored. Thus, AI, Business Intelligence, Statistical Analysis System (SAS) and several milestone projects were early initiatives with analytics based on statistical methods and mathematical models. Website log processing was a significant milestone in the field.

Analytics in the field of education has been gradual, it took some time to settle in. It still has a long way to go. In developed countries, it is gaining traction in schools and mainly higher education institutes whereas in developing countries, it is yet to be explored. The credit to popularise the term Learning Analytics specifically goes to the International Conferences on Learning Analytics and Knowledge (LAK), the first of which was in 2011 and described learning analytics as mentioned in the previous section.

Figure 2: Research Areas in Learning Analytics and Knowledge (LAK) Conferences Organized by SOLAR Annually

So far, research studies on LA as shown in Figure 2 have focussed mainly on higher education, students at risk of dropping out or underperforming on learning resource recommender systems.

Learning Analytics: Importance

Learning Analytics (LA) is widely used for several purposes. As it resolves numerous concerns in education related to administration and teaching-learning, it is gradually becoming popular with researchers, practitioners, educators, teachers, and other stakeholders in education. With its usage, wide acceptance, and its association with technology, it is easy to understand its importance in education. As LA relies heavily on data-driven decision-making and statistical measurement and modelling, it is scientific, systematic, and pragmatic. It is used for several purposes as per the need and requirement proving its relevance and significance in the field.

LA facilitates in the identification of students at risk to enable the provision of positive and timely interventions to improve retention of those at-risk students. Thus, it helps to improve the drop-out rates also. It is possible to assess students learning by understanding patterns in the performance and thereby, predicting behavioural and academic performances. Once the learner's characteristics and requirements are identified, they can be recommended learning material as per their requirement and level. Courses can be designed and tailored as per the needs of the learners. It will further lead to pedagogic improvements. It is also possible to measure the time-on-task with the on-line courses. Such measurements of time-on-task may provide further insights into the course as well as learners. Feedback based on this analysis can be provided that can further help a learner academically to improve learning outcomes.

Benefits of LA are not limited to students only. It not only maximises student learning, skill acquisition, and student-retention but also eases teachers' task with the method and knowledge. It also facilitates educators, teachers, and course-providers in improving teaching. Gradually teachers can identify the most suitable method for a particular student. It is possible to procure feedback from the students about the course and the methods used to further improve and update them. Educators, teachers, and course providers can easily track students' progress through log-records and hits. Data trails left behind by learners provide sufficient information that teachers need for further planning, efforts, and input to be prepared for the students benefit. Once the pattern in the performance is identified, further deliberations become clearer and more specific. LA directs and channels the efforts for personalised learning and individual experience though ethical use of learners' data remains a concern.

Thus, LA provides scientific data-base with trails left behind by users. Most of the learning management systems (LMS) have in-built analytics that can facilitate further correlation and reference. So, LA may be used to find a pattern in content usage, content quality issues and adaptive learning. While teachers can utilise these patterns and data with a deeper insight for different purposes, students can work to maximise their outcome with personalised learning. Besides the benefits for students, teachers, and educators, it may be useful for administrative purposes also keeping in view the cost-involvement along with students' learning experiences. It aids curriculum mapping, behavioural prediction, learning intervention, measurement, reporting, and many other tasks for the purpose of education which is not possible otherwise with only human efforts.

Learning Analytics: Components

As the book considers the definition of LA provided by SOLAR, the three components included can be easily observed from the definition itself. The definition discusses 'the measurement, collection, analysis, and reporting of data about learners and their contexts,' indicating the first two components, namely, data and analysis. Furthermore, the two components are used, 'for purposes of understanding and optimising learning and the environments in which it occurs,' indicating some action based on the data and its analysis. Thus, the three crucial components of LA are — Data, Analysis and Action, as shown in Figure 3. For LA, data, raw or classified, is the primary requirement. Analysis is the further process of using statistical modelling and mathematical methods to transform data for deeper insights. The last component of action is the eventual goal of the LA process. It may be an ongoing cycle for a while. Appropriate implementation of these three components during the process can solely determine the quality of output that LA provides.

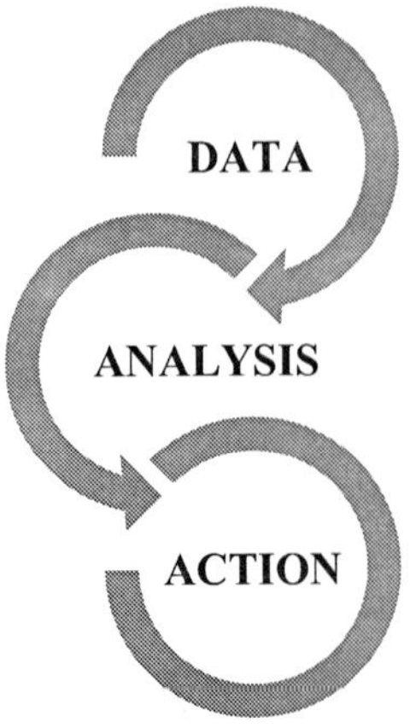

DATA

ANALYSIS

ACTION

Figure 3: Components of Learning Analytics

The data of LA is a set of information measured and collected in learning environment to improve the learning outcomes of students. Some LMS may be involved in the teaching learning process that records the students' performances. Data can be triangulated with other relevant information about students from stakeholders such as parents and administration. Therefore, data collection may extend beyond the LMS.

Though LA is closely associated with data mining and big data, but if an LA project is run in a classroom scenario, practitioners, researchers, teachers, or educators may not have to deal with that huge data. Still, machines are required because processing data is possible only through some technological intervention. If it is run as a MOOC or using Moodle at a higher education level where thousands of students are enrolled, it may generate big data. Even in a school set up across grades with various divisions or may be in a longitudinal case, the data may be generated to support student learning which is discussed next. Now, data may be analysed descriptively or predictively. The descriptive data analysis is reactive and allows the understanding of the past, consequently, its possible influence on the future. The predictive data analysis is proactive – influencing the present and, therefore can influence the ongoing learning process. Data may be analysed descriptively or predictively depending on the nature and requirements of a study and its purpose.

With the last component, the cycle of LA can be completed with further follow-up. If action is not taken, then the entire exercise and efforts of data collection and analysis become futile. Sometimes, data is descriptive or predictive. Action will inform ultimately about the degree of correct analysis and further improvements. As the action is data-driven, it will provide a deeper insight with outcome of the entire effort. The end-process will inform the purpose for which the exercise was performed. The purpose may be to identify students at-risk, quality of the content, feedbacks to improve learning outcomes, or even may be unsuccessful teaching-learning method. The output received at the end of the process after the action is taken will narrate the entire LA process. Thus, the three components of LA are not only inter-connected and inter-dependent but also go together for LA to function as seen in Figure 3 previously.

Learning Analytics for School

Learning Analytics (LA) has become immensely popular in higher education with both researchers' and practitioners' efforts and experiments. It may be due to attachments of the researchers and practitioners to higher education with relatively easier access to implementation. Though lately, efforts have been made to introduce and popularise LA at the school level, yet it needs to go far in school level education. It is clear from the above discussion that LA uses available data from the database of different sources for analyses and further action to support different stakeholders in teaching and learning process. The process involved remains universal for every level.

At schools, different pedagogical subjects have different approaches and teaching methods to deliver the content. If maths is more about problem-solving, logic and reasoning, science is more about information, facts, knowledge, practical and experiments. If social studies involve knowledge, facts and information of history, geography and civics, studies of languages are more about skill development and aesthetic sense. Approaching school subjects with LA can be different from taking up LA at higher education level, though the process and components remain the same. Therefore, it is utmost important that a need analysis of the content and method should be carried out before implementing LA components and further strategies in a school classroom.

According to Viberg et al. (2018), little evidence was found supporting LA in higher education. In their observation, the four propositions were, whether learning analytics i) improve learning outcomes, ii) support learning and teaching, iii) are deployed widely, and iv) are used ethically. Their results based on 252 papers demonstrated through several LA studies that overall, there was little evidence showing improvements in students' learning outcomes (9%) as well as learning support and teaching (35%). Similarly, little evidence was found for the third (6%) and the fourth (18%) proposition. The highest percentage (35%) was for learning support and teaching, and (9%) to improve learning outcomes which leaves a lot of room for researchers and practitioners to popularise and implement the concept worldwide, especially to improve learning outcomes. The work provides a huge scope for researchers to verify LA not only at the higher education level but also at the school level.

Learning Analytics and Analytics-Based Feedback

Learning Analytics (LA) is an evolving field in which sophisticated analytic tools are used to improve learning and education. In last decade of LA surge, there have been lesser empirical studies at school level education as the majority have been conducted with undergraduate or college students in the Western countries. Other segmented definitions of learning analytics include definitions that focus on processes and activities (Brown, 2011), on purpose (Ferguson, 2012), and on distinguishing learning analytics from academic analytics and educational data mining (Siemens and Long 2011); Siemens and Baker, 2012). The way learning analytics is defined by SOLAR as mentioned in the beginning, it is encompassing, covers different forms (data sets) and functions (uses), works as a cohesive and integrated whole, and is intended to serve the needs of the academy at a variety of levels (van Barneveld, Arnold, and Campbell, 2012).

In line with the purpose of LA, Analytics-based Feedback (AbF) focuses on improving learning outcomes based on previous performances of the learners. The pattern of errors and mistakes committed by the learner is key to improvement. Constant and continuous feedback for improvements may make learners more conscious during the next performance. Once the mistakes and errors are addressed, gradually, the learning outcomes and performance may improve. Here, technology may play a crucial role in providing analysis of the previous performance. This is further discussed in the conceptual framework of the study. Therefore, Analytics-based Feedback is suggested to improve learning outcome as a research area.

Analytics-Based Feedback (AbF)

In a traditional classroom, usually teachers circle the errors and mistakes of a student while checking the notebooks or answer-sheets with a red pen. Students also look at their errors, observe and realise the mistakes. The next very important step of follow-up or feedback is not taken up 'consciously' from both the ends. Feedback is any information about a person's performance of a task, etc. which can be used as a basis for improvement. Therefore, Analytics-based Feedback (AbF) is hereby defined as

> *... any information about a person's performance of a task resulting from the systematic analysis of data with the help of statistics which provides meaningful patterns that can be further used as a basis for improvement in performance.*

The model developed for AbF is presented in Figure 4. The model presents the use of AbF to improve the learning outcomes of the students. The stakeholders of the process are students, teachers, schools or institutes and parents. As, a teacher assesses the performance of a student, the teacher also analyses the performance and provides feedback. The teacher must analyse the frequency of the same error in the entire performance and take note of it.

Assessment of performance may be online or offline but feedback should be provided. Students are to be provided with feedback this observation and should be 'consciously' making an improvement on that category of errors. With every assessment, teachers are to take note of the frequency and constantly remind students of the error or use positive reinforcement in

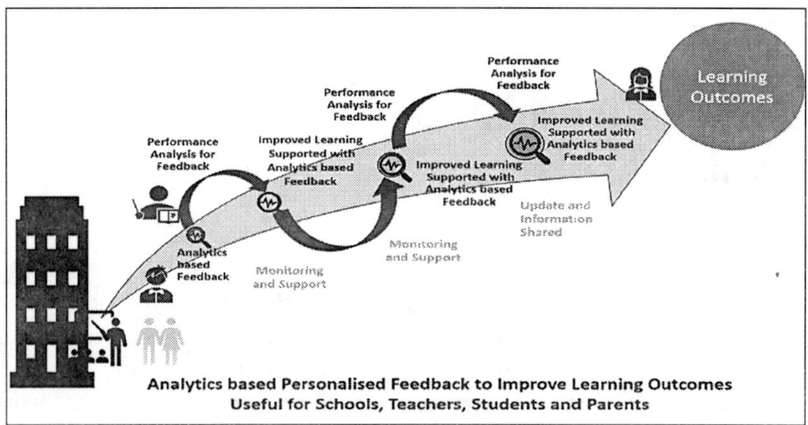

Figure 4: Model of Analytics-based Feedback Developed During the Study

case of improvement. The school or institute's role is to provide necessary online support and infrastructure. As the third stakeholders in AbF, parental support should be sought as the data is generated in online educational content, assessment and necessary permissions should be taken. It personalises learning for the student as the feedback is intended for an individual learner, whose performance has been assessed. Besides providing AbF, teachers must consider and understand the adequacy, usefulness, timing, and quality of feedback.

Summary and Suggestions

With the introduction of artificial intelligence and machine learning in the field of education, learning can not only be improved but also measured, monitored, and tracked. Learning Analytics can be used to understand, improve, and modify the learning based the data gathered about student learning. AbF allows stakeholders to gain actionable insights about the learning process and determine the course of action. Looking at the data from different educational theories and implications' perspective is as important as knowing the technology and its mindful utilisation.

2

Language Teaching-Learning and Learning Analytics

Language remains at the centre of human evolution and civilisations. It has provided the basis of communication and sharing in a social set-up. It has created the possibilities of symbolising and coding the inner thoughts, emotions, and feelings through expressions for mutual understanding. Over time, the world has witnessed the emergence and extinction of several languages. Similarly, language has led to the development of both, community and identity. Post-industrial revolution in the late 19th century and at the dawn of the 20th century, several technological advances have been invented and introduced to the world. With the advancement of technology, language has also evolved and numerous philosophies, theories and concepts related to language have been established. New languages have emerged. Gradually, technology took over the world like never before. It has made an impact in almost all walks of life. Engineering, pharmacy, space science, management, automobiles, or any other aspect of living, no field has remained untouched. Similarly, the field of education has also gone through numerous changes in the last few years. Language-learning has greatly transformed as well.

Learning Analytics for English Language-Learning

Learning Analytics (LA) has provided empirical evidence in pedagogical interventions during the last decade. With rapid technological advancements, technology is certainly indispensable for language teaching. For pedagogical interventions in language teaching and learning, LA has been substantially used in several studies at higher and school education, especially in higher education. Language teaching and learning deal with the development of the four language skills, i.e., Listening, Speaking, Reading, and Writing. Several software programmes have been developed by researchers and practitioners to experiment with LA in language education. Relevant literature has been presented in the upcoming chapters on language-learning with LA. It mainly involves the development of language skills through student engagement, monitoring, feedback and assessing their comprehension and understanding to identify potential problems and then resolve them. Lately, language skills have been the main concern in language teaching with LA.

Issues related to skill development have been the main concerns for educators, teachers and learners of language teaching and learning. Similarly, the rise of Computer-assisted Language Learning (CALL) and Mobile-assisted Language Learning (MALL) provide sufficient evidence on rise of technology in Language-learning. When a language is taught as second one, the use of technology not only facilitates the students but teachers as well. In India, English language is taught as a second language which is the focus of the present study. The apt use of various technological tools aids the process of English language teaching-learning in a more effective and efficient manner. Software developed to target a particular skill can facilitate the language learner in a more focused way. Several case studies have been conducted worldwide to present empirical evidences on the same. The project VITAL (Visualisation and Tools to Monitor Online Language-learning and Teaching) in Europe, a study by Rienties et al. (2018) in the Virtual Learning Environment (VLE) at Open University of UK, the study with the software Got it Taal (Language) to teach Dutch, *Wi*READ project in a Singapore high school, project book More! of Austria, and many more works have been focusing on using LA in language teaching.

The research studied the Learning Progression of English Language (L2) where continuous and constant feedback were provided based on the analytics of the performance in BICS and CALP abilities of students. The study utilised the available analytics tools to understand and map the learning progression of English language. As Learning Analytics studies and researches are conducted dominantly in the higher education and not so frequent in school education, also discussed in the works of Viberg et al. (2018), the study was intended to be conducted in school education with English language for empirical evidences. Further, the studies so far have focused on student retention, time-on-task, to identify at-risk students early and other purposes; the current work tried to study if the English Language-learning progression associate with improved learning outcome with Analytics-based Feedback (AbF). Thus, the research intended to study the learning progression of ESL when students were provided Analytics-based Feedback (AbF) on their previous errors and mistakes committed. Thus, understanding the significance and rise of LA in language teaching have provided sufficient impetus for the present study to be conducted in transforming India.

Language-Learning

Learning is envisioned as a development of progressive sophistication in understanding and skills within a domain. Language is one such domain which is instrumental to express and communicate ideas, thoughts, and views in the society. Language-learning begins with birth and goes on for a lifetime. Any language-learning revolves around four basic skills of Listening, Speaking,

Reading, and Writing (LSRW). Several theories have been around regarding acquisition and learning of language with these skills. These language theories are in-turn also supported or countered by theories of learning. Some of the theories advocate about an innate capacity to learn and acquire language whereas others base their argument on experience and consider it to be social phenomenon with structures. Further, theories of learning adopt these hypotheses to suggest and approach language-learning.

The famous Swiss linguist Ferdinand de Saussure approaches the theory of language-learning from two quite different perspectives. One perspective revolves around the idea that any language is a system of signs calling it a semiotic system or a semiological system. The other perspective propounds that any language is also a social phenomenon which means language comes from the community – consequently is, a product of the language community. Saussure presented language to be a structured system and insisted the significance of signs and phonology. It was asserted so as language can be viewed synchronically for existing at any time and diachronically for changing in the course of time. He coined two significant terms 'parole' and 'langue.' 'Parole' is a speech of the individual person and 'langue' is underlying system of speech activity. His suggested theories are still regarded as the setting off points of linguistics, popularly known as Structuralism to his contemporaries. Accordingly, when the theory based on the role of society and experience with structuralism began to gain much attention from linguists and language theorists in the early twentieth century, an anti-thesis appeared on the screen.

In contrast to Saussure's theory of Structuralism in language, Phonology and Sign Language theory, on the other hand, it was propounded that language is innate, universal, and wired. According to the famous American linguist Noam Chomsky, Saussure's contemporary, language is an 'innate facility', capability and understanding. He grounded his theory on the very idea of Universal Grammar that every language contains similar structures and rules. It means that every child acquires language in a similar fashion effortlessly. He asserted that humans are born wired to acquire language. He based his Nativist theory on the Language Acquisition Device (LAD) which is an implicated mental instinctive capacity enabling everyone to acquire language from infancy. Thus, he states,

> . . . languages are infinite pertaining to the sequence of word forms (strings) and grammar. These word forms organize grammatically correct sequences of words that can be pooled over a limited lexicon of each independent language. So, LAD is tasked to select from an infinite number of grammars the one which is correct for the language that is presented to an individual, for example, a child.

Though Chomsky argues that linguistics and language are cognitive sciences, there is inadequate evidence from neuroscience and language acquisition research to support this innate theory and Universal Grammar. The theory has been challenged for its claim that language is the manifestation of a random mutation in the human genome. Despite the criticism, supporters of generative grammar believe that Saussure's structuralism has been reformed and replaced by Chomsky's modern approach to linguistics. Thus, Saussure and Chomsky's invaluable works related to language acquisition and learning remain indispensable to the field. Similarly, learning theories propounded by different educationists and theorists about the approach also influence the teaching-learning of a language.

Behaviourist theorists like Thorndike (1921), Watson (1925) and Skinner (1957) influenced language-learning with strategies involving stimuli–response. They asserted the stimulus–response with operant conditioning and reinforcement for habit-formation by imitation was assumed to be at the centre of language-learning. Skinner particularly maintained positive reinforcement and feedback for the learner's response. Bloom and Gagnè insisted on constant repetition for effective reinforcement. As a result, behaviourists considered language teaching-learning to be more of habit formation where faults and mistakes were viewed as learners' errors and not as products of the teaching-learning process. Analogy was preferred over analysis in a linguistic and cultural set-up. Later, the behaviourist approach has been criticised for its approach to language teaching-learning as to habit but not as an interest. This neglects many other significant dimensions like motivation, attitude etc. Similarly, the structuralist view presented situational language teaching and American audio-lingual methods where the focus was entirely on producing correct sentence patterns and error-free grammatical structures. Thus, language was more about phonemes, words, syntax, and morphemes rather than significant comprehension.

The modern linguist Chomsky countered these assumptions about language teaching-learning and presented the innate ability and Universal Grammar as in-born capacities to learn language. Later, Constructivist views appeared on the screen where two schools of constructivism i.e., Cognitive constructivism by J. Piaget and Socio-cultural constructivism Lev Vygotsky presented language-learning as active interaction with in surroundings and environment. While Piaget focused on cognitive dimension, Vygotsky emphasised the role of social context and inputs. The constructivist approach emphasised on communication and internalisation.

Thus, these theories left an impact on language teaching and learning and as also on language teaching. Earlier, with behaviourism and structuralism, language was taught with an approach of imitation and rote-learning. Grammar was taught with structures and situational learning approach. With cognitive constructivism and social constructivism, further avenues have opened approaches for a particular language to be taught as first, second or third language. Certainly, these established theories make an impact on the approach of teaching and learning a language in a classroom set-up against the natural one. The two arguments of language aspect are if it is acquired or learnt. It has also led to a discussion on the mother tongue, its significance and role in an individual's life. Along remain the inquiries around a second language, the third language and other foreign languages. Besides all the discussion, language remains at the centre of all the learning as it supports the understanding and comprehension of every other subject.

English Language Teaching-Learning

Approximately, more than 1.5 billion people speak the English language across the globe. Over the years, it has become a common international language, especially as the language of business and professional studies. It has also received the status of an 'Official Language' in various countries. As the language widely dominates across the globe, it is taught in the entire world either as a first, second or third language. With advanced technology, English language teaching-learning is also changing profoundly. Throughout, language teaching learning has remained under the influence of different learning theories, be it behavioural, structuralism, constructivism, cognitivism, or socio-cultural. As these theories have been the guiding force behind teacher's training for pedagogical purposes and thereafter the classroom practices, they have also influenced teaching-learning of English language.

English is taught worldwide as a first, second, or third language. Many aspirations of a learner are associated with the learning of this language. Therefore, motivation and attitude to learn English language plays a significant role here. Similarly, the learning styles and habits of learners are also significant factors here. For a long span, behaviourism and structuralism dominated English language-learning where imitation and rote memorisation were encouraged to learn the language in the case of second or third languages. Reinforcement was also used. Rubin (1975) provided fourteen characteristics of a good English language learner where the learner had to act according to the expectations. English language-learning was mostly teacher-centric.

Lately, constructivism has swept the world with its active and participatory approach to learning language. Learning is viewed as a progressive non-linear process with the active involvement of the stakeholders in the teaching-learning course. The theories by Piaget and Vygotsky promote cognitive and social factors in learning the English language. Constructivism approaches English language-learning with a holistic view and prefers a 'process approach' with 'top-down' and 'bottom-up' approaches as per need. The English language learner is the constructor of its own knowledge and thereby actively participates in language-learning. With self-regulation, learning remains at the focal of the entire English language-learning. As Vygotsky (1978) explains Zone of Proximal Development (ZPD), it is 'actual level as determined by independent problem-solving' supported by 'level of potential development as determined through problem-solving under adult guidance or in collaboration with more capable peers.' Thus, any English language learner goes on to learn and acquire the language within an individual's capacity but with scaffolding and social support, further language development takes place and improves. Therefore, peer-group support, teachers as facilitators and surroundings are indispensable for English language teaching-learning, specially to increase the competence of language learners. As discussed in the previous section about the four skills of language learning, Listening, Speaking, Reading, and Writing, they form the basics of English language teaching-learning too. Thus, it becomes a requisite for educators and teachers to strategies their teaching-learning methods around these skills and refine them accordingly. The discussion of each skill has been presented below.

Listening Skill

The first skill in language is listening, which is key to absorbing all the information as a listener. Interestingly, it begins with the infancy stage where infant responds to the sound and voices. Hearing is the first sense that begins to develop and further leads to all other language development. It is a mix of imitation, reaction and response to activities taking place around the child. As the child grows, difference between hearing and listening gets clearer. Though the first step is hearing but listening is being aware of information received, paying sufficient attention to it and responding according to situation need. Thus, hearing may be voluntarily or involuntarily but listening is always voluntarily with some interest and purpose. The active listening is taught gradually and thereby getting the desired action and response from the listener. Furthermore, at school and in a learning environment, listening skills are developed – as a result, communication skills are polished.

Lundsteen (1979) analysed the major components of listening as 'previous knowledge, listening material, physiological activity (hearing sensation and perception), attention or concentration and being highly conscious at the time of listening and beyond.' Here, listening can serve various purposes in different situations like mere listening to attend, to imagine something or to seek answers through previous knowledge, compare, interrogate, or recode to reply. Listening may also be literal or for figurative thinking further. These components can be simply taken as the pre-cursor to the communication process. Thus, listening involves more than mere hearing.

Listening is primary to learning any language and several strategies can be used to improve listening skills and language acquisition. Interestingly, listening to others first is the key to learning a language fast. Focus and concentration are significant components as well as strategies of listening skills. The more a person is focused, the better their listening and understanding will be. Students can be motivated to use the target language more for listening and listening to the target language should improve. Here, the teacher as a facilitator plays a significant role because it is they who must use the target language first. Usually, the use of the mother tongue to teach English forces the grammar-translation method on learners which hampers listening skills, the most basic and essential of all the skills in language-learning.

The study has focused on understanding literal meaning, comprehension listening, summarising and response during the study for listening competency. Components like listening material, focus and concentration were emphasised.. Listening tests, focus, recap, and repeat, learning style-wise listening, no interruption, pen, and paper handy for note-taking are some of the strategies which the study has used during the intervention. Listening tests in the study are also prescribed as a part of assessment of speaking and listening skills.

Speaking Skill

The second significant soft skill is speaking in English which involves the production of verbal sounds according to the context and understanding of the listener. Speaking may be a response or initiation of a conversation to convey ideas, information, expression, or exchange of facts. English language teaching-learning mainly revolves around enabling the language learner to be able to speak the language fluently and efficiently. Earlier, task-based teaching was mainly used where the learner was expected to converse given a certain situation. Though the learner would learn the terms associated with that condition, it would become difficult to deal effectively using language in a real-life situation. It may be noted that speaking English language is more about developing the confidence and competence to use the language in daily life as per the need and requirement.

Unfortunately, speaking has hardly been the focus of the English language teaching-learning process as much as writing. The entire focus shifts to writing the language in the most accurate manner. Yet, speaking the language is the first interaction of any learner with someone else or a job aspirant seeking a job. Thus, speaking English is not only about the competency to produce the language but also the ability to communicate cohesively and coherently. Therefore, learning to speak the English language is also about using the language efficaciously in daily life whenever needed and not merely academically.

Teachers as facilitators need to focus on certain learning outcomes while teaching speaking skills to learners. An English language learner must possess a definite ability to speak after finishing school level education. Before the components of speaking skills are discussed, it is important to understand that there are specifically three components of any speech and they are speaker, listener, and the utterance itself; what has been uttered, who has uttered and to whom. So, it is equally important for the listener to understand the idea behind what was intended to be conveyed.

There are mainly five components of speaking skills, comprehension, grammar, vocabulary, pronunciation, and fluency, as discussed by Harris (1974). Each component significantly contributes towards fine communication skills and the lack of just one can entirely impact successful communication. The study investigated all the components of speaking skills while assessing and providing treatment. Several strategies were used to improve speaking skills. However, one of the main suggestions was to listen first as listening is the primary step towards learning any language. Students were encouraged to record their own speeches and conversations then listen to them again for their own insights into their spoken language skills especially fluency and pronunciation. They were encouraged to use the English language as much as possible, read, acquire vocabulary, and become acquainted with their own learning style.

Reading Skill

Reading is fundamental for acquiring knowledge, as information and facts are obtained from written words, primarily books. Therefore, it is essential and mandatory to acquire reading habits from a young age. Though reading habits at a young age can be primarily formed only based on interest but teachers as facilitators may use several strategies to generate it like stimulating curiosity through story-telling, or riddles. The habit may start as leisure, engaged during free time but gradually it will help the learner not only to acquire strong language as also enhance vocabulary which is an indispensable aspect of English language-learning. Reading for leisure·forms the strong habit of reading that further helps towards academic reading, which is to understand concepts and information needed to be further processed. It helps not only to understand concepts and information mentioned in books but opens avenues to a whole new world of knowledge and wisdom.

Reading may be categorised as oral or loud, silent, critical, extensive or intensive. In a usual English language classroom, a teacher can be observed asking students to read aloud to the class – that is how students are engaged with their textbooks. Traditionally, teacher asks students to note their new words and explains the text with word-meanings. Around the year, silent reading can be steadfastly observed, which is equally important to understand the text for an individual learner. Today, reading is not limited to mere literature but includes articles, facts, and information to interpret the text. School level education is a comprehensive preparation for job opportunities and careers which await at the end of academic terms. Extensive and intensive readings must also be included in the curriculum during this preparation.

It is important to understand the two reading categories or components, namely extensive and intensive. Extensive reading is intended for the delight and pleasure of the reader's interest. The purpose is mainly to enjoy various writings of interest. With this aim, stories, comics, novels, folk-tales etc. are some of the works that are read extensively. The book may be a work of fiction, imagination, or any genre of interest. A specific comprehension of the reader is not held accountable as different interpretations and understanding of the values and messages are allowed. Nevertheless, it is not the same with intensive reading. The word intensive itself means 'in-depth'. It is centred around understanding the text and mainly related to academic reading. It may be for knowledge, information gathering or for further interpretations and calculations. Academically, more intensive readings of a subject lead to specialisations. Thus, in a classroom, both readings are to be encouraged for the cognitive development of the learner.

Besides extensive and intensive readings, there are certain techniques or strategies to improve these reading. Skimming and scanning are two such techniques that facilitates learners to read with a purpose. Skimming is to gain a comprehensively condensed and overall understanding of any provided text. It is to mainly glance with rapid reading through title, headings, theme, graphical or pictorial presentation of the text. It is to get the first impression of the work after looking at the material. For instance, if someone picks up a travelogue, instead of reading all of it, someone may prefer to know only a particular the place written about, sites to visit and pictorial presentation of the work. If it impresses, then reader may choose to read all of it. This is skimming and therefore, it is important to put up an attractive title and sub-headings along with interesting pictures. Scanning is specifically to look for certain information in the given text. These two techniques are important to learn for the students as it facilitates reading comprehension.

The study focused on oral loud reading, silent reading, pronunciation while reading, extensive and intensive reading. Strategies like skimming and scanning were taught as strategies of reading comprehension. Oral loud reading and silent reading were also important components of reading skills that formed part of the treatment for the reading aspect of the study.

Writing Skill

The most complex and abstract aspect of English language-learning is writing skills. Since the enrolment of a learner in the school, writing remains at the center of all the academic learning with utmost focus. As it is the highest order of all the skills of language learning, teachers attempt to strengthen this skill with all the efforts. Writing skills are also taught under two categories of creative writings and academic writings. If creative writings require individual interest, dedication and teacher's guidance and support, academic writings focus on production of knowledge, facts, and information. Academically, every other subject in centrally-run schools is teaching all other subjects through the medium of English language. Along with English, Mathematics, Sciences and Social Sciences are also taught with the same medium of instruction. In this way, writing becomes an integral aspect of all learning with the English language at the centre of it with academic writing being emphasised.

During school education, English language-learning with academic writing essentially contributes to learning of higher order skills needed for professional success. The most significant components to develop for writing skills are grammar, spelling, punctuation, format, vocabulary, and syntax. Long with these components, study also focused further on Time and Tense, numerical writings, title-writing, capitalisation, full-stop. Addressing questions and content understanding are important deliverables required for effective academic progress. Writing mainly can display and assess their understanding of the content and subject. During the study, notebooks, online and offline assessments and learning-style wise improvement was observed and strategized for the treatment in a blended learning environment.

Thus, the four skills of the English language are deeply inter-connected and interdependent. One skill cannot be comprehensively learned in isolation that is, without acquiring the other. Listening is the first and foremost skill to be acquired and learned. The rest of the skills are like climbing a ladder, one on top of the other as shown in Figure 5.

Speaking is not possible without listening; reading and writing are abstract but not possible without the first two. However, writing is at the top of the learning ladder but the rest of the three skills are at its base. Every skill of language-learning augments the other. Every intended component of English language-learning should be strategized accordingly and it supplements the entire teaching-learning process.

English Language Teaching in India

The English language is one of the 'Official Languages' of India. Though, during British India, the official languages were English, Hindi and Urdu, while adopting the Indian Constitution in 1950, Hindi was adopted as

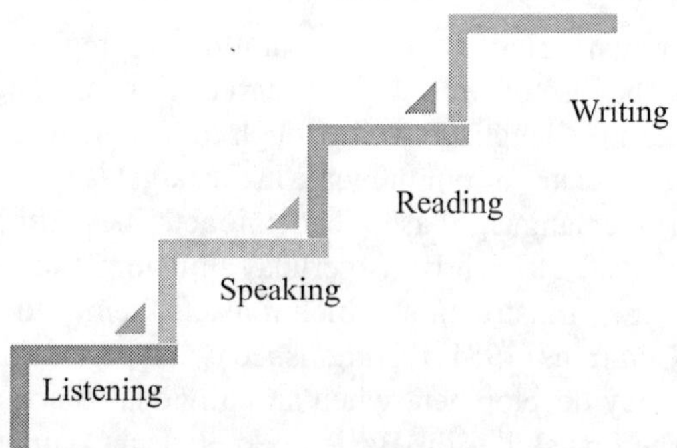

Figure 5: Four Skills of English Language in the Order of Acquisition

official language. Yet due to language constraints all over India, English was continued to be used by Parliament with a view to be phased out in favour of Hindi over a fifteen-year period. Hindi as the only official language was opposed in many parts of the country. In 1948–1949, University Education Commission had recommended a Three-language formula citing the examples of other multi-lingual countries, which was eventually adopted by the Parliament of Indian Government in 1968. English found the status of official language of India.

Originally, the Education Commission of 1964–1966 recommended a Three-language formula as a language-learning policy proposal, which was followed by some debate in the country. The formula proposed for the study of three languages, Hindi, English and one regional or modern language of choice. The formula was sought due to regional demands from non-Hindi speaking states of Southern India, mainly Tamil Nadu. Presently, Tamil Nadu does not follow this Three-language formula. Though the Education Commission of 1986 also reiterated the 1968 formula, recently 'New Education Policy 2020' has pushed away remarkably from the English–Hindi approach of 1968 by emphasising the mother tongue of the learner.

Before the 'New Education Policy' 2020 English language was compulsory for the schools either as a second or third language. All English medium schools used English as the medium of instruction and the curriculum and syllabus were provided in the same language. Though schools followed behavioural and structural model of teaching English language, but lately, constructivism and cognitive approach began to take over the previous approaches to teach the language. English textbooks prescribed by the National Council of Educational Research and Training (NCERT) are followed up to the Higher Secondary Stage of schooling. Other subjects of English medium schools also have their textbooks in the target language. Thus, English, as a common global language, will continue to be the medium of communication in India.

Teaching English Language at Higher Secondary Stage

The Higher Secondary stage is the preparation for higher education and graduate studies that is towards a first degree. English language learners (ELL) need to learn the language well enough to be able to access academic content as also be efficient to communicate in the target language in the school environment and other language based academic activities. Although, ELL may be able to communicate efficiently in everyday situations, they may struggle to acquire the language of instruction, which impacts their academic success in school settings. Cummins (1981) distinguished two types of skills required for language proficiency development when an individual is acquiring a second language (L2). The first skill is the Basic Interpersonal Communication Skills (BICS), which allows students to have face-to-face communications. The second is Cognitive Academic Language Proficiency (CALP). The CALP is necessary for a child's academic language development. BICS and CALP are the skills needed for a child to be successful at the grade school level.

At the Higher Secondary stage of school level education, English language teaching is supported by main textbooks and supplementary readers. The CBSE in India began with Assessment of Speaking and Listening at the Higher Secondary stage also which looks after the BICS aspect of language-learning. Categorically, BICS is about listening and speaking whereas CALP is more about reading and writing. Thus, BICS and CALP remain two categorised skills required for language proficiency development while acquiring a second language (L2). The Basic Interpersonal Communication Skills (BICS) allows students to have face to face communications with listening and speaking whereas Cognitive Academic Language Proficiency (CALP) is necessary for a child's academic language development focusing more on reading and writing. Cummins (2017, p.65) further elaborates that BICS is the conversational fluency in a language while CALP is students' ability to understand and express, in both oral and written modes, concepts and ideas that are relevant to success in school education. Later, the terms conversational/academic language proficiency were used interchangeably with BICS/CALP. The two concepts have been discussed below under separate headings.

Basic Inter-personal Communication Skills (BICS)

BICS are the English language communication skills mainly used for social interaction. These skills are used on an everyday basis to interact with people in the community, social set-up, and groups. BICS skills are also needed in schools where the medium of instruction is English. Still students generally prefer to use their mother-tongue to interact among themselves and BICS skills of English language suffer due to this habit. Students continue to do so unless they are either motivated to use the language or they realise the significance of communication skills in the target language for professional development. Once the importance is known, peer-interaction, usage of the language on the daily basis can also strengthened BICS skills. As BICS are not too demanding cognitively, gradual learning of the language may take a few months up to a year or two depending on learner of the language. Since Assessment of Speaking and Listening has been regularised, conversational language has also been given attention in the English language classrooms. Understanding of the language along with fluency, coherence, cohesion, pronunciation, vocabulary, and grammar are some of the significant aspects that the language user must pay attention to while gaining a working proficiency. As discussed earlier about the four basic skills of language, LSRW, BICS is listening and speaking with understanding and its proficiency should never be confused with CALP being academic language.

Cognitive Academic Language Proficiency (CALP)

CALP refers to the academic learning of the English language dealing with academic listening, speaking, reading, and writing. In simpler terms, it is English language for academic purposes. It is learned to understand and comprehend the given content in an academic setting. When BICS is more conversational, CALP needs to have some previous knowledge of some content. The language structure is more complex and involves intricate possible technical vocabulary including jargon. Therefore, it demands cognitive understanding from the learner. When BICS is dealing with only two skills of language, CALP uses all of them in an academic setting. It also takes a longer time to master and therefore, school level education is mere preparation for all the required CALP skills. Letter writing, speeches, literature, and many other academic endeavours are part of CALP. It involves grammar, vocabulary, punctuation, syntax, with other significant aspects of language. Though Cummins details CALP yet insists that it takes a longer time to be learned as compared to BICS. Therefore, curriculum and syllabus planners may consider this carefully while planning any English language curriculum.

Conceptual Framework

Present standards and curricula in education tend to cater learning horizontally as well as vertically. Thus, learning is conceived as a sequence or continuum of increasing expertise. A vertical conceptualisation of learning is inherent to the idea of learning progressions, thus, supporting a more developmental view of learning. It is obvious to learning that students do not precede in lock step that they do not move forward at the same rate or with the same degree of depth due to their individuality. Student learning is differential and may lie at different points along the vertical progression. Learning progressions can be understood as a sequence along which students can move progressively in the learning for a better performance. The notion of continuity and coherence are implicit in progression. Here, learning is not regarded as distinct events, but rather as a trajectory of progress that connects knowledge, concepts, and skills within a particular domain. With clear associations in different points of the progression, teachers can recalibrate their teaching to any missing precursor understanding or skills revealed by assessment. They can further determine what the next steps are to move the student forward from that point.

It is expected that after understanding the trajectory of learning once, and thereafter receiving scaffolding and feedback from the teacher, students may improve in BICS and CALP of English as a second language with the tools of Learning Analytics (LA). As LA has wide operations with different purposes, the study used Analytics-based Feedback (AbF) to improve learning outcomes. The purpose of this study was to analyse the learning progression made using

Analytics-based feedback as a tool of learning analytics (LA) for ELL. In the paragraphs below, conceptual clarifications are provided.

The present research work revolves around two main concepts. The two concepts are LA - AbF, and English Language-learning progression to be mapped through BICS and CALP levels of students. LA has a wide spectrum of its potential usage, like, time-on-task, virtual teaching, augmented teaching, student at risk and retention, feedback, so on and so forth. The study focussed on improving learning outcomes with the help of Analytics-based Feedback (AbF) and its conceptualisation has been discussed in detail earlier. This section further elaborates more on blended learning, flipped classroom as strategies under AbF, stakeholders of the study, other components like learning style, study habits, motivation, attitude to study English language, and socio-economic status observed during the study.

Parents are also to be informed regularly of the performances and improvements, if any, constantly. They can also participate in online monitoring of the student. It personalises learning for the student as the feedback is intended for an individual learner, whose performance has been assessed. Besides providing the AbF, teachers also should consider and understand the adequacy, usefulness, timing, and quality of feedback as mentioned earlier while explaining the AbF model. Gradually, it must be learnt how the students prefer to receive AbF. Once the AbF are provided, students were to improve on the errors and mistakes and if repeated, teachers are to gently remind them about the same. Once they begin to make efforts and improve on their previous performances progressively, they may take interest to further improve on their assessment. Thus, this study used AbF as a strategy in a blended learning environment.

Blended Learning

Blended learning, in simple terms, integrates online and offline instructional methods to customise the learning experiences of students. It is also known as hybrid learning or mixed-mode instructions. It is to be understood and

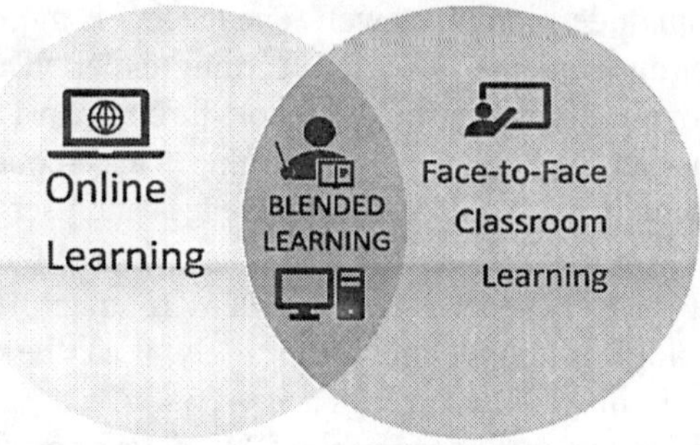

Figure 6: Blended Learning with Online and Offline Support

prioritised that it is a teaching-learning process that needs the support of classroom teaching or online teaching. Both the methods were used with the intension of improving learning experiences. The technology used should support the content which is intended to be taught. Students not only get teacher support, but peer support, easy and flexible access, personalised experiences, and better exposure, improves soft skills and engagement.

The method provides more flexibility for learners as well as teachers to use technology and digital platforms along with face-to-face classroom teaching as shown in Figure 6 for a blended learning environment.

Blended learning can engage a learner in a better manner to also save time. The purpose of both methods remains to engage the learner in a more focused manner. Blended learning balances the extremity of online and offline modes of instruction. There are six to seven models of blended learning, such as, Face-to-Face Driver, Rotation, Flex, Labs, Self-blend, and Online Driver. One of the most popular versions of blended learning is the Flipped Classroom, which was strategized for this study.

Flipped Classroom

A flipped classroom is a sort of blended learning strategy which focuses on the student's active participation and engagement. It allows the facilitator to blend students' exposure to content with different exercises. In a flipped classroom, students may get to watch online lectures or content, collaborate with peers, engage in discussions to understand concepts before actual face-to-face classroom interaction. In a traditional classroom, the teacher may introduce content with some activities to engage students but in a flipped classroom, students have experienced the content and may have their doubts or seek further in-depth knowledge. The model shifts instructions from the teacher's hand to the students' active understanding. The study used flipped classrooms as one of the strategies to facilitate learning.

Learning Management System Developed on Moodle

Blended learning environments need the support of some online content with offline classroom underpinning as well. The teacher is more of a facilitator of education engaging students in varied learning experiences. The study was designed to provide online learning support through an LMS developed on Moodle for Class XI English language-learning. This e-course on Moodle was developed keeping in view the cost effectiveness and user-friendly interface. Moodle allowed up to 50 users for free then. Moodle Cloud solutions was found to be apt for K-12 teaching-learning environment. It does not demand complex technological knowledge; accordingly, it can be easily designed. It also provides in-built analytics of logs and views.

The figure 7 is the dashboard of the LMS developed. The e-content was developed and shared on the LMS via YouTube which also provides analytics

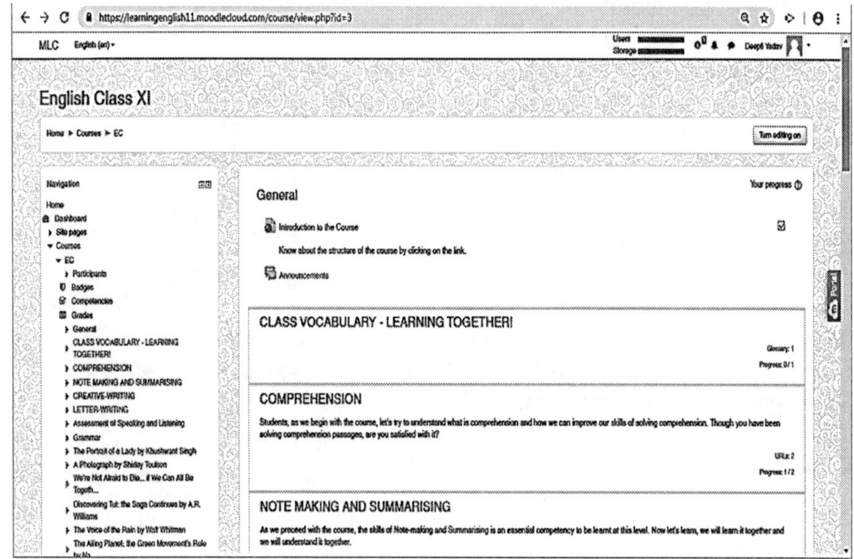

Figure 7: Dashboard of the LMS, E-Course at Moodle for Class XI

of the videos viewed. Similarly, Google Forms were used for the purpose of assessment as it is simple, thereby easy to analyse each submission and provide personalised feedback. The LMS provided a common platform to design the course to put all the content together. The log entries and completion of the tasks and sections could be easily tracked to view for every enrolled student. The LMS also provided complete log-entries date and time-wise for each user.

Thus, an interactive online environment was provided to the learners and teacher for AbF and performance assessment.

Stakeholders of the Study

Usually, in any intervention, the researcher-teacher and students are the two stakeholders of the intervention who actively participate in a study. But, Learning Analytics encompasses the entire facilitation and learning, and it also considers the context in which the learning is taking place. Therefore, school and parents also become significant stakeholder of the teaching-learning process. The motivation to improve the learning outcome is received from all the sides rather than just teacher. Parents play a significant role in a child's life and cannot be ignored according to the process of Learning Analytics. As data ethics and privacy is a great concern while conducting a LA studies, the parental permission become a pre-requisite before enrolling any student in the online course for any purpose. It is the parents who are expected to provide the required web facility in home learning environment. Thus, parents became a part of the LA study.

Similarly, it is the school that provides the blended learning environment along with parents. Consequently, school authorities become a part of the required support. Thus, as shown in Figure 8, it is also important to include the school authorities and parents to support the teaching-learning process while the purpose is to study AbF for the English language-learning progression.

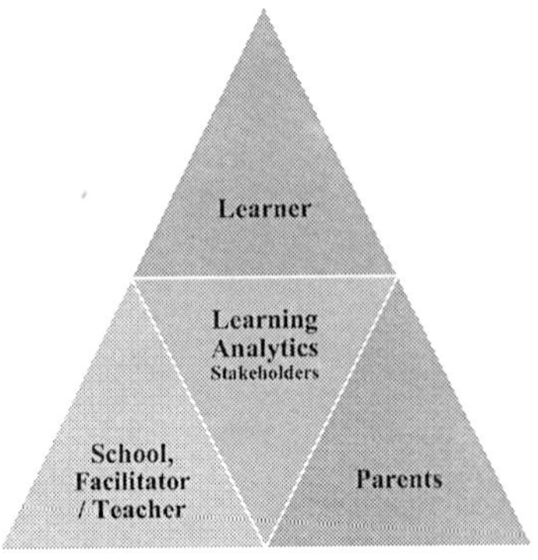

Figure 8: Stakeholders of the Study

Other Components

Any learning is an outcome of a sum of experiences and conditions. Learning progression cannot be studied in isolation of other variables, which are also responsible for learning outcomes. A few variables were also selected to understand the progression in ESL. Therefore, the study also chose to observe some background variables in addition to AbF, BICS, and CALP in the context of this work on Analytics. The other background variables studied were Learning Style, Study Habits, Motivation, Attitude, and background key variables such as Gender and Socio-Economic Status. After assessing the learners for their respective learning style, the Analytics-based Feedback was based on their respective style, learners were also counselled for their Study Habits, Motivation and Attitude toward language-learning. Thus, the present research was conceptualised as a study of Analytics-based Feedback with respect to BICS and CALP of ESL in relation to other background variables viz. Learning Style, Study Habits, Motivation, Attitude, and Background Key Variables of Gender and Socio-Economic Status. The other components of the study and their relation with English language-learning and AbF is discussed below.

1. Learning Style

Every person is a product of heredity and environment. It leads to individual differences with certain features and factors. These natural individual differences account for varied performances and success of learners in any subject area. It is also applied to language-learning for second language learners as they begin to learn the target language later than their first language acquisition. Also, first language is acquired whereas second language take certain efforts on the part of learners. Thus, these differences are natural and bound to accrue. It is essential for the facilitators to acknowledge and accept such natural individual differences like intelligence, competence, physical characteristics, personality, gender, interests, aptitude, and many other aspects. Due to individual differences, learning styles of the learners also differ and vary. If the feedback to improve second language is to be provided, it cannot be the same for all. These individual differences should to be taken into consideration for personalising learners' specific feedback on language. The AbF, thus provided, may offer better facilitation to the learners, and make teaching-learning process more effective and productive.

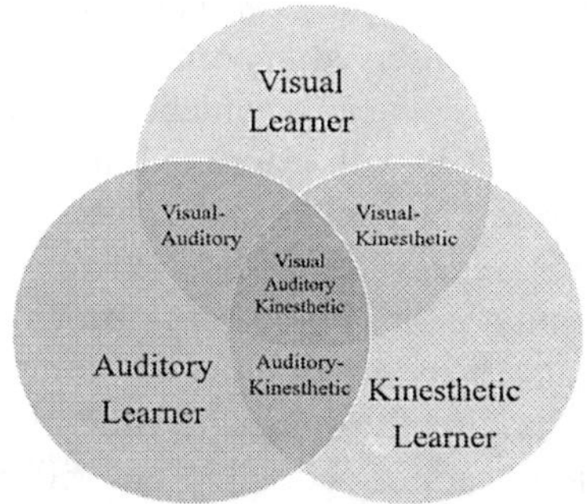

Figure 9: Different Learning Styles Related to Each Other

Though there have been several theories and concepts on learning styles floating around for more than thirty-five years, a consensus has not arrived yet. It was psychologist, David Kolb in 1984 who first proposed his theory on learning styles accounting for genetics, experiences, and environment. Many other theorists have suggested their own understanding and experiences regarding learning style since then. Despite the differences in the available theories of categorisation and assessment, it is agreed that individual differences persist due to different learning styles. The study had been delimited to the three fundamental learning styles as visual, auditory and kinaesthetic. The feedback provided to students with different learning styles were based on these three. It was also observed that an individual does not rely solely on only one style of learning but use all the ways and senses to learn, acquire knowledge and experience things as shown in Figure 9.

A learner may have one dominant learning style and another secondary style but it is through all the senses that a learner makes the attempt to gain knowledge in the environment as seen above. Therefore, AbF was based on these strategies to motivate learners to first acquaint themselves with their learning styles and then, improve all the possibilities of gaining knowledge and language. Students were introduced to their respective dominant learning styles and were suggested to open up avenues of learning further to improve. It also helped in personalising feedback for the respective learning styles to improve learning outcomes and further study the learning progression.

2. Study-Habits

Study-habits are simply the everyday conduct or behaviour towards learning which have eventually formed over the years since formal education began. Study-habits which are formed and shaped over the years, the nature of such habits can be beneficial or harmful. Psychologically, it is known that these study-habits play a dominant role in academic success. As a learner spends approximately six-to-seven hours at school, only a fraction of the explicit part of study-habits can be observed in academic performance. When a learner plans the learning, much is better known about study-habits. These habits include every practice associated with learning. It may be related to examination, time-management, space arrangement of the place of study, note-taking, or even health.

Several other routine habits also make an impact in the long run over study-habits. For instance, procrastination is a habit related to delaying things, but it may affect the study-time or achieving the study-target. Somewhere, it is directly related to time-management. Thus, little habits formed over the years of schooling are difficult to change either due to negligence or possible lack of guidance. At times, students are unaware of their own habits or despite being aware, are not able to find a solution. They need counselling to ensure steady progress.

Study-habits, good or bad, can be assessed with some tools. As the stakeholders of study are not limited to teachers and students but parents too, these study-habits cannot only be assessed but improved with proper observation and with dedicated attentive care of learners' parents and teachers together. Improvement in the learning outcomes should be observed in a holistic manner for a permanence rather than merely for one time on paper. Literature review related to study-habits also provides empirical evidence of the relationship between good study habits and better academic achievement. Therefore, it was conceptualised if learners can be provided with the feedback and counselling on their study-habits by analysing their inventory. Subsequently, with gradual work on these habits 'consciously' in a short span of time, some change in the learning outcomes were observed.

3. Motivation

Motivation is defined as 'enthusiasm for doing something' according to the Cambridge Dictionary. This fervour to do something may be internal or external. When an individual is motivated from within, the person is said to be intrinsically motivated. On the other hand, if someone needs to be motivated from other external sources, it is called extrinsic motivation. An individual acquires the mother tongue naturally due to the need of socialising and community from a especially young age. It is the intrinsic motivation behind learning the native language. Hindi, other regional or tribal languages and dialects are pre-dominant due to the diversity and multi-lingual culture in India. There may be several reasons for a learner to take up a second or third language. Family, social-setup, or peer-interaction may be some of these incentives. Any other language besides the mother tongue is gradually learned and mastered. English is taught as a second language across the country. It is taught from pre-school to learners in an English medium school set-up. A child is either extrinsically or intrinsically motivated to learn the second language based on their individual differences and background.

Motivation plays an extremely essential role in learning and mastering a second language. This impetus can be understood as the guiding drive or force to achieve anything conveyed through behaviour and efforts. The forces or drives may be social, emotional, cognitive, or even biological. Motivation can be one of the major driving forces behind learning English as a second language as observed during literature reviews.

During the study, it was an area of observation if after learning about their respective learning style, study habits and counselling related to their own performance improvement, how students would feel about English language-learning and AbF. Receiving the feedback regarding their performances and consciously working on the errors and mistakes may motivate them for better performance and improvement, or otherwise. Such motivational strategies may push students to regulate their own learning behaviour and improve their study habits. Self-regulation is seen as a strategic tool to bring change in learning behaviour and motivation can be one of the significant factors in doing so. Therefore, the study observed and measured the motivation level of students pre- and post-study. It would also help in understanding the role of motivation in learning English as a second language.

4. Attitude Towards English Language Learning

Cambridge Dictionary defines attitude as 'a feeling or opinion about something or someone, or a way of behaving that is caused by this.' Collins' Dictionary defines attitude as 'Your attitude to something is the way that you think and feel about it, especially when this shows in the way you behave.' Thus, attitude is a general predisposition towards a certain phenomenon either positive or negative. It is the required impetus for language-learning too. Students usually have a pre-notion either positive or negative towards language learning, especially English as a second language. It has an enormous impact on the teaching-learning process subsequently also on learning outcomes as revealed during the literature reviews.

In a multi-lingual setting, the attitude towards English language learning can be highly divergent. At the Higher Secondary level, students have already formed their attitude about a particular subject and know their preferences. They have selected their subject streams too, knowing their preferences for career choice, and therefore, the subjects are already prioritised. Here, attitude towards English language-learning may affect the participation as well as experiences for the study. The pre-set notions and attitude at this age can only be influenced if any sort of feedback improve their chances and performances for their careers. So, the students experienced blended learning environment for English language-learning and different other strategies like flipped classroom, a virtual environment, LMS etc. with AbF. Understanding the significance of attitude towards English language learning, the pre and post of the attitude towards English language-learning with the treatment was observed, measured, and studied. It was also to study the change in the attitude towards English language-learning with the AbF, if any.

5. Socio-Economic Status

Socio-economic status is a specific measure of sociological and economic present condition of an individual. It is in comparison to other community members' sociological and economical position in the society. English language-learning in a classroom setting is a natural process of teaching-learning the target language. The environment is same for all the learners. The difference in the background is due to their genders and socio-economic status. As the study has been strategized for a blended learning environment and flipped classroom at times, it is important for the learner to be equipped with necessary technological facilities.

Due to diverse backgrounds, differences may be observed in the performances of the students. It may be due to various facilities provided by the parents in the home environment of learners. Differences in the parents' educational qualifications and occupation may also affect the performance of the learner. Without the required infrastructure, the study may not run smoothly. The socio-economic differences may lead to varied access to the online content despite the offline efforts in the classroom. Working level, income, education, and occupation of parents are considered while calculating the socio-economic status. It may generate a difference among the sample of the study chosen as English language learners of Class XI. Therefore, while conducting the study, Socio-Economic Status was studied as an independent variable of the study. It was to analyse the differences in the achievement of the learners in the English language, if any. Therefore, Socio-Economic Status had been selected as one of the components of the study.

Summary and Conclusion

Though Learning Analytics (LA) is conceived as a substantial tool in higher education, yet it needs more empirical studies and further researches, especially in early and school education and thereby improving learning outcomes. The investigation presented in the book focuses on the usage of Analytics-based Feedback in school education and thereby defines it. The aim of the work was to explore analytics-based feedback to improve learning outcomes in English as a Second Language (ESL). The objective was to study the learning progression in terms of achievement in ESL's Basic Interpersonal Communication Skills (BICS), Cognitive Academic Language Proficiency (CALP) and other background variables of the learners in successive trials when analytics-based feedback is provided based on previous performance.

3

Rationale with Literature Review

Learning Analytics

While working on any study, a literature review is indispensable and essential to develop insights and understanding of the past, present and expected developments in the field. Though LA has been gripping researchers and academicians, alike, worldwide, India is still observing the field mainly at the higher education level. The in-depth literature review helped in understanding the gaps and strategising empirically to tap school level education to improve learning outcomes. The previous chapters delved into the introduction of the book with learning analytics, AbF and other relevant details. The current chapter presents a review of relevant literature. It presents current trends, advancements, and findings related to LA in schools, LA in language education, language-learning progression, and other related variables of the study. The key broad area covered in the review is learning analytics. It has been divided into three parts, first delving into learning analytics, second delving into language and other components and lastly delves into overall scenario in India. It deduces a conclusion of the literature review and the relevance of the review to the present study.

Learning Analytics

This section presents a review of studies on Learning Analytics. The reviews have helped to understand the research trends in the field of learning analytics.

Yang, Yao, Lu and Zhou and Xu (2020) conducted a unique study with Learning Analytics. The researchers made an automatic analysis of students' in-classroom behaviour to evaluate the effect of teaching. In their work, they analysed the students' concentration degree with the teacher or teaching content. Specifically, they detected students' faces, track faces and analyse the students' behaviour, i.e. raising or downing faces and corresponding head orientations to the teacher, teaching content or not with the help of classroom videos. Besides, texts were also obtained from the teacher's speech and the course topics taught in the class were extracted. Audio features of the teacher's speech were extracted and analysed. Finally, the correlation of the students' degree of concentration with the course topics, audio features were analysed. This analysis helped teachers to explore find the effective teaching characteristics to better improve students' concentration degree better.

Critical Appraisal: The study was an example of extreme penetration of technology into human learning. Concentration and focus being inner relative behaviour could be subjective and relative. Study researched upon the concentration degree but could have also suggested measures to improve concentration.

Ferguson (2019) built on the extensive work of an ongoing series of international workshops on ethics and privacy in learning analytics (EP4LA). The associated guest editorial (Ferguson, Hoel, Scheffel and Drachsler, 2016) reviewed the eight papers in the section and identified a series of learning analytics challenges with ethical dimensions. These challenges could be clustered under six headings: duty to act, informed consent, safeguarding, equality and justice, data ownership and protection and privacy and integrity of self.

Critical Appraisal: Study delved into significant aspects and challenges of LA. Any study to be conducted has to have considered these issues before planning and executing any.

Harrak, Bouchet and Luengo (2019) presented a work focussing on feedback on the quality of questions. According to this study, the analysis of student questions could be used to improve the learning experience for both students and teachers. They investigated questions (N = 6457) asked before the class by first-year medicine/pharmacy students on an online platform, used by professors to prepare for Q&A sessions. The long-term objectives were to help professors in categorising those questions and to provide students with feedback on the quality of their questions. To do so, a coding scheme was developed and then used for automatic annotation of the whole corpus. They identified student characteristics from the typology of questions they asked using the k-means algorithm over four courses. Students were clustered based on question dimensions only. Then, they characterised the clusters by attributes not used for clustering, such as student grade, attendance and number and popularity of questions asked. Two similar clusters always appeared (lower than average students with popular questions and higher than average students with unpopular questions). They replicated these analyses on the same courses across different years to show the possibility of predicting student profiles online. This work showed the usefulness and validity of their coding scheme and the relevance of their approach to identify different student profiles.

Critical Appraisal: This LA study familiarised us with the significance of the quality of questions by students and how these could be utilised further.

Liu, Froissard, Richards and Atif (2019) worked on data collected through Moodle and how it can be further used with the help of some plug-ins. As Moodle, an open-source Learning Management System (LMS), collects a large amount of data on student interactions within it, including content, assessments, and communication, some of these data can be used as proxy indicators of student engagement, as well as predictors for performance. However, these data were difficult to interrogate and even more difficult to action from within Moodle. Therefore, they described a design-based research narrative to develop an enhanced version of an open-source Moodle Engagement Analytics Plugin (MEAP). Working with the needs of unit convenors and student support staff, they sought to improve the available information, the way it was represented and create affordances for action based on this. The enhanced MEAP (MEAP+) allowed analyses of gradebook data, assessment submissions, login metrics and forum interactions, as well as direct action through personalised emails to students based on these analyses.

Critical Appraisal: Moodle had been providing for plug-ins but students needed to be sent personalised emails for direct actions for evaluations. Thus, it had to be understood if Moodle and the plug-ins served the purpose, entirely.

Saint (2019) recognised the potential of data science methods for the analysis of temporal processes. To explore this potential, his research aimed to 1) improve the measurement of SRL by deriving micro-level processes from trace data; 2) analyse these micro-level processes for temporal associations; 3) explore how such temporal associates between micro-level processes are correlated with learning strategies; and 4) assess the impact of formative data-driven feedback on these SRL processes. They undertook two preliminary studies and found that certain temporal activity traits relate to performance in the summative assessments attached to the course, mediated by strategy type. In addition, more strategically minded activity, embodying learner self-regulation, generally proved to be more successful than less disciplined reactive behaviours.

Critical Appraisal: Study could have provided for the strategy type used for summative assessments attached to the course.

Atapattu and Falkner (2018) explored the association between video interactions and non-visual (i.e., verbal) content focusing on language and discourse features of lecture video contents. The primary focus of previous video learning analytics studies was on analysing video interaction behaviour using views, the *explicit* factors. According to their results, a number of discourse features, like, lexical diversity and causal connectives demonstrated a statistically significant correlation with video interactions. Their results demonstrated that descriptive features like sentence count, word count, sentence length, syllable count and speaking rate positively correlated with video interaction peaks. The research forwarded a significant step towards understanding hidden patterns of language and discourse that could impact the video interactions of MOOC learners.

Critical Appraisal: Study could have discussed and elaborated upon the strategies used to observe the association. Every content type has its own advantages and disadvantages. Certain other factors also make a difference for the video contents which may be considered as extraneous factors.

Nguyen, Huptych and Rienties (2018) conducted extensive research in learning science where they attempted to establish the importance of time management in online learning. They focussed on the temporal characteristics of learning by allowing researchers to capture authentic digital footprints of student learning behaviours. Nonetheless, students' timing of engagement and its relation to learning design (LD) and academic performance received limited attention. This study investigated to what extent students' timing of engagement aligned with instructor learning design and how engagement varied across different levels of performance. Their findings revealed a mismatch between how instructors designed for learning and how students studied. In most weeks, students spent less time studying the assigned materials on the virtual learning environment (VLE) compared to the number of hours recommended by instructors. The timing of engagement also varied, from in advance to catching up patterns. High-performing students spent more time studying in advance, while low-performing students spent a higher proportion of their time on catching-up activities. By incorporating the pedagogical context into learning analytics, it was attempted to understand students' engagement and their behaviour influenced by the way instructors design for learning.

Critical Appraisal: An orientation for all the stakeholders was needed for such a study. A mismatch between the stakeholders while conducting the study would put the outcomes into the doubts.

Viberg, Hatakka, Bälter and Mavroudi (2018) based their analysis on 252 papers on learning analytics in higher education published between 2012 and 2018. Learning analytics can improve learning practice by transforming the ways it supports learning processes. The main research question was: What was the current scientific knowledge about the application of learning analytics in higher education? The focus was on research approaches, methods and the evidence for learning analytics. The evidence was examined in relation to four earlier validated propositions: whether learning analytics i) improve learning outcomes, ii) support learning and teaching, iii) are deployed widely and iv) are used ethically. The results demonstrated that overall, there was little evidence that showed improvements in students' learning outcomes (9%) as well as learning support and teaching (35%). Similarly, little evidence was found for the third (6%) and the fourth (18%) proposition. Despite the fact that the identified potential for improving learner practice was high, they could not later see much transfer of the suggested potential into higher educational practice over the years. However, the analysis of the existing evidence for learning analytics indicated that there was a shift towards a deeper understanding of students' learning experiences in recent years.

Critical Appraisal: This work delved mainly if LA was making substantial footprint over learning. The LA works studied were mainly theoretical as seen from the inferences. Therefore, more empirical studies and evidences were needed to support the notion of LA's usefulness for education and its stakeholders.

Dvorak and Jia (2016) analysed the relationship between students' online work habits and academic performance. Data were collected from logs recorded by a course management system (CMS) in two courses at a small liberal arts college in the U.S. The three aspects of students' online work habits, timeliness, regularity and intensity were measured. The data originated from two courses with a combined enrolment of 78 students. The format of the classroom meeting with students was a combination of lecture and discussion. It was found that students with high prior GPAs and high grades in the course work on their assignments early and even more regularly. It was also found that the regularity of work habits during the first half of the term predicted grade later in the course, even while controlling for the prior GPA. Conclusively, the CMS data offered insights into the drivers of student success. The work suggested that publicising habits of successful students with other fellows could engender positive peer effects. It was established for the hypothesis that study habits as measured by students' online behaviour are correlated to their achievement in the course.

Critical Appraisal: Study habits were analysed with online behaviour and habits against some standardised tool. Therefore, some online habit inventory could have developed and administered to understand the study habits in some standardised manner.

Gašević, Dawson and Siemens (2015) offered a discussion reflecting the impetus for building the field of learning analytics. Though counting of certain types of activities that learners performed with some online learning tools can be correlated with their academic performance, the true test of time for learning analytics is evaluating the long-term impact on student learning and teaching practices. Learning analytics that do not facilitate effective learning and teaching are susceptible to the use of trivial measures such as increased number of log-ins into an LMS, as a way to evaluate learning progression. In order to avoid such undesirable practices, it is necessary to involve the relevant stakeholders, be it learners, instructors, instructional designers, information technology support and institutional administrators – in all stages of learning analytics and the culture that the extensive use of data in education carries.

Critical Appraisal: The study discussed one of the most important aspects of LA's survival for the long term. Big data studies patterns out of a magnanimous amount of data generated whereas LA needs to look into improving the learning of an individual. As an early indicative study, it suggested avoiding trivial issues of login and mere temporal analysis.

Kovanović, Gašević, Dawson, Joksimović, Baker and Hatala (2015) presented a paper giving the results of a study that examined the effects of different time-on-task estimation methods on the results of commonly adopted analytical models. The primary goal of this paper was to raise awareness of the issue of accuracy and appropriateness surrounding time-estimation within the broader learning analytics community and to initiate a debate about the challenges of this process. For this study, the data were collected from a 13-week long masters' level, fully online course in software engineering offered at a Canadian public university. Conducted at the postgraduate level, the course focussed on challenges in the area of software engineering with research intensive and focussed on contemporary trends. The data were obtained from Moodle's PostgreSQL database and consisted of 167,000 log records produced by 81 students from six offers of the course. Researchers conducted an experiment using 15 different strategies for time-on-task estimation. A series of multiple linear regression analyses were conducted given that standardised regression coefficients are easy to interpret and directly comparable. Several practical implications from the results of this study were that above all was the need for more caution when using time-on-task measures for building learning analytics models. Given that today's students are more easily distracted than prior generations due to the availability and affordances of digital technologies it was strongly argued that time-on-task estimation, its issues, limits and reliability challenges warranted further consideration. With the rising amount of student distraction by digital technology, researchers should be aware of the role that noise in the LMS trace data can play in developed analytics.

Critical Appraisal: Technology seemed to try harder due to significant distraction with digitalisation of age. Time-on-task studies can estimate and measure the time spent on the content but human behaviour consists of several other innate factors which have been a great concern for learning.

Aguiar, Ambrose, Chawla, Goodrich and Brockman (2014) derived measurements of engagement from students' electronic portfolios and show how these features can be used effectively to augment the quality of predictions. One very fitting application for these techniques was that of predicting student attrition. For this study, researchers selected a range of classification methods such as Naïve Bayes, Decision trees, Logistic regression, Hellinger distance decision trees and Random forests suitable to work with imbalanced datasets. Researchers utilised a 10-fold cross validation technique. Information gain (IG) (Quinlan, 1986), gain ratio (GR) (Quinlan, 1993), chi-squared (CS) and Pearson's correlation (CR) were used as the feature selection methods. The key findings revealed that out of a set of several academic performance, demographic and ePortfolio features, the number of ePortfolio hits displayed, based on multiple metrics, showed the strongest correlation values to the outcome (student was retained/not retained). The performance of the prediction models that used only ePortfolio data was consistently better than that of models based on academic performance data alone. Using only academic performance data and a leave-one-out cross validation setup, researchers were able to identify 11 of the 48 students not retained past their first semester (out of the 429 students in the course). By adding the ePortfolio features, the model's performance dramatically improved and researchers were able to label 42 of the 48 students correctly while incurring very minor losses in accuracy regarding the retained group.

Critical Appraisal: Student engagement was measured with ePortfolios which could be considered a significant step for student retention. Number of students identified improved the number of students significantly.

Andergassen, Mödritscher and Neumann (2014) investigated potential correlations between learning results and learning management system (LMS) usage during exam preparation, focusing on practice and repetition. The study was based on 250 million log-file entries used to analyse student interactions within specific courses and overall, in the LMS. The results showed positive, albeit modest, correlations between usage variables and final exam grades. The findings for practice and repetition indicated that it was more advantageous to transfer learning to new tasks than to again repeat the same items a number of times. The study not only looks at single usage variables but also examines the distribution of the descriptive and dependent variables and uses visualisation techniques and quantiles to deal with outliers.

Critical Appraisal: A significant number of log-files entries were used to draw conclusion. Moderate correlations were observed between usage variables which indicated several other variables influencing the learning. The study could have observed and studied those too.

Buerck and Mudigonda (2014) presented an experience report based on a study of academic institutions of higher learning for improving student performance and retention. They intended, firstly, to identify the procedures that an instructor, the departmental administrators and the advising staff had to follow to ensure that intervention activities that encourage help-seeking and involvement on the part of students are optimised. Secondly, it was to improve communication with students about their participation and performance in the course and guide them to helpful resources. It was found that academic institutions intending to undertake Learning Analytics initiatives need not start with an all-out approach requiring the deployment of tools and analytical procedures subsumed under the Big Data paradigm. Rather, they can use a multi-phased approach where they may undertake small LA initiatives centred around one or a few courses, utilise existing LMS-based tools to determine, given the current constraints and technology-based affordances, the optimal set of communication, intervention and help-providing procedures so that student performance and retention are maximised. Then, based on what they have learned through this experience, they can determine the next steps needed for scaling their initiative to encompass more courses and eventually determine a path for a more complete implementation of LA.

Critical Appraisal: The study had rightly pointed out regarding multi-phased approach with small LA initiative instead of Big Data paradigm. Somewhere, learning seemed to be unprioritised with big data revolving mainly around data generation and utilisation instead to improving learning.

Chiu and Fujita (2014) explicated a method through an illustration study. It was observed that the online forums, synchronous and asynchronous offer huge and exciting data opportunities for analysing how people influence and effect one another through their interactions. The study addressed several difficulties with Statistical Discourse Analysis (SDA) and illustrated them on 1,330 asynchronous messages written and self-coded by 17 students during a 13-week online educational technology course. Both individual characteristics and message attributes were linked to participants' online messages. It was observed that men wrote more messages than women about their theories. The results showed that both individual characteristics and the micro-sequence context of recent messages' cognition and social meta-cognition affected the likelihoods of subsequent new information and theorising. Informal cognition facilitates more formal cognition. Meanwhile, social meta-cognition, in the form of questions and different opinions, had the strongest effects on subsequent new information and theoretical explanations.

Critical Appraisal: The sample size of the study was too small for the study though data generated asynchronously could be enormous.

Dunbar, Dingel and Prat-Resina (2014) described how data from institutional, learning and what we call 'developmental' analytics can be incorporated into course and curricular design by using a purposefully built analysis tool that permits the exploration of data relevant to course/curriculum design. The disconnection between data collection and analysis across academic and administrative units within institutions of higher education made it challenging to incorporate diverse data into curricular design. Understanding the factors related to student retention and success was unlikely to occur by focusing on only one unit at a time. By promoting course design informed by data from diverse units, it was more likely to understand important connections that could encourage more effective and holistic change. Facilitating evidence-based course design should begin with a faculty-driven process to identify how best to explore data across units for integration into the traditional course/curricular design. This Browser of Student and Course Objects (BoSCO) was being built in a faculty-driven process and can be used as a bridge between the analytics space and the course/curriculum design environments, therefore encouraging faculty to use analytics for course and curricular design.

Critical Appraisal: Currently, academic analytics and learning analytics are seen as two different segments of analytics. The study observed the disconnection between the two with respect to curriculum design which is mostly academic.

Gilmore (2014) applied Goffman's presentation of self in everyday life to analyse online and offline student participation in two online subjects. Mixed-methods were used to produce a fuller account of students' experiences. Second-year university students from both a discursive subject and a computational subject: Psychology and Engineering were recruited. The data were collected using LMS activity logs, student self-reporting questionnaires, Content analysis of the discussion board activities and in-depth semi-structured interviews. It was concluded that the study helped to illustrate the engagement of students at the front stage, with whom and under what circumstances. In-depth interviews explained the reason behind the drop in front stage participation. Students who were disconnected from online classmates in the front stage were regularly discussing content backstage offline at work or with family members and partners revealed through questionnaires and interviews. It was found that backstage data has the sufficient potential to add depth to the interpretation of front stage data or the lack thereof. Learning analytics and conventional research methods, could be brought together to improve engagement in online education and research learning as a whole.

Critical Appraisal: The study brought forward the significance of blended and collaborative learning. Despite the availability of online course, there was a drop in the front stage participation.

Gray, McGuinness, Owende and Carthy (2014) reviewed factors that could be used to predict academic performance, but which were currently not systematically measured in tertiary education. The study was focussed on psychometric factors of ability, personality, motivation and learning strategies. Their respective relationships with academic performance were enumerated and discussed. Regression and correlation were used for statistical interpretation. It was concluded that lack of independence, linear additivity and constant variance in the relationships between psychometric factors and academic performance suggested increasing relevance of data mining techniques, which could be further used to provide some useful insights on the role of such factors in the modelling of learning process.

Critical Appraisal: Study could have provided more and better insights on how these factors can be placed while modelling the learning process. The conclusion regarding the relationship between psychometric factors and academic performance had been established by various studies which was confirmed with respect to data mining.

Gunnarsson and Alterman (2014) explored the feasibility of using student promotions of content, in a blogosphere, to identify quality content and implications for students and instructors. The data were collected from two cases and thus data analysis came from two classes: the first with 107 students and the second with 50 students. There was a mix of undergraduate and master's students in both courses. The first class had weekly writing assignments completed in a class blogging environment. The study used data collected from the second class (50 students) to confirm the key results of the first study; despite a smaller set of promotion types, the key results were verified. The comments were graded by three undergraduate students. The comment and peer review forms were simpler – just asking if the comment or peer review met expectations – the graders could give a 0 for 'not completed', 1 for 'not good' and 2 for 'good work'. The data compiled the promotion statistics of 92 students. The use of peer promotions was explored as a tool to filter for high quality content. The data showed that students willingly used the tool and that the application of the tool provides the desired results – the promoted content was of significantly higher quality than content that was not promoted and content that was repeatedly promoted was of higher quality than content that had fewer promotions. These results had been verified by two different case studies. Other results showed that good and poor promoters could be identified. Both classifications of promoters had value: by focusing on good promoters, the reliability of quality assessment could be improved; by focusing on poor promoters, the instructor was in a better position to identify students who may be struggling. Research showed that students actively and voluntarily promoted content, identified quality material with considerable accuracy and used promotion data to select what to read. It explored the benefits of knowing which students were good and poor predictors of quality content and what instructors could do with this information in terms of feedback and guidance.

Critical Appraisal: This study apparently drew the line for content promoted and not promoted keeping in view the quality of the content. Therefore, the success and failure of LMS largely depends on the quality of content it offered. But the study provided no guidelines on how to decide if the content is good for promotion with higher quality.

Hecking, Ziebarth and Hoppe (2014) presented an analysis of resource access patterns in two recently conducted online courses. One of these was a master level university lecture taught as a blended learning course with a wide range of online learning activities and materials, including collaborative wikis, self-tests and thematic videos. The other course was offered in the form of massive open online courses (MOOC). In order to gain deeper insights into the usage of learning materials, researchers adapted methods from social network analysis and applied them to dynamic bipartite student-resource networks built from event logs of the students' resource access. By investigating the overlaps between the student–resource clusters, it was possible to identify a small set of learning material also used by more than one group of students. The analysis showed that students whose oral exams were scheduled later than those of other programmes also had different patterns of resource access during the exam preparation phase. Since the MOOC had not such a strong emphasis on group work, the students seemed to focus more on the same resources. Another interesting insight gained by the tracing of bipartite clusters during the time of the Content management course (CMC) was that the continuous interest pattern was dominant in the first weeks of the course. It was interesting to see that from week 7 on the resource access of course participants became more diverse as the course activity started to rise again after weeks of decline. By a deeper investigation of the clusters, it could be shown that there were periods in the course when students tended to access only a few resources and hence could not be allocated to a cluster.

Critical Appraisal: It was observed that MOOC content could not keep up the enrolled students engrossed throughout. After the initial weeks of rolling out the course, there was a dip during the middle of the course. Besides several other challenges, keeping up the enrolled students going with the course seemed to be another daunting and challenging task during LA work.

Jayaprakash, Moody, Lauría, Regan and Baron (2014) presented the goals and objectives of 'The Open Academic Analytics Initiative' (OAAI), depicted the process and challenges of collecting, organising and mining student data to predict academic risk and reported results on the predictive performance of those models, their portability across pilot programs at partner institutions and the results of interventions on at-risk students. For the data, sample from fall 2010 and spring 2011 were used for training the 9,938 classifiers; fall 2011 was reserved for testing purposes with 5,212 samples. Experiments were conducted to test the predictive performance of the classifiers. Researchers used Platt's (1999) sequential minimal optimisation (SMO) algorithm, chi-square, one-way ANOVA, post-hoc analysis and logistic regression models for the outputs. The research findings of the OAAI were initial evidence that predictive models can be imported from the academic context in which they were developed to different academic contexts while retaining most of their predictive power. There may be benefits associated with customising imported predictive models using local institutional data as a means to enhance their predictive power further. The research tested the portability of Predictive models and the success of intervention strategies in improving at-risk student outcomes. The results were promising as they pointed to a higher portability of learning analytics models than initially anticipated.

Critical Appraisal: The results were promising for the study but did not provide any intervention strategies as an exemplar. It would have been helpful and guiding for future studies if a few were suggested.

Kovanovic and Gašević (2014) focussed on the development of a learning analytics framework for inquiry-based digital learning. Building on the Community of Inquiry model (CoI) – a foundation commonly used in the research and practice of digital learning and teaching – this research was designed based on the existing body of knowledge. The primary means of conducting the research were quantitative methods and the investigation of empirical data from real-world, fully online, blended and massive open online courses. It included collecting trace data and online discussion transcripts from several courses and manually coding the messages in accordance with the cognitive-presence coding scheme. The data were then used for the development of a text analytics system for (semi) automated message coding. The results indicated several classes of features useful for this classification task. For example, when a message showed indicators of several phases of cognitive presence, rules of the cognitive presence coding scheme stated that a message should be coded to the highest exhibited phase.

Critical Appraisal: Study provided that the potentials were limited for pedagogical interventions due to manual coding but did not seek solutions or suggested implications for that.

Monroy, Rangel and Whitaker (2014) presented a scalable approach for integrating learning analytics into an online K-12 science curriculum. The research included examples of data visualisation based on teacher usage data along with a methodology for examining an inquiry-based science program. With more than one million students and fifty thousand teachers using the curriculum, a massive and rich dataset were continuously updated. This repository depicted teacher and student usage and offered exciting opportunities to leverage data to improve both teaching and learning. Data were used from a medium-sized school district, comprising 53 schools, 1,026 teachers and nearly one-third of a million curriculum visits during the 2012–2013 school year. This growing dataset also posed technical challenges such as data storage, complex aggregation and analyses with broader implications for pedagogy, big data and learning. The purpose of implementing the study was to increase teacher and student use of the curriculum through improved design. The strategy was meant to answer three key questions about the curriculum; firstly, how can they incorporate the LA data into a broader effort to understand how a digital curriculum is used? Secondly, how can they leverage the LA data to support teachers and administrators? Thirdly, how can they integrate the LA data into the evaluation of the curriculum's impact? It was concluded that LA has the potential to bring important changes to K-12 education research and development if implemented with a pedagogically sound, mixed methods strategy. It was also learned that LA data painted an incomplete picture of what teachers do in their classrooms with the curriculum. By bringing in more traditional measures of use, such as surveys, interviews and classroom observation, researchers were able to contextualise some of the findings gleaned from the LA data.

Critical Appraisal: As an early attempt at LA in school education, it was clearly observed that LA data presented an incomplete picture of classroom transactions. Later studies suggested bringing in traditional measures rather than providing solutions to overcome these hindrances.

Scheffel, Drachsler, Stoyanov and Specht (2014) proposed a first outline of a five-dimensional framework of quality indicators for learning analytics to aid standardise the evaluation of LA tools. The work was initiated due to lack of available evaluation standards defining quality indicators of LA tools. It was a study of group concept mapping (GCM) with experts from the LA domain to identify a list of quality indicators. After creating a point map, a cluster map including cluster labels, experts' ratings on importance and feasibility of the statements, taking the rating maps, the ladder graph and the go-zone graphs into account, the first outline of the framework was proposed with the five criteria and quality indicators: first, *Objectives* (*Awareness*, *Reflection*, *Motivation*, *Behavioural Change*); second, *Learning Support* (*Perceived Usefulness*, *Recommendation*, *Activity Classification*, *Detection of Students at Risk*); third, *Learning Measures and Output* (*Comparability*, *Effectiveness*, *Efficiency*, *Helpfulness*); fourth, *Data Aspects* (*Transparency*, *Data Standards*, *Data Ownership*, *Privacy*) and; fifth, *Organisational Aspects* (*Availability*, *Organisational Change, Implementation*, *Training of Educational Stakeholders*). As most participants of the study work at a university and are more research- than practice-oriented, the author thought of it to be interesting to see if the framework and its quality indicators would change, in case (high) school teachers or more practice-oriented university faculty were involved in the process.

Critical Appraisal: The above-mentioned quality indicators can be useful to anyone who would be planning LA tools. But these indicators may have been further specified for school teachers or university staff. School teachers' involvement was limited, therefore above indicators may serve university level more than school education.

Worsley and Blikstein (2014) presented in their study that learning analytics and educational data mining were introducing a number of new techniques and frameworks for studying learning. The scalability and complexity of these novel techniques had afforded new ways for enacting education research and had helped scholars gain new insights into human cognition and learning. Nonetheless, there remained some domains for which pure computational analysis was currently infeasible. One such area, which was particularly important were open-ended, hands-on, engineering design tasks. These open-ended tasks were becoming increasingly prevalent in both K-12 and post-secondary learning institutions, as educators were adopting this approach in order to teach students real-world science and engineering skills (e.g., the 'Maker Movement'). This study highlighted findings from a combined human–computer analysis of students as they completed a short engineering design task. The study uncovered novel insights and served to advance the field's understanding of engineering design patterns. More specifically, this study used machine learning on hand-coded video data to identify general patterns in engineering design and develop a fine-grained representation of how experience relates to engineering practices. Finally, the study concluded with ideas on how the specific findings from this study could be used to improve engineering education and the nascent field of 'making' and digital fabrication in education. It was also discussed how human–computer collaborative analyses can grow the learning analytics community and make learning analytics more central to education research.

Critical Appraisal: LA's early adaptation was in higher education and not in K-12. Yet the study discussed both the levels on one plateau. Engineering and school education pedagogy are entirely different and different views must be inserted related to the observation of both.

Ye and Biswas (2014) worked on the early dropout and low completion rate problem in MOOCs. Data were analysed from video lectures, weekly quizzes and peer assessments from the ten-week Pattern-Oriented Software Architectures (POSA) MOOC course. Two discrete variables were the dropout week (when a student watched less than 10% of the remaining lectures and stopped submitting assignments) and the final grade (normal certificate or distinction) upon completing the course. The results showed that finer-grained temporal information increases the predictive power in the early phases of the course by Vanderbilt University. The efforts were towards going beyond traditional methods and demonstrated the advantages of extracting more fine-grained features for analysis and early prediction.

Critical Appraisal: The LA work clearly pointed towards the serious problem of drop-outs from an online course. This situation was worrisome as LA seemed to put in efforts towards data stories rather than improving learning outcomes.

Brooks, Thompson and Greer (2013) investigated three case studies about applying information visualisation techniques to lecture capture video systems. The principal goal was to better understand how students used these systems and what visualisations made for useful learning analytics. Three different methods were applied to viewership data aimed at understanding student re-watching behaviour, temporal patterns for a single course and how usage can be compared between groups of students. For the case studies a second year undergraduate Chemistry course was examined using traditional lectures to 546 students in multiple sections. Examinations and assignments between sections were the same. Only 333 watched video content for at least five minutes with a participation rate of 61%. The results led to gain insight into how learners used lecture capture, how this aligned with activities over an academic term and how student populations differed in their use of lecture capture systems. Applying visual analytics to 'big data' problems was not without caveats – the effects of parameters for charts including time offsets, resolution on heartbeat data, aggregation into bins for heat maps and histograms and determining the right data to process made discussion and prototyping essential steps in the process. How to provide visual learning analytics to different stakeholders was also an issue that was carefully considered. The work was aimed at instructional designers and instructors who were deeply interested in their courses. It was interesting also in showing visualisations to students and instructors to help them gain insight into their learning and teaching and how that related to usage of technology like lecture capture.

Critical Appraisal: The study is a clear example that content can be created and presented but interest cannot be generated from outside but within. Students did not go through the content entirely which is evident from temporal analysis. It also reminds technology of human connection for teaching.

Dimopoulos, Petropoulou, Boloudakis and Retalis (2013) presented a new assessment tool, called Learning Analytics Enriched Rubric (LAe-R). Based on the popular assessment technique of rubrics, LAe-R contains 'enriched' criteria and grading levels that are related to data extracted from the analysis of learners' interaction and learning behaviour in an e-learning environment. As the assessment of students' performance in online learning environments is a challenging and demanding task for teachers, Moodle's platform offers several assessment tools. LAe-R has been developed as a plug-in for the Moodle LMS. The findings of a case study showed that LAe-R is a quite usable tool highly appreciated by teachers and students. LAe-R was developed with the aim to support teachers in their ongoing summative assessment tasks, using a variety of Learning and Interaction Analysis Indicators (LIAI) embedded in criteria. Despite its advanced assessment features and customisation options, the tool was fondly accepted and adopted by educators.

Critical Appraisal: Although Moodle has simple settings but for a novice to create a course on this platform would require a number of trial-and-error attempts. It also provides free space for a very limited data which may get exhausted too soon with a limited number of participants. LAeR is a plug-in assessment tool whereas the study mentioned that Moodle already has assessment tools. It was a tool created despite having several already available tools.

Ferguson and Shum (2012) reviewed some of the 'tectonic forces' reshaping the learning landscape. They introduced five categories of analysis though not entirely exhaustive in nature. The first two categories were inherently social, while the other three can be 'socialised', i.e. usefully applied in social settings. First, social network analytics where interpersonal relationships define social platforms; second, discourse analytics where language is a primary tool for knowledge negotiation and construction; third, content analytics where user-generated content is one of the defining characteristics of Web 2.0; fourth, disposition analytics where intrinsic motivation to learn is a defining feature of online social media and lies at the heart of engaged learning and innovation; and lastly, context analytics where mobile computing is transforming access to both people and content.

Critical Appraisal: Largely, the paper presented a larger landscape of LA use providing five categories. It wasn't exhaustive in nature if they're analysed now with several other aspects like academic analytics coming into mainframe.

Kruse and Pongsajapan (2012) proposed a student-centric, inquiry-based model of analytics that puts the tools and premises of analytics into the hands of students, empowering them as metacognitive agents of their own learning and understanding. In their thought paper, they emphasised that the future of learning analytics is concurrently full of possibility as well as in need of caution. As Universities are keen to see what analytics can do for them, conversations on analytics are enthusiastic and lively. Nonetheless, the path many analytics implementations are taking may not be a sustainable one, with ethical concerns and questions of meaningful effect bringing much-needed sobriety to a conversation that might otherwise lead higher education astray with hype. Their article proposed a new focus for analytics and that focus is both simple and traditional – student learning. By rejecting the flashy appeal of big data and refocusing on the lifelong learning of our students, analytics will be an approach worth championing in its true sense.

Critical Appraisal: The thought paper looked at LA as a possibility for universities and not school education. This was emphasising student learning but never realising that it begins at a young age and with formal education, in schools. As an early thought, it rightly pointed out the over-emphasising of big data rather than usefulness for students.

Lauría, Baron, Devireddy, Sundararaju and Jayaprakash (2007) used analytics in improving student retention by identifying under-performing students early and making necessary interventions to ensure that they improve their academic performance and graduate at the University of Alabama, Sinclair Community College and Northern Arizona University. The methodological framework consisted of six phases, namely collect data, rescale/transform data, partition data, balance training data, train models and evaluate models using test data. A data sample corresponding to fall 2010 undergraduate students was gathered from four different sources: Students biographic data and course related data; Course management (Sakai) event data and Sakai's Grade book data. Datasets were joined and data were cleaned, recoded and aggregated to produce an input data file of 3877 records corresponding to courses taken by students. The research concluded with an emphasis on the need of introducing the model development approaches that can be used in practical settings to predict academic performance and carry out early detection of students at risk.

Critical Appraisal: Being one of the early efforts on LA, the work suggested for a model much needed at that time. It worked mainly on secondary data so the interpretation can be relative regarding student at risk with data of student enrolment.

Feedback with Learning Analytics

This section presents a review of the studies on Feedback with LA. The review has helped to understand the research trends in the field of Feedback with Learning Analytics which is the focus of the study.

Cavalcanti, Diego, Mello, Mangaroska, Nascimento, Freitas and Gašević (2020) presented a substantial research based on feedback. According to the work, feedback is a crucial element in helping students identify gaps and assess their learning progress. In online courses, feedback becomes even more critical as it is one of the resources where the teacher interacts directly with the student. However, with the growing number of students enrolled in online learning, it becomes a challenge for instructors to provide good quality feedback that helps the student self-regulate. In this context, this paper proposed a content analysis of feedback text provided by instructors based on different indicators of good feedback. A random forest classifier was trained and evaluated at different feedback levels. The results achieved outcomes up to 87% and 0.39 of accuracy and Cohen's κ, respectively. The paper also provides insights into the most influential textual features of feedback that predict feedback quality.

Critical Appraisal: The paper has contributed significantly towards the role and importance of Feedback in a classroom situation. Somehow, it also points out towards a good student-teacher ratio as the complexity increased with more online students and thereafter the quality of feedback. It indicated positive contribution of feedback for the improvement of learning but with a condition of the relevance and quality of such feedback.

Iraj, Fudge, Faulkner, Pardo and Kovanović (2020) also researched on the essential element of feedback in the field of Learning Analytics. According to the researchers, feedback is a major factor of student success within higher education learning. However, recent changes – such as increased class sizes and socio-economic diversity of the student population – challenged the provision of effective student feedback. Although the use of educational technology for personalised feedback to diverse students had gained traction, the feedback gap believed to exist: educators wondered which students responded to feedback and which did not. In this study, a set of trackable Call to Action (CTA) links was embedded in two sets of feedback messages focusing on students' time management, with the goal of (1) examining the association between feedback engagement and course success and (2), to predict students' reaction to the provided feedback. We also conducted two focus groups to further examine students' perception of provided feedback messages. Our results revealed that early engagement with the feedback was associated with higher chances of succeeding in the course. Likewise, previous engagement with feedback was highly predictive of students' engagement in the future and also that certain student sub-populations, (e.g., female students), were more likely to engage than others. Such insight enabled instructors to ask 'why' questions, improved feedback processes and narrowed the feedback gap. Practical implications of their findings were observed to be relevant.

Critical Appraisal: The research focussed on feedback gaps and how to reduce them to predict students' engagement further. It also examined students' perception of the provided feedback to improve the feedback quality. The study emphasised factors such as socio-economic diversity and student population. Though this study pointed towards female engagement more than others, the overall effect of feedback was observed to be positive.

Wang and Eberhard (2020) made a presentation about a teaching staff's journey of incremental use of technologies to support students' learning. A programme was designed for a cohort to work through the courses together; the cohorts come from diverse backgrounds. English was a second language for most of the students. The researchers wanted to use some of the techniques from the flipped classroom approach and turned the paper-based tutorial worksheet into online quizzes using the quiz function in the LMS. Researchers noticed a big improvement in the classroom, students were more engaged and they felt comfortable answering questions in class. The quiz statistics also allowed researchers to focus their energy in class on topics and areas where students were more confused and skip the topics students understood well. Students' feedback on these preparation quizzes was positive. After the success of utilising existing technology to change how the author supports students, the author was introduced to another tool, On Task. The author obtained student data from these online quizzes, as well as other learning analytics data from LMS (e.g., participation, page view, test results). Through further analysis, the author was able to use the On Task tool to provide detailed and individualised feedback to the students on the topic areas that they may be weaker on and provide guidance to these students. The individualised feedback was expected to help students to improve their academic performance and attainment. Students could potentially feel more valued, as the feedback they received was generated according to their own personal assessments, consequently enhancing their engagement.

Critical Appraisal: The study utilised the Flipped classroom to engage students in the English language-learning with LMS, where feedback played a key role to improve the performance further. The study also observed the positive effect of feedback on the language learners with individualised learning and attainment. Student feedback was also positive. Thus, it was interesting to observe a similar situation in different demographic conditions.

Mori, Sakamoto and Mendori (2019) aimed to improve learner's activities by feedback based on learning history. They developed a real time viewing status feedback system on LMS. The system collected page transition of the teaching materials during the lectures. The system gave the collected information visually to teachers and students. The students could confirm how many students were viewing the previous or subsequent pages or same page as the teacher. Through this study, they confirmed that the collected information affected students learning activities.

Critical Appraisal: The study used learning history of students to provide feedback and confirmed that there was an effect of feedback. But it neither informed about the quality of feedback nor the feedback from the students. Providing the feedback and learning content had to be simultaneously compared with improvement in the learning outcome driven by analytics of data and student achievement. Therefore, the present study tried to collect student feedback too.

Vigentini, Liu and Lim (2019) explored tools used to provide feedback at scale, through a workshop at LAK which shifted the attention to data-driven approaches to support the provision of feedback and the students, especially considering how they perceived the feedback and what they did with the feedback received. The workshop aimed to bring together scholars and practitioners to find a common ground for showcasing interesting examples of effective feedback and explored what and how data can be used to improve the process and richness of feedback for both learners and educators. Key outcomes were a better understanding of approaches and existing cases of good practice.

Critical Appraisal: The theoretical paper provided insight into the data-driven approach to use feedback and how was it perceived by students and what they do with them. Feedback may be a constructive step towards student learning provided how is it acted upon further.

Jørnø and Gynther (2018) established that actionable insights currently are viewed from what they had labelled a data-informed decision-making perspective. It was argued for greater consideration of the roles of perspective and action. It matters who has acted to produce the data. Insights are a significant way of creating a feedback loop in a system or actor's action competency and capabilities. It also matters what the producer's intermediate and ultimate goals are to collect the data. Insights are 'actionable' because it is possible to act upon them as feedback information to promote a better result. 'Actionable insights' are constituted by actions. Assuming a sole goal in a multivariate organisation with many different actors (i.e., increasing retention or outcome) skews the feedback cycle and transforms learning practices that are ends in themselves into means to institutional ends, not unlike the scorned practice of 'teaching to the test'. They focussed on the importance of the feedback loop between action capabilities, data, and end goals in relation to actionable insights.

Critical Appraisal: 'Actionable insights' provide valuable information for teachers in the classroom. They trigger the feedback cycle and are significant means to execute the purpose of improving learning outcomes.

Shum, Sándor, Goldsmith, Bass, and McWilliams (2017) detailed the methodology about designing a writing analytics application, by which informally expressed rubrics are modelled as formal rhetorical patterns. It was a capability delivered by a novel web application so designed. As reflective writing was still a novel genre to compose in for many students and researchers alike, even tutors may be inexperienced in its assessment. As such conditions set a challenging context for automated solutions, natural language processing might help address the challenge of providing real time, quick formative feedback on draft writing. Preliminary tests conducted on an independently human-annotated corpus were encouraging. It showed improvements from the first to second version, but with a wide scope for improvement. A range of issues, like, the prevalence of false positives in the tests, areas for future technical improvements, the issue of gaming the system and the participatory design process that has enabled work across disciplinary boundaries to develop the prototype to its current state were discussed. Thus, the potential of providing instant formative feedback on draft writing was identified for student work that would otherwise receive no feedback due to the limited availability of educator time.

Critical Appraisal: The educator's time and management of feedback remained a matter of concern in this study and it's observed to be important element of timely feedback. Also, improvements with feedback were observed but with wide scope of improvements. It meant that proper planning should always be considered while deliberating on learning improvements with feedback.

Berland, Baker and Blikstein (2014) investigated the relevance of educational data mining (EDM) or learning analytics to provide a basis for quantitative research on constructionist learning. For constructionist learning environments, it is of particular importance that learners be given process feedback to help them learn and build what they want to build. Supporting the analysis of learner data, EDM also well suited to give feedback in learning situations, through providing a basis for understanding where and when students need support. Real time feedback has long been a hallmark of constructionism which supported the study. They explored potential collaborations between researchers in the EDM and constructionist traditions; supporting the understanding of learning in a range of learning interactions, educational data mining and learning analytics methods supported the provision of automated feedback to learners.

Critical Appraisal: The study supported and emphasised the significance of feedback in a constructionist learning environment but provided for automated feedback to learners. The quality of feedback may get affected being irrelevant or out of context when the feedback is automated irrespective of the errors and mistakes committed by the learner.

Papamitsiou and Economides (2014) sought to identify and formalise temporal parameters as predictors of performance ('temporal learning analytics' or TLA) and examine students' temporal behaviour during testing (i.e., in terms of time-spent). The goal was to specify a functional set of parameters that would be embedded in an adaptive assessment system in order to contribute towards the personalisation of feedback services. The model explained the results from the first case study that was the almost 63% variance (R2) in Actual Performance (AP). In the model, Total Time to Answer Correct (TTAC) and Total Time to Answer Wrong (TTAW) were the temporal factors that had a statistically significant effect on AP. Self-reported data gathered through questionnaires into the system's initial results highlighted a detected trend that TTAC and TTAW had a significant direct positive and negative effect on AP respectively. They both had a significant direct positive effect on (un-)certainty. Moreover, Goal Expectancy (GE) was a determinant of TTAC and TTAW and (un-)certainty was a determinant of AP as well. In a sense, (un-)certainty seemed to increase student efforts to answer the questions. In addition to this, the detected indirect effect of GE on (un-)certainty indicated that students' perception of preparation influenced their cautiousness.

Critical Appraisal: The study is an early attempt to personalise the feedback with online assessments. It attempted to involve students for improving outcomes by timely analytics of the responses given during the assessment. It had increased certainty as well as uncertainty of the effect of achieving the goal expectancy. Though an early attempt for assessment – it opened up several other avenues of using feedback and evaluation as a medium to improve learning outcomes.

Ebner and Schön (2013) developed two apps for testing competences in multiplication developed at Graz University of Technology. They estimated the competence level of every user and adapt to their individual development in this domain. In the foreground they gave feedback in a compact and clearly arranged way to the single student and the teachers of classes. The analysis of the data during a longer term depicted that the process of testing and giving feedback has a positive effect on learning. LA brings new insights into the classroom. The research was started with the expectance to improve the diagnostic of some problems with the multiplication table and multi-digit multiplications. The results showed that automated precise testing and feedback can be seen as an individual assistance and an effort to an effective learning process. Looking at the unique feature of LA, their first attempts would be in language education. As a trainer is implemented to measure the reading competences of school children, there are some simple partial competences which could be observed, measured, and perhaps trained without appreciable investments – and without additional stresses and strains for the teachers. They were finally able to summarise that LA is an important step to give the learners precise feedback. This shows how teaching of tomorrow can support and promote each individual learner exactly at the stage needed.

Critical Appraisal: Study positively supports the role and significance of learning analytics with feedback not only for students but for teachers as well. The app was developed at the university and used at the school which is an excellent example of bringing together the need and service in education. However, the app was developed for teaching Mathematics, which has a fixed set of steps and rules relatively as compared with language. The study also claimed to have a venture in language education, but language teaching is different from Mathematics. Therefore, it would be interesting to observe the outcome of the present study and compare it further with this one.

Anjewierden (2012) conducted a study with the aim of adapting to contribute to make learning environments better and easier to use for students. An example of a learning environment that is pedagogically interesting and well-engineered is *Betty's Brain*. According to the review of the work the current version of *Betty's Brain* took many years and much iteration to develop, with contributions from researchers with different backgrounds. Something similar was the case for the 'process' of achieving adaptation. This 'process' also takes time and perhaps even more importantly, it requires researchers with different backgrounds working together. There was also a pedagogical angle, identifying patterns that were interesting and associating patterns with feedback. There was a need for 'pedageers', a contraction of pedagogical engineers. A pedageer, as a singular noun, does not exist, but one can think of pedageering as the science of designing learning environments that result from thoughtful cooperation between researchers with a pedagogical or an engineering background. The studies with the collision and electrical circuit environments were conducted in secondary schools in The Netherlands. The researchers had to book computer rooms in these schools, install the software, negotiate with system managers to obtain the necessary permissions and perform other logistical operations. The students had to move from the classroom to the computer rooms. In other words, integrating inquiry learning into the school curriculum was nontrivial. Several secondary schools in The Netherlands gave tablets to their students and for most science subjects study books were available for these devices. Later, students did not have to move to a special computer room anymore and the use of educational software could consequently be more easily integrated into the curriculum. If inquiry learning environments were made available on these tablets, the implications may be significant, for both science education and inquiry learning. Not a few hundred, for the collision and electrical circuit environments, but thousands of students would have easy access. The social relevance for making learning environments adaptive could increase likewise. During the research it was observed that students used the feedback from the agents based on the quality of the models they created. Researchers did not know how students used the feedback and an analysis of the process data provided an explanation. Another direction for future research is finding patterns related to pedagogical concepts like 'floundering' and '(un)systematic' behaviour.

Critical Appraisal: The study experimented with the famous *Betty's Brain* version and provided significant implications for science education and inquiry learning. But it neither kept a track of the feedback given to students that the system provided nor made a follow up what students did with that feedback. The study also brought out infrastructural hindrances in conducting such studies in a developed country like Netherland though later it was resolved by providing students with tablets.

Leelawong and Biswas (2008) presented the idea that teaching others is a powerful way to learn as it is intuitively compelling and supported by research literature. Researchers developed computer-based, domain-independent *Teachable Agents* that students could teach using a visual representation. The students queried their agent to monitor their learning and problem-solving behaviour. This motivated the students to learn more so they could teach their agent to perform better. This study presented a teachable agent called *Betty's Brain* that combined learning by teaching with self-regulated learning feedback to promote deep learning and understanding in science domains. A study was conducted in a 5th grade science classroom which compared three versions of the system: first, a version where the students were taught by an agent, second, a baseline learning by teaching version and third, a learning by teaching version where participant students were given feedback on self-regulated learning strategies and other domain content. The results indicated that all three groups showed learning gains during a main study where students learned about river ecosystems, but the two learning by teaching groups performed better than the group that was taught. These observed differences continued in the transfer study, but the gap between the baseline learning by teaching and self-regulated learning group decreased. However, there were indications that self-regulated learning feedback better prepared students to learn in new domains, even when they no longer had access to the self-regulation environment.

Critical Appraisal: It was another study that used *Betty's Brain* for 5th graders to teach Science with self-regulated learning which affirms the usage of educational technology to teach Science. The study had shown learning gains in the three self-regulated learning group but not as high as the other two teaching groups. But this gap reduced gradually also indicating that the feedback better prepared students to learn in new domains.

Learning Analytics in School

This section presents a review of studies on Learning Analytics in schools. The review has helped to understand the research trends in the field of Learning Analytics at the school level education which is the focus of the study.

Crossley, Karumbaiah, Ocumpaugh, Labrum and Baker (2020) built on prior research by leveraging natural language processing (NLP), click-stream analyses and survey data to predict students' mathematics success and math identity (namely, self-concept, interest, and value of mathematics). Specifically, they combined NLP tools designed to measure lexical sophistication, text cohesion and sentiment with analyses of student click-stream data within an online mathematics tutoring system. Then, they combined these data sources to predict elementary students' success within the system as well as components of their math identity as measured though a standardised survey. Data from 147 students were examined longitudinally over a year of study. The results indicated links between math success and non-cognitive measures of math identity. Additionally, the results indicated that math identity was strongly predicted by click-stream variables and the production of more lexically sophisticated and cohesive language. In addition, significant variance in math identity was explained by affective and cognitive variables. The results indicated that NLP and click-stream data could be combined to provide insights into non-cognitive constructs such as math identity.

Critical Appraisal: The study presented a deeper insight into click-stream data with Mathematics identity but Mathematics aptitude is another significant dimension related to the variables involved. A cross-sectional study could also have presented more insights related to the study.

Lewis, Anderson and Carroll (2020) explored a system that attempted to maximise high school students' sense of choice when selecting elective subjects. The researchers proposed that individual schools can tailor the combinations of subjects they offered to maximise the number of prospective students who can study their preferred subjects, potentially increasing enrolment numbers and academic outcomes while also reducing administrative overheads. They analysed the underlying computational problem encountered in this task and describe a suitable AI-based optimisation algorithm that was made available for free download. Some outcomes of using this method on a small number of case study schools were also discussed.

Critical Appraisal: Using AI to assist students for selection of elective subjects was a creative idea. This presented the choices visually to the students.

It also suggests that technology is clever but its users should be not only clever but creative too in order to explore the possibilities. A pilot study is always needed before implementing the technology for the main study.

Ahmad Khanlari, Gaoxia Zhu and Marlene Scardamalia (2019) presented an exploratory study which aimed to assess the extent to which elementary-school students within knowledge building communities work productively with ideas across content areas. The knowledge building pedagogy, with its 12 principles and associated technology, Knowledge Forum®, provided multifaceted support for linking ideas across disciplines and communities. Toward that end they examined 'crisscrossing topics' – student use of concepts from multiple content areas – to explore the extent to which students think and theorise across disciplinary boundaries, use concepts found in curriculum guidelines at and beyond their grade level and generate cross-topic notes that advance discourse. Results showed that elementary school students engaged in knowledge building can extend knowledge boundaries and bring a considerable range of conceptual content to their work, resulting in productive discourse threads that contribute to community knowledge.

Critical Appraisal: The study identified knowledge building communities to work with students but did not define or specify the role of the teacher. Though, how the discourses shaped the understanding of conceptual content and how it was assessed, the study could have delved deeper.

Holstein, McLaren and Aleven (2019) delved on the notion that involving stakeholders throughout the creation of new educational technologies can help ensure their usefulness and usability in real-world contexts. Their article presented a detailed case study of the iterative co-design of Lumilo, a wearable, real-time learning analytics tool for teachers working in AI-enhanced K-12 classrooms. In the process, they argued that the co-design of LA systems requires new kinds of prototyping methods. They introduced one of their own prototyping methods, REs, to address unique challenges of co-prototyping data-driven algorithmic systems such as LA tools. Their work presented the first end-to-end demonstration in the literature of how non-technical stakeholders can participate throughout the whole design process for a complex LA system – from early generative phases to the selection and tuning of analytics to evaluation in real-world contexts. They concluded with a summary of methodological recommendations for future LA co-design efforts.

Critical Appraisal: AI should be a tool to reduce a teacher's workload and wearing another gadget to keep track of learners may be viewed critically by teachers themselves. Also, it was a methodological paper whose practical implications are yet to be explored and yet unforeseen.

Liu, Liu, Pan, Zou and Li (2019) observed that little research on problem-based learning (PBL) existed for disadvantaged middle school students, especially students who were considered at risk of failing academically. To promote inclusion and success for all learners, they shared their study on at-risk students using learning analytics. They examined the science knowledge of a group of at-risk middle school students as they used a multimedia-enriched PBL environment. The results showed that these students significantly improved their science knowledge after they were engaged in PBL learning. While there were no differences in the scores between the genders, the gain scores from pre- to post-tests in science knowledge for the girls were larger. Visualisations were used to present the findings from qualitative data. Such research provided much needed insights on the effect of PBL for all students.

Critical Appraisal: The study is a substantial effort to help at risk students of failing academically. It was also observed that it was to promote inclusion which remains unclear if the students were physically disadvantaged, socially, or otherwise.

Wei, Cutler, Macfadyen and Shirazi (2019) presented an argument that the evolution of learning analytics (LA) systems and tools offered unprecedented opportunities to make use of insights from learning data to promote effective teaching and learning practices. However, a significant gap still exists between what is possible and what is being applied in practice. Little is known about instructors' interests and concerns in relation to implementing LA for supporting classroom practices. Their study aimed to address the gap by identifying tertiary teachers' interests and concerns regarding the implementation of LA in teaching and learning. Interviews and surveys were used to collect responses from faculty members of a large research-intensive university. Findings revealed tertiary instructors' degree of familiarity with LA and their attitudes to, interest in and concerns about using LA tools in various contexts. Discussions about how to take actions to enhance teaching and learning practices with the implementation of LA were provided.

Critical Appraisal: The study has pointed out what LA field has been observing for a decade. The gap between LA researchers, practitioners and the end-users i.e. teachers and educators has widened. Several suggestions have been offered to reduce the gap already and the study has supported the notion with a survey among the tertiary instructors. It would have been beneficial if the problem faced by those instructors could have been discussed and addressed accordingly.

Zheng, Fancsali, Ritter and Berman (2019) presented a study related to predictive modelling in the Mathematics subject at the school level with assessments. They extended predictive models of math test scores and achievement levels from existing literature and specified six categories of models that incorporate information about student prior knowledge, demographics and performance within the MATHia intelligent tutoring system. Linear regression, ordinal logistic regression and random forest regression and classification models were learned within each category and generalised over a sample of 23,000+ learners in Grades 6, 7 and 8 over three academic years in Miami-Dade County Public Schools. After briefly exploring hierarchical models of this data, they discussed a variety of technical and practical applications, limitations and open questions related to their work, especially concerning the potential use of instructional platforms like MATHia as a replacement for time-consuming standardised tests.

Critical Appraisal: The standardised tests shall remain standardised for their purpose and utility. These tests may be conducted online but Mathematics being logical and numerical, their properties remain the same.

Cejnar and Kao (2018) described a novel real-time learning analytics tool providing teachers and educators feedback on actual computer usage in order to improve teaching and policies. As Australian K-12 classrooms have adopted 1:1 computer use, however, academic results have been inconsistent arguably due to a lack of ICT skills and distraction. They used an app transmitting student activities to a cloud-based Artificial Intelligence (AI) algorithm to analyse in real-time students' classroom use of computers. Data from 549 students from 4 schools were collected over 9 months aged between 7–12 years. The results depicted that computers were used for 20 minutes per lesson; overall 17% was Off-task, but for 20% of students, a full 30% was Off-task. Distractibility Index (DI) combining Off-task with task switching was steady in years 7–10, but dramatically improved in years 11–12. Distractibility was reduced by a significant 31% in a subgroup of students given feedback of their DI data. The findings demonstrated the feasibility, utility and objective measurement. The student interest in using feedback and the consequent persistent reduction in distractibility was the most exciting result achieved and supports the well documented utility of timely formative feedback for self-regulation and learning.

Critical Appraisal: The study is a good example of timely feedback improving consistency and self-regulation. It is to be observed that the study was conducted in an environment where the computer ratio was 1:1 and despite the fact that students lacked ICT skills with a certain amount of distraction. Therefore, the study is an example and a reference case for infrastructure ratio as well as the lack of ICT skills.

Ferguson (2018) undertook a project to map the school's data landscape in partnership with a secondary school in Sydney Australia. A diverse set of contexts was identified including ethics, legislation, teaching and learning, decision-making and planning in addition to the data sources and stakeholders producing and consuming data. Thus, a high-level data landscape was mapped and ideas for how to extend the work were shared with the school. Their brief report illustrated an emerging methodology for mapping data landscapes in schools.

Critical Appraisal: Though the study was taken up to deduce a methodology for school level learning by generating high-level data landscape but an understanding among teachers is the need of the hour to promote LA at school level.

Liu, Stamper and Davenport (2018) described a generalisable approach for a more efficient yet rich sense-making of temporal data during student's use of intelligent tutoring systems. During the study, a multi-step approach was used that involved coarse-grain temporality, learning trajectories across knowledge components. It was to identify and further explore 'focal' moments worthy of more fine-grain, context-rich analysis. The data were collected from a classroom study in which students engaged in a Chemistry Virtual Lab tutoring system. Participants were 59 students at a high school in the greater Pittsburgh area who were enrolled in a honours' chemistry classes. They participated in four Stoichiometry modules of the ChemVLab+ educational tutor over the course of three weeks. The captured videos were exported from Camtasia for each session, resulted in one mpeg4 screen video for each unique student and session of ChemVLab+ use. The learning trajectory visualisations were assessed and the work served as illustrative examples of how this generalisable approach can assist to handle large volumes of rich data at multiple levels of granularity. It was proposed that this analytic approach could be useful, more broadly, to any branch of learning analytics research wherein data from multiple sources or modalities can be integrated for analysis.

Critical Appraisal: The study focussed on individual learning but does not delve on at-risk students or drop-outs or lagging students. Also, the duration of the course is too short to draw any conclusions from it.

Divjak and Vondra (2016) presented a study where far less research and prediction about the role and implementation of learning analytics in pre-tertiary education (schools) is available compared to higher education. The research was conducted in primary and secondary schools in Croatia. The research interrogated the possibilities of applying learning analytics in the pre-tertiary educational sector and the similarities and differences between higher education and pre-tertiary education related to the implementation and usefulness of learning analytics. It examined the specific challenges of ethics and privacy issues of LA in pre-tertiary education, the most useful data sources about learners in pre-tertiary education and to integrate data from face-to-face classroom with data from LMS and other e-sources. Considering the research gap in the pre-tertiary learning analytics area, the users' needs identification was conducted in two phases: collecting the set of their possible questions and assessing their relevance for different user groups. Based on students' and teachers' needs, further analysis of availability and reliability of data performed. Finally, taking into account the results of this analysis, different dashboards for different users were designed. Besides, students (learners) were also interested in impact of various factors on student achievement, such as family social status, school equipment and design, working atmosphere, school practices, team work, absences from school, time spent on independent work etc.

Critical Appraisal: The study delved on too many areas like classroom data and LMS data, factors affecting students' achievement, privacy issues, user's need identification and many others like designing dashboard etc. in a vague form. All these issues may be tackled together in an orderly and systematic manner.

Ferguson, Brasher, Clow, Cooper, Hillaire, Mittelmeier, Rienties, Ullmann and Vuorikari (2016) presented a policy document to help European policymakers for high-quality, innovative ways of learning and teaching through LA. For the school level education, some inventory of tools, practice and policies were proposed. The tools suggested were *ASSISTments, Bettermarks, Bingel, Cito LUVS, Civitas Learning, Cognitive Tutor software, Conexus – Vokal, FFT Aspire, itslearning, Metacog, Schoolzilla, SNAPP and VitalSource CourseSmart*. These assessment tools were described according to their roles of analytics, data source, supply model, ethics and privacy.

Critical Appraisal: The policy document suggested a number of online assessment tools which may be made available to teachers for online assessment but assessment of life skills need teacher presence and assistance. Also, data privacy and publication has remained a greater concern even at higher education level whereas school level has the complexities of dealing with children below legal age.

Rodríguez-Triana, Vozniuk and Gillet (2016) carried out a Go-Lab European project devoted to promote STEM (Science, Technology, Engineering and Mathematics) education by means of pedagogical guidelines based on blended Inquiry-Based Learning (IBL), authoring tools for rich open educational resources and online labs. They analysed the orchestration needs of expert teachers in inquiry learning and STEM and provided a set of Learning Analytics (LA) apps to address them. They designed and built three sample apps to address the identified main awareness needs of the Go-Lab teachers. These apps target common scenario where each of the students does their individual work. The three LA apps – Online Users, Student Time Spent and Submitted Reports which, based on the context description, provided visualisations of the student activity to support teacher awareness and reflection. Real-time awareness tools were well received by the teachers both in terms of usability and applicability. They stated that the tools helped them to monitor the progress of the students in the classroom but they could be also useful in order to have evidence of the work done at home. However, during the evaluation it was noticed that some students were not happy about others seeing their progress. Here, the questions of students' data privacy are worth investigating.

Critical Appraisal: When data privacy has remained a greater concern globally, it would be interesting to observe how the education sector tackles the same, especially, when children without their parents' consent cannot take decision and need their approval for all their activities.

Segedy, Kinnebrew and Biswas (2015) presented their work on developing and evaluating *coherence analysis* (CA), a novel approach to interpreting students' learning behaviours in open-ended computer-based learning environments (OELEs). CA focuses on the learner's ability to seek out, interpret and apply information encountered while working in OELEs. To validate their approach, researchers applied CA to data from a recent classroom study with *Betty's Brain*. Results showed a clear relationship between CA-derived metrics, prior skill levels, task performance and learning. Taken together, these results provided insight into students' Self-Regulated Learning (SRL) processes and suggested targets for adaptive scaffolds to support students' development of science understanding and open-ended problem-solving skills. In addition, it was investigated whether or not CA-derived metrics would reveal common problem-solving approaches as a set of distinct behaviour profiles from the study data. Ninety-nine 6th grade students from four mid-Tennessee science classrooms participated in the study. The participating school was an academic magnet school with competitive admission requirements. This study was conducted over a period of approximately 6 weeks. Pre-tests and post-tests were conducted. Results showed some support for both hypotheses: CA-derived metrics were predictive of students' task performance and learning gains and students' prior skill levels were (weakly) predictive of some of the CA metrics. It suggested a link between task understanding and effective open-ended problem-solving behaviours of the participants. In addition to testing these hypotheses, a clustering analysis was applied to characterise students based on their CA metrics and this provided insights into common problem-solving approaches used by students in this study.

Critical Appraisal: A substantial teaching agent *Betty's Brain* has been laudable agent since its inception. The duration of the study could have been little longer to provide stronger evidences. It has been established that higher self-regulation among students is required to utilise the potential of *Betty's Brain*, therefore, SRL acts as pre-cursor to the outcome of the study. Only if, *Betty's Brain* could develop the interest among learners, it would have greater significance for teachers and students.

Lang (2014) proposed a rationale for the use of Inverse Bayesian estimation to summarise and make predictions about student's behaviour in adaptive educational settings. The relative impact of contextual factors and internal student factors on student performance was used for the time series data across a range of possible dimensions. The data set consisted of 448 students aged 12–14 years. Their answers to math problems concerning the Pythagorean Theorem formed the data. Three variables, correct/incorrect responses, student confidence and the partial credit metric were analysed using the Inverse Bayesian model. It is concluded that learning analytics has the potential to expand the metrics used within education. The plurality of measurements can allow some deeper insight and more diverse understandings of learning.

Critical Appraisal: Though the study draws mainly upon time series data but does not mention the duration frame for how long the observation was made. The study made a potential contribution to expand LA in education.

Pardos, Baker, Pedro, Gowda and Gowda (2014) investigated the correspondence between student affect and behavioural engagement in a web-based tutoring platform throughout the school year and learning outcomes at the end of the year on a high-stakes mathematics exam in a manner that was both longitudinal and fine-grained. Affect and behaviour detectors were used to estimate student affective states and behaviour based on post-hoc analysis of tutor log-data. For every student action in the tutor, the detectors gave an estimated probability that the student was in a state of boredom, engaged concentration, confusion, or frustration and estimates of the probability that the student was exhibiting off-task or gaming behaviours. Data were used from the ASSISTments math tutoring system and found that boredom during problem solving is negatively correlated with performance, as expected; however, boredom was positively correlated with performance when exhibited during scaffolded tutoring. A similar pattern was unexpectedly seen for confusion. Engaged concentration and surprisingly, frustration were both associated with positive learning outcomes. In a second analysis, a unified model was built that predicted student standardised examination scores from a combination of student affect, disengaged behaviour and performance within the learning system. This model achieved high overall correlation to standardised exam score, showing that these types of features can effectively infer longer-term learning outcomes.

Critical Appraisal: Human feelings and emotions are relative and difficult to measure on a scale for an accurate outcome. Yet the study attempted to explore students' performance correlation with their moods and mental conditions. It is highly critical that frustration can be positively associated with positive learning outcomes.

Baker (2013) proposed some action principles for schools, local education agencies (LEAs) and state education agencies (SEAs). It was suggested how the emerging fields of learning analytics and educational data mining can be used to improve their practice. Action Principles for Schools were to provide formative data to teachers on student learning, to predict which students are at risk for dropping out, identify learning topics that are being learned less well within school and capture and respond to changes in student engagement. Some action principles for local education agencies were also proposed, like, identify specific areas of excellence and high success in teaching practice, identify students who could benefit from enrichment programs, develop internal expertise in learning analytics, develop data management and sharing plans to support partnerships with university researchers in line with legal obligations and identify exemplary teachers and schools for providing incentives. It was suggested after researching that teachers using the system review student homework before class and are able to change the focus of classroom activities based on student understanding and providing feedback. Learning analytics provided the opportunity to utilise very fine-grained data. Across entire years for a specific student, LA has been an excellent opportunity for better understanding learners and learning.

Critical Appraisal: It was one of the significant papers that insisted upon exploring LA in school education. It offered the larger picture of LA in school education building the foundation for higher studies, later in a students' formal education. It also pointed out intricacies involved in LA like data privacy at school level. Besides, Baker also pointed out the gap between LA practitioners, researchers, educators, teachers and end-users, i.e. students.

4

Learning Analytics, Language and Other Components

Literature Review

The second part of the review presents the studies on learning analytics and language. The review has helped to understand the research trends in the field of analytics with respect to language.

Learning Analytics and Language

Friedl, Ebner and Ebner (2020) focussed on the development of a prototype of a mobile application for Android and iOS, in which different learning applications for language acquisition were offered on the basis of learning analytical measurements provided by experts in the field. By logging and collecting interactions of the user, it was possible to create a variety of statistical evaluations and thus respond to the needs and weaknesses of students. For the evaluation of the application, a user experience test was carried out, whereby the child-friendly operation of the application was tested. Due to the very positive feedback, the design was found to be good and can therefore was suggested to be further developed.

Critical Appraisal: The study supported the mobile-assisted language-learning (MALL) and provides positive feedback about the strategy used. Though the study had used mobile applications but it also raises concerns over usage of mobile phones by younger population.

Lecailliez, Flanagan, Chen and Ogata (2020) proposed a smart dictionary integrated into an e-book reading platform. It allowed the learner to search and note word definitions directly with the purpose of reducing context switching and improve vocabulary retention. Finally, it was proposed that learner interactions with the system could be analysed to support EFL teachers in identifying possible problems that arose through dictionary use while reading.

Critical Appraisal: A solution had been offered with a smart dictionary on the reading platform itself which would have supported and eased out EFL teachers' strategy by providing probable solutions. An online smart dictionary or a word-pool was thought of to be created for the present study while citing this literature review.

Hilliard (2019) described the development and use of a learner corpus for materials development in an advanced English as a Second Language (ESL) writing course. Using corpus software, student essays were evaluated for frequency and errors of transition words in four separate genres and student examples were used to create classroom materials to target underused and misused transitions. After using these classroom materials, students more frequently produced the targeted transitions but still made some mistakes. This raises issues for further materials development, showing that a learner corpus can inform a continual cycle of evaluation and implementation for more successful student outcomes.

Critical Appraisal: As the study used corpus software and used student examples to create classroom materials, somewhere individual learning is compromised and also mistakes and errors are not common and differ from learner to learner.

Reinders (2018) described what learning analytics is, how it can work in practice, as well as its potential benefits and drawbacks for language-learning and teaching. Although LA and Educational Data Mining (EDM) offer significant potential for language research, there can be benefits of their implementation in a teaching context too. Reinders talks about synchronous using classroom management tools. Administratively speaking, a lot of tedious work can be handled by learning management systems. Pedagogically speaking, such systems allow teachers to monitor student engagement in ways that, especially in large classes, may be difficult to achieve otherwise. Asynchronous analytics can offer a number of other administrative benefits, like, the potential for increased transparency; significant pedagogical benefits, support can be targeted more precisely, both temporally and individually, resources can be allocated. The author concludes that just as with synchronous analytics, asynchronous data can be made available to students to give insight in to their progress over the duration of a course or an entire program, potentially increasing students' sense of control over their own learning. It is also helpful to open up a discussion with others, to identify common questions/areas for investigation as it is unlikely that one person will be able to figure out both the practical and technical aspects of using analytics. Although many free and relatively easy tools are available, it is often useful to work as a team and to think of learning analytics as a form of action research/detective work, where it is helpful to draw on knowledge and skills from different people as well as to cover different areas in the school environment. LA, both in its synchronous and its asynchronous forms, offers genuinely exciting opportunities for insights into the language-learning process that were previously unattainable.

Critical Appraisal: Though the researcher used synchronous data later making it available to students for insights, asynchronously, the role of facilitator remains questionable. Language is one domain of learning where a number of learning theories have supported and insisted on the significant role of facilitator.

Rienties, Lewis, McFarlane, Nguyen and Toetenel (2018) used a student activity-based taxonomy with a module design, combining principles of learning analytics and Big Data with learning design adopted by the Open University UK. In this study, they explored if learning design decisions made by language teachers influenced students' engagement in the Virtual Learning Environment (VLE). The learning designs of four introductory and intermediary language education modules and online engagement of 2111 learners were differentiated using weekly learning design data. The learning analytics study highlighted the potential affordances for Computer Assisted Language Learning (CALL) researchers to use the strength of learning design and big data to explore and understand the complexities and dynamics of language-learning for students as well as teachers. The Hausman test was used to differentiate between fixed effects and random effects models. The results supported the assumption of correlation between observation errors and predictors. Using fixed effect models, the findings indicated that 55% of the variance of weekly online engagement in these four modules was explained by the way language teachers designed weekly learning design activities.

Critical Appraisal: The study exemplified language teaching in an Open University set up. It would have been also interesting to study and observe drop outs of the course, delving deep into the student's feedback.

Admiraal and Bulterman-Bos (2017) carried out a case study with five secondary language teachers using online performance data of their students to adapt their lesson plans and teaching in the next lessons. The research questions were about the kind of learner data that teachers use for their teaching practice; the way teachers use learner data in their instructional practice; and the way these classroom instructions evaluated by students. The 7th Grade, 114 students from a secondary school participated. In the computer room at school, students completed online Dutch language tests. The software Got it Taal (Got it Language, https://www.thiememeulenhoff.nl/got-it) was used for the language tests in the domain of reading, spelling and grammar of Dutch language. Data collection included students' language test scores, lesson preparation forms, reports of the 12 team meetings and a start-up meeting, video recording of the 55 lessons and interviews with five teachers, one mentor and 47 students. The teachers used various feedback during their lesson, ranging from individual and additional tasks via working in pairs (mostly one poor performing student with one high performing student) to whole class instruction based on the learner data from the online tests. It was revealed that students were generally not very satisfied with an individual approach of their teacher during the lessons. Neither the poor performing students nor the high performing students evaluated an individual teaching approach positively as they felt that they get too much attention making them conscious in a group. It was due to the place in a special position or did not learn much from this approach about particular topics of Dutch language.

Critical Appraisal: The study should have oriented teachers as well as learners about the strategies and approach before plunging into the study. Pairing up two students with one high and one poor performing student but it should have been further studied if they gel up well for their learning. The review had different opinion than other study regarding the strategy it had used for the study but also points out the lacuna it had while conducting it. It helped to understand the significance of orientation before conducting a study.

Peng (2017) tried to explore English teaching and learning modes based on learning analytics in the Big Data Era in college. Under the theories of second language acquisition and learning analytics, it is held that it is important and indispensable to apply learning analytics to college English teaching and learning based on the two typical cases of wide application of 'Corrects a Cool Web' at colleges and universities and the pilot project—the blended teaching and learning method conducted at the University of Electronic Science and Technology of China. The paper concluded with some implications based on the two typical case analyses of learning analytics mentioned above that the intellectual technology brought about profound and strategic breakthroughs in foreign language teaching and learning. It proposed that researchers and teachers should try to explore more college English teaching and learning modes in the Big Data Era. Evidently, all the data-based activities facilitated students to learn English more actively and the reliable data and results made teachers and students more convinced about LA.

Critical Appraisal: The paper proposed to explore more English colleges in the Big data era which provided an implication that there was a need to have sufficient number of online education infrastructure. LA is assumed to be only for online education for big data but LA with offline or blended learning remains unexplored. The paper emphasised on big data but left the implications for blended learning unexplained.

Tan, Koh, Jonathan and Yang (2017) harnessed the affordances of learning analytics (LA) dashboards and visualisations to enhance 21st century (21C) pedagogical and learning strategies and outcomes. As they observed a knowledge gap in use cases and empirical understandings of student experience, especially in the K-12 schooling sector and in Asian education contexts, they addressed this knowledge gap in two ways. First, they presented an iteration design of a computer-supported collaborative critical reading and LA environment, *Wi*READ and its 16-week implementation in a Singapore high school. Second, they foregrounded students' evaluative accounts of the benefits and drawbacks associated with *Wi*READ's LA dashboard, which pointed to a number of potentialities and perils. They drew on a subset of data generated from quasi-experimental study that evaluated the impact of WiREAD's collaborative critical reading and LA dashboard affordances on student learning outcomes (3 WiREAD classes, N=116). It was compared to a control group (3 classes, N=92) using a combination of pre/post-tests and self-reported questionnaires and qualitative feedback forms and focus groups conducted at the start and end of the 16-week innovation term. It was concluded that student accounts of the LA dashboard revealed positive benefits to learning in terms of fostering greater self-awareness and self-regulatory learning natures, improved learning motivation and engagement and nurturing connective literacy among students. Simultaneously, the 'double-edged sword' nature of peer-referenced visualisations for stimulating competition, causing undue and felt pressure and triggering complacent behaviour in learners was foregrounded. These students' perceptions arguably revealed different expectations of the EL activities and the techno-pedagogical design of WiREAD. WiREAD is one of the first LA-focussed learning environments trialled in the Singapore secondary schooling context involving 116 students and three EL teachers. This paper significantly contributed empirical evidence on how students made sense of and accounted for the promise and perils of LA dashboards and visual analytics. At the same time, the findings reported in this paper remind LA designers to be aware of the restrictive effects of one-sized-fits-all approaches to assessment.

Critical Appraisal: The study provided an empirical evidence to conduct an experimental study for language teaching and individual learning. But it dealt with only reading aspect of language teaching while listening, speaking and writing remained untouched.

Volk, Kellner and Wohlhart (2015) presented a study where the online learning platform www.more-online.at for English learning is analysed for the purposes of understanding and optimising the learning behaviour of students. In Austria, up to 20,000 students use this platform per day for doing their English-homework. For English education at lower secondary education level, this online platform functions as an additional tool to the course book More!. This online course encompasses 40 Cyber Homework units which includes 159 exercises. Each Cyber Homework unit consists of some specific competence areas such as reading, writing and speaking, a set of interactive exercises. The study tried to understand the learning process and learning outcome of students interacting on this online platform. Google Analytics was used in order to obtain a general overview of the platform's usage and to track the behaviour of website visitors. The results showed that the usage behaviour is strongly influenced by the factor time and the time and activity structure of a school year in an e-learning environment. The findings about the temporal aspects of user's behaviour provided first insights into how students and teachers interact with the platform and provide a valuable basis for future research.

Critical Appraisal: Google Analytics is mainly used for business purpose and its most of the settings adhere to that. Though there are many studies with using Google Analytics but its use in education is yet to be simplified for teachers and educators. Also, the study smartly used available data but individual learning and assessment accordingly could have been a dimension under concern.

Dowell and Graesser (2014) highlighted the advantages of using theoretically grounded automated linguistic tools to identify pedagogically valuable discourse features that can be applied in collaborative learning, intelligent tutoring systems (ITS), computer-mediated collaborative learning (CMCL) and MOOC environments. The results suggested that students' covert cognitive, affective and social processes can be monitored by analysing their language and discourse. An interdisciplinary approach combining psychological theories of discourse comprehension with computational linguistics methodologies holds the prospective for enabling extensively improved learning environments by providing real-time detection of student's and group's performance. This information can be used further to develop student models and provide adaptive learning supports.

Critical Appraisal: The work presented was mainly theoretical and needs empirical evidence to support the notion.

Tran and Duong (2013) conducted a study to investigate students' attitudes towards English language-learning (ELL) and the use of self-regulated learning (SRL) strategies at a college in Dak Lak, Vietnam. This study involved 241 non-English majors taking part in answering MSLQ questionnaire. They were mainly second-year students consisting of 133 females (55.2 %) and 108 males (44.8%). There were 201 (83.4%) participants having learned English over seven years and 40 (16.6%) participants having learned English from three to seven years. Their last self-reported academic achievements were grading as grade A (23.7%), grade B (51.4%), grade C (18.7%) and grade D (6.2%). The participants had to study English in four terms in total, three of which were General English and one of which was English for specific purposes. The results from one-way ANOVA revealed that significant differences existed between academic achievements with English anxiety, organisation and environmental management strategy usage. It also showed that although the participants had positive attitudes towards ELL, they were likely to have low engagement in SRL. Number of years of learning English did not account for the participants' change of attitudes to ELL. Academic achievements were also found to be significantly related to cognitive learning and environment management strategies. Additionally, academic achievements and attitudes towards ELL were positively correlated to SRL, yet only attitudes towards ELL were predictors of SRL.

Critical Appraisal: The study primarily revolves around self-regulated learning for ELL but observed that despite the positive correlation between academic achievement and SRL, attitude towards ELL remained unchanged. It would be interesting to study and compare the same with the present study.

Swalander and Taube (2007) completed a study how SRL, reading attitude and family reading background relates to reading ability. The sample included 4018 eighth graders from Sweden. Using a reading literacy test and little research was conducted on English language learners (ELL) students, achievement and SRL. Results suggested that the results obtained by ELL students on their achievement tests are impacted by their language background. ELL students perform lower in achievement tests in the area of mathematics, reading and science depending on their proficiency levels in English. The biggest impact occurred in the area of reading achievement because this was the area that required the most linguistic ability to understand. Whereas in the areas of mathematics and science the linguistic demand was lower and the influence of language was not as great. Thus, the current study explored the relationship between SRL and achievement on ELL students. The study suggested a need to pursue researches as there were just a few studies that had been done with students from other cultures studying self-regulated strategies.

Critical Appraisal: The sample of the study was sufficient to draw the conclusion. Language is fundamental to learning associated with other cognitive subjects to be studied. The study mentioned two contradictory statements when it was mentioned that 'ELL students perform lower in achievement tests in the area of mathematics, reading and science depending on their proficiency levels in English' and self-contradicting 'in the areas of mathematics and science the linguistic demand was lower and the influence of language was not as great'; it was difficult to draw a conclusion due to these vague statements.

Learning Analytics and Motivation

This section of the chapter presents a review of the studies on learning analytics and motivation. The review has helped to understand the research trends in the field of analytics with respect to motivation.

Wang and Zhan (2020) conducted research with aims to study the assumed relationships between learner characteristics (learner beliefs, anxiety, motivation) and self-regulation in the online English learning context. It was carried out by conducting structural equation modelling analysis to examine their relations. Researchers adopted the previous questionnaires with sufficient reliability as instruments to evaluate students' online English learner beliefs, learning anxiety, learning motivation and online self-regulated English learning. The valid responses collected from 425 Chinese undergraduate university students enrolled in an online academic English writing course provided the data source. The results indicated that learner beliefs positively predicted, while learning anxiety negatively predicted, online self-regulated English learning. Online English learning motivation was a mediator in these associations. The findings suggested that stronger learner beliefs of self-efficacy and perceived value of English learning promoted learning motivation and self-regulation. In contrast, higher learning anxiety, such as test anxiety and fear of negative evaluation, harmed learners' motivation and their online self-regulated English learning.

Critical Appraisal: Study provided sufficient insights into the role of motivation for self-regulated learning. It also provided empirical proofs for the role of test anxiety and learner's belief to boost the motivation. But in an online learning environment, if this was only for English language-learning or lack of ICT skills also can contribute to test anxiety or relief, remains questionable.

Nagy (2016) showcased a school-wide Student Effort Tracking project which has been implemented in two Sydney high-schools over eight years. The project has successfully supported the improvement of student motivation for learning in all cohorts, creating high-quality data-driven conversations between students, teachers and parents. Rather than nurturing a joy of lifelong learning, this 'results-driven focus' emphasises distinct ability-divisions which promotes 'fixed mind-sets' in students, teachers and parents. The result created an academic climate where failure was seen as a reinforcement of inability, rather than a challenge to be overcome. This climate also increased students' anxiety levels, often with a detrimental effect on their performance and wellbeing. Instead of comparing students with each other based on their effort, rather than their achievement alone, they subtly shift the systemic 'success-focus' onto qualities which promote a growth mind-set in all students in place of fixed mind-set. It developed important 'non-cognitive' character traits such as persistence and resilience among students. The engagement and continuing professional development of teachers were also critical to embed and sustain the project.

Critical Appraisal: The study presented a longitudinal effort over eight years to promote a growth mind-set among students as well as teachers. Only if there could have been some comparison with other schoolers who were not a part of Student Effort Tracking project, results could have not only empirical evidences but later the project could have been implemented for a wider reach.

Ali, Hatala and Winne (2014) aimed to investigate how the learning strategies and achievement goal orientations of students relate to their academic behaviours and performance in the context of an online learning system. The study also developed and validated a relational model between student learning strategies and achievement goals. The research question aimed to find how learning motivation and achievement goals relate to a student's study logged activities in online collaborative environments such as MOOCs. The ability to predict students' goal orientations from their online activities would support user-level course adaptations and early interventions to support learning. Researchers used the Motivated Strategies for Learning Questionnaire (MSLQ; Pintrich & DeGroot, 1990) and the Achievement Goal Orientations (AGO) instruments for gauging students' self-reported learning strategies and goal orientations. The undergraduate students who took part in this preliminary study were 376. Students' learning strategies were measured using the Motivated Strategies for Learning Questionnaire, which included 44 items on student motivation, cognitive and meta-cognitive strategy use and self-regulation. The goal orientations were measured using a 3X2 Achievement Goal Orientation questionnaire. A second study was conducted on 34 participant undergraduate students one semester later. The second dataset was used to validate researchers' models from the first study. Four new scales from the MSLQ data were also theorised to measure the mastery approach, mastery avoidance, performance approach and performance avoidance goal orientations. Student activity data were collected from an online software engineering course. The data were analysed using parametric linear models including correlations, canonical correlations analysis and multiple regression analysis. Researchers analysed theorised scales using both confirmatory and exploratory data analysis approaches. The confirmatory analysis of the preliminary study suggested that the MSLQ datasets could reveal the following achievement goal orientations of students: mastery approach, mastery avoidance and performance approach goal orientations. The preliminary results showed empirical support for building new models to get secondary information from the datasets collected for some other primary purposes. The provision of secondary information can enhance the understanding of a phenomenon on one hand and can allow for the reuse of precious datasets for additional purposes on the other.

Critical Appraisal: In order to validate the data from the first study, 34 participants as sample were taken which seemed to be not in proportionate with 376 participants sample in the earlier one. The study provided empirical evidence with the MSLQ providing greater insights into the tool and its utility.

Jahedi (2012) undertook a study to explore and identify the relationship between motivational beliefs (self-efficacy, intrinsic value, test anxiety) and self-regulated strategies (cognitive strategy and self-regulation) and academic achievement (marks obtained by students in four tests conducted during that academic year) of school students. Thus, relationship between motivation and self-regulated learning components was examined. The study also found out whether motivational beliefs and self-regulated learning components influenced academic achievement. Additionally, the study sought to identify gender difference on motivation and self-regulated learning components and the influence of the parents' education on motivation, self-regulated learning strategies and achievement of their children were studied. The research question examined if there was a significant relationship between motivational belief components (self-efficacy, intrinsic value and test anxiety) and self-regulated learning components (cognitive strategy use and self-regulation) among students; if motivational belief components (self-efficacy, intrinsic values, and test anxiety) influence academic achievement; if self-regulated strategies components (cognitive strategy use, self-regulation) influence academic achievement; if motivational beliefs components differ in boys and girls; if self-regulated strategies components differ in boys and girls; if there an influence of parents' education on their children's motivational beliefs components; and if there was an influence of parents' education on their children's self-regulated strategies components. Data were collected from 8th standard students in group of 12 to 15 years of English medium schools in Pune city. Students responded to self-report Questionnaire: Motivated Strategies for Learning Questionnaire (MSLQ). Statistical Techniques such as Pearson's product moment correlation, t-test and ANOVA were used. The major findings showed that there was significant correlation between motivational beliefs components and self-regulated learning components of the students. The findings from the second and third research question showed that all components of motivation and self-regulated learning strategies influenced the academic achievement of students.

Critical Appraisal: The study did not mention the sample size. The study could have either worked upon correlational aspect between motivational beliefs components and self-regulated learning components of the students providing better and deeper insights or the components of MSLQ i.e motivation and self-regulated learning strategies influencing academic achievement.

Turingan and Yang (2009) investigated the self-regulatory processes employed by Korean and Filipino college students. The MSLQ was utilised to assess the self-regulation of learning skills and the motivational orientation of students. The participants of the study were 185 Korean and 209 Filipino college students. Results of this study indicated that Filipino students had a higher level of skills to self-regulate their learning compared to their Korean counterparts. Thus, Filipino students had a higher level of skills in terms of cognition, meta-cognition and management of resources than Korean students. Due to the diversity in the classrooms, it was necessary to understand the relationships between the notions of learning and the utilisation of learning strategies. Cultural diversity also revealed differences in styles of thinking and values. Some of the differences were that Korean people emphasised the role of parental supervision in the academic life of their children. Furthermore, Koreans were more predisposed to have tutors helping in the learning process of their children. On the other hand, Filipino students relied on the school system.

Critical Appraisal: The study could have compared the two groups with respect to their cultural backgrounds and difference but comparing the two with respect to motivation seems incomparable. It was certainly due to the cultural differences. The study provided an insight not to compare the two different backgrounds for motivational beliefs. Though the review under this section has established the utility of MSLQ.

Language and Other Variables

This section of the chapter presents a review of the studies on language and other associated variables. The review has helped to understand the research trends in the field of language-learning, learning style, learning habits, attitude, motivation, and socio-economic status.

Language-Learning

This sub-section presents a review of the studies on language-learning. The review has facilitated to understand research trends and concepts in the field of language-learning.

Cho, Lee, Joo and Becker (2018) attempted to evaluate the effects of employing mobile devices in language-learning and tried to explore these questions about mobile technology use in language-learning through meta-analysis. Based on the explicit inclusion and exclusion criteria, 22 d-type effect sizes from 20 studies were calculated for the meta-analysis in the study. The random-effects model was adopted and the estimated average effect was 0.51 (se = 0.10). The overall effect of using mobile devices on language acquisition and language-learning achievement was a moderately positive. This result confirmed that the use of mobile devices could facilitate language- learning.

Critical Appraisal: After the CALL (Computer-assisted Language-learning), MALL (Mobile-assisted Language-learning) has been on the rise and reported. The study gave insight into an opportunity to observe the same if students prefer to use their mobiles or computer to access the content.

Cummins (2017) distinguished between basic interpersonal conversational skills (BICS) and cognitive academic language proficiency (CALP) and thus, drew attention to the very different time periods naturally required by immigrant children to acquire conversational fluency in the school language when compared to grade-appropriate academic proficiency in the second language. The distinction made also highlighted the challenging educational consequences of conflating social and academic language. The BICS/CALP distinction was embedded within a broader framework that specified the role of societal power relations in framing both the organisation of educating and teacher-student identity negotiation. It is debated that the distinction is consistent with a wide range of research and has also proven very effective in making positive changes in educational practices and policies in relation to culturally and linguistically diverse students.

Critical Appraisal: Cummins established and distinguished between BICS and CALP but did not offer any observations on technology-assisted language teaching which plays a significant role in modern and advanced education.

Khatib and Taie (2016) tried to investigate the status of the BICS and CALP dichotomy in the second language acquisition (SLA) literature following Kumaravadivelu's suggestion concerning creating a 'pattern which connects'. The BICS/CALP dichotomy as proposed by Cummins has over-time attracted the attention of many educators, language pedagogues, syllabus designers and various educational systems involved in the education of minority migrant children. Though attracted criticism, this distinction has resolved some of the enigmas concerning the second language acquisition. Nevertheless, its relationship with SLA on the whole has remained under-researched.

Critical Appraisal: The paper focussed more on a theoretical mode rather than offering some empirical evidences on Cummins' BICS and CALP. Though, it was insisted that SLA with BICS and CALP dichotomy remained under-researched but there are several other studies that pointed out on essential element of technology assistance with it.

Harsono (2015) wrote an article describing teaching/learning materials development for English for Specific Purposes (ESP). The description included the definition, the principles, the procedure and the practical undertaking of the material's development.

Critical Appraisal: The paper assisted in providing some insights into learning material development but needed some greater details onto online education related to language.

Heritage and Bailey (2014) presented an article that addressed the theoretical and empirical issues related to the development and evaluation of language-learning progressions. The authors explained how learning progressions aligned with newly introduced content standards can form a central basis of efforts to describe the English language required in school contexts for learning, instruction and assessment. Learning progressions, in contrast with standards, can show incremental growth and are placed to support teachers' formative assessment practices with K-12 students who are acquiring English as an additional language. Extending learning progressions that have taken hold in some other areas of student learning to language-learning and development requires conceptualising in two dimensions, firstly, in what ways language progresses and secondly, how language growth can be supported by educators. The authors illustrated both considerations of dimensions with the examples of a new language-learning progression and formative assessment initiative which are based on the characterisation of explanations generated by students with an extensive range of experiences with the English language.

Critical Appraisal: The article presented a deeper insight into mapping the learning progression but didn't aid much with respect to other extraneous or intervening variables. Language is not learnt in isolation but contextually too. Here, formative assessment was discussed but summative assessment remained uninformed.

Language-Learning and Learning Style

This sub-section presents a review of studies on language-learning and learning styles. The review has facilitated an understanding of research trends and concepts in the field of language-learning and learning styles.

Islam (2020) investigated the effect of the jigsaw technique on reading comprehension with students' learning styles. The aims of this research were to analyse whether the students who were taught by using jigsaw had better reading comprehension scores than taught by using conventional technique, to analyse whether the students who were different with learning style had different reading comprehension scores and to analyse whether there was any interaction between jigsaw and learning style in students' reading comprehension score. This research was quasi-experimental design with experimental and control groups of tenth grade. The instrument used questionnaire and reading comprehension test. This study used the independent t-test and two-way ANOVA. The findings showed mean of experimental groups was 76.40 and control group was 68.00. Therefore, it may be said that the students who taught by using jigsaw have better reading score than those who taught by using conventional technique. In accordance with second research problem, the significance value was .084. It meant the students with different learning style had different reading comprehension scores. Concerning the third research problem, the result of the analysis of jigsaw and students' learning style presented significance value of 0.319. It meant that there was no interaction between jigsaw technique and learning style in reading comprehension.

Critical Appraisal: The research emphasised on a Likert scale on lesser than five points in its suggestions for an easier administration. It implicated that the study did not conduct a pilot study or used the tool loosely.

Pawlak (2020) built upon the previous cognitive-interactionists approach and investigated the impact of English learners' proficiency, gender and learning style on the occurrence, nature and outcomes of negotiation in two tasks, which differed with respect to the presence of an information gap. Results provide some evidence for the mediating role of gender and learning style but not proficiency, with task type being an important mediating variable.

Critical Appraisal: The study pointed out that learning style played a mediating role in the presence of an information gap which would be interesting to observe for the present study.

Wong (2015) explored the English language-learning and teaching style preferences in English for Academic Purposes (EAP) classrooms at the community college level in Hong Kong. The present study adopted a mixed method approach involving both questionnaire surveys and semi-structured interviews, in attempt to investigate the factors influencing learning styles and teaching styles, and the relationship between them. It aimed at providing valuable information for curriculum design and teacher training in order to offer Hong Kong community college students adequate and effective academic English language-learning support. A total of 637 students and 10 EAP teachers from two community colleges in Hong Kong participated in this research. The findings of this study showed that the community college students in EAP classrooms had multiple learning style preferences. A plethora of factors such as cultural and educational backgrounds were related to their development of learning styles. This research also explored the nature of teaching styles and the possible variables, including students' English language proficiency and their learning styles, influencing their teaching styles in EAP classrooms.

Critical Appraisal: The study primarily looked into learning style preferences. Learning style may be formed naturally or worked upon over a period of time for specific purposes. Study neglected conversational skills which may have an influence over language acquisition and academic language-learning.

Gülbahar and Ilgaz (2014) chose Moodle LMS as an e-learning environment and analysed it through SAS (Statistical Analysis System) Level of Analytics. According to the analysis, some practical ideas were developed. However, as Learning Analytics was assumed to be based on quantitative data as per researchers, qualitative insights were also gained through various approaches which can be used to strengthen the numerical data by providing detailed facts about a phenomenon. Thus, in addition to focusing on the learner, for research studies at the course, program and institutional level, the researches on LA should include instructors and administrators in order to reveal the best practices of instructional design and fulfil the premise of effective teaching. The work concluded that instructional materials could be offered based on students' learning styles; and tutors' teaching styles could be aligned with students' learning styles.

Critical Appraisal: The study followed a mixed method approach but did not provide a clarity how the online content and instructional designs were to be managed according to the learning styles. It offered more of a theoretical aspect of designing instructions according to learning styles than some practical insights.

Karthigeyan and Nirmala (2013) conducted a study with the purpose to identify the predominant learning style preference of English language learners in higher secondary schools with respect to demographic variables like gender, locality, nature of school board and grade in which they are studying. The Perceptual Learning Style Preference Questionnaire (PLSPQ) developed by Joy Reid was adapted by the researchers and the reliability of the questionnaire was established. The questionnaire was administered to 582 students. The data were analysed using descriptive and percentage analysis. The data analysis showed that the primary and secondary learning styles of the students were visual and auditory learning style.

Critical Appraisal: The study made a good attempt at identifying the learning styles of the students but with a sample of 582 students, none of them recognised as kinesthetic or tactile learners raised doubts over the sound administration of the tool. Earlier Islam (2020) suggested to use a Likert scale lesser than five whereas this tool has Likert scale on five points.

Yassin (2012) investigated the learning styles of ESL students (students who learn English as a second language). The focus of this study was on ESL Arab Gulf (Saudi Arabia, Oman, Kuwait and the United Arab Emirates) students who study English as a second language in Intensive English Language Centers (IELCs) in the United States. The study explored the ESL Arab Gulf students' learning style preferences and how they are affected by different variables such as cultural background, gender and language level in IELCs. ESL Arab Gulf students were administered the VARK Learning Styles questionnaire. It measures several sensory types of learning styles such as visual, auditory, kinaesthetic and tactile. The participants in this study were from Saudi Arabia, Oman, United Arab Emirates and Kuwait. The finding of this quantitative research study showed that ESL Arab Gulf students' learning styles were affected by their cultural backgrounds and their gender as well. The results of this study showed that matching teaching styles to ESL Arab Gulf students' learning styles impacted the ESL Arab Gulf students' academic success positively. It helped students to achieve higher TOEFL scores more than the students who had different learning styles from their teachers.

Critical Appraisal: The study used VARK which categorises learning styles into four categories of Visual, Aural, Reading and Writing and Kinesthetics. Interestingly, the reading and writing are skills and can be further added to the modes of visual or aural or kinesthetics.

Chen (2009) investigated the relationships between grade level, perceptual learning style preferences and language-learning strategies among Taiwanese English as Foreign Language (EFL) students in grades 7 through 9. Three hundred and ninety junior high school students participated in this study. The instruments for data collection were the Perceptual Learning Style Preference Questionnaire (PLSPQ) and the Strategy Inventory for Language-learning (SILL). Results showed that statistically significant relationships were found to exist between grade level and kinaesthetic learning style preference ($p = 0.001$), tactile learning style preference ($p = 0.047$) and individual learning style preference ($p = 0.02$). Results also showed that statistically significant relationships were found to exist between grade level and the use of memory strategies ($p = 0.005$), cognitive strategies ($p = 0.02$), metacognitive strategies (p = 0.000), affective strategies (p = 0.000) and social strategies (p = 0.000). The implications are that it is critical for classroom teachers to be more aware of the differences in their students and ensure that their courses present information that appeals to students at different grade levels.

Critical Appraisal: Chen (2009) also used PLSPQ by Reid. It was mainly to investigate the relationship between learning styles and learning strategies.

O'Brien (1989) developed 'The Learning Channel Preference Checklist' (O'Brien, 1988), a questionnaire designed to develop this awareness. Teachers can administer the Learning Channel Preference Checklist and follow it up with an interpretive discussion. There is total thirty items and ten items for each sub-category. The tool was appropriate for school level education. Students are asked to rank each statement according to how it generally relates to them. There are no right or wrong answers. Students' final cluster scores will indicate what their learning styles are, i.e., Visual, Auditory or Kinesthetics.

Critical Appraisal: The tool has three dimensions of learning style and thirty items on a three-point Likert Scale. The tool was found to be relevant and administrable for the study.

Language-Learning and Study Habit

This sub-section presents a review of studies on language-learning and study habits. The review has facilitated an understanding of research trends and concepts in the field of language-learning and study habits.

Vyas and Choudhary (2016) conceived and formulated their research work on a very wide canvas of adolescents in India. The study was in the context of students' socio-economic status and its relation with study habits of adolescent students. The investigators undertook the study in government as well as private schools located in Delhi, the capital of India. Normative survey method was used from grade 9 with 450 samples to gather the data. 'Palsane and Sharma's Study Habit Inventory', (PSSHI) and Socio-economic Status Scale (SESS) were the tools. Data were analysed using Mean, SD, one-way ANOVA, *t*-test and Correlation techniques. The study revealed that there was no significant difference observed in study habits of male and female adolescent students. Further, there was no significant difference in study habit scores of adolescents of different socio-economic strata except low SES. It was inferred that gender influences study habits of adolescents who fall under same low SES. A positive low correlation was observed between the study habits and socio-economic status. It was suggested that since the students from low SES had poor study strategies, they must be helped by the teacher to plan some effective study strategies to achieve their projected potential.

Critical Appraisal: The study observed an influence of socio-economic status on gender wise study habits. Researchers suggested for the teacher to plan study strategies instead they could've suggested a few concrete and concerted steps to move forward.

Kumari and Chamundeswari (2015) investigated the relationship between achievement motivation, study habits and academic achievement at the secondary level using a survey method. A sample of 457 students was selected at the secondary level. The tools used were the Achievement Motivation Scale (Beena, 1986), Habits Inventory (Gopal Rao, 1974) and a researcher-made Academic Achievement Test to assess students' achievements. The results of the statistical analyses depicted a significantly positive correlation between achievement motivation, study habits and the performance of students. A significant difference was also observed between students of different categories and gender of the sample pertaining to achievement motivation, study habits and academic achievement.

Critical Appraisal: It is not clear if the study was conducted to study the relationship or observe the differences between the variables.

Pandey and Singh (2015) aimed to find out the differences between study habits and academic achievement of rural and urban first-generation learners and subsequent generation learners. The sample selected were 16 schools from East Delhi/ NCR by convenience sampling. Further, from each school 20 students were selected, first generation learners and subsequent generation learners, 10 each. The Study Habit Inventory by Palsane and Sharma (1989) was used. It was shown that there was a significant difference observed between study habits as well as the academic achievements of rural and urban first-generation learners and subsequent generation learners. The result of this study had implications not only for teachers, students and parents but also for educational planners, various financial agencies and boards. As the first-generation learners face more problem related to studies as compared to subsequent generation learners, it is important for the first-generation learners to improve their study habits which eventually improve their academic performance.

Critical Appraisal: Representative sample seemed to be too less from each school. The study could have suggested measures to improve the study habits of first-generation learners.

Siahi and Maiyo (2015) carried out their research work to seek the relationship between study habits and academic achievement of students. In the descriptive correlation study, survey design was employed. The sample included the 9th grade students at Spicer Higher Secondary School and stratified random sampling was used to select the respondents. Tools used were the habits inventory by Palsane and Sharma and school examinations records were used to construe the achievement score. Interpretation and recommendations of the findings were according to the computed Pearson's Product Moment Coefficient of Correlation. Results of this study showed a positive correlation (+ 0.66) between study habits and academic achievement. The results implied that the study habits are directly correlated with academic achievement – therefore due attention to the habits are required to improve academic performance.

Critical Appraisal: For the purpose of this survey, only a single school was selected. Survey studies need to have a substantial number of samples to draw a constructive conclusion.

Nadeem, Puja and Bhat (2014) conducted a research to study and understand the Study Habits and Academic Achievement of Adolescents girls in Jammu and Kashmir. The sample was 400 randomly selected students from two ethnic groups, Kashmiri and Ladakhi. The investigators had used Palsane and Sharma's Study Habits Inventory (PSSHI) to collect data. The statistical techniques used were percentage, S. D., Mean and t-value to analyse the data. The result confirmed that there was a significant mean difference observed between Kashmiri and Ladakhi adolescents about their study habits and academic achievements.

Critical Appraisal: There may be several other extraneous variables affecting the difference but those factors also could have been mentioned and studied. Some measures could have been suggested to overcome the difference and improve study habits for academic achievement.

Yazdani and Godbole (2014) studied the relationship between academic performance and achievement motivation and study habits together in high school students in Hyderabad. The sample was drawn of 400 students consisting of boys and girls of 7th and 8th grade. Two tools were used in the study. Habits inventory by M. N. Palsane (1989) and achievement motivation scale by Deo Mohan (1992) were used. Data were analysed by using mean score, standard deviation, Pearson's correlation and regression. The result showed that there was a significant positive relationship between achievement motivation and study habits to academic performance. The result also depicted the extent of contribution of achievement motivation and study habits to academic performance. Therefore, it was concluded that achievement motivation and study habits had proved to be positively correlated with academic performance of students and it can help them for better performance and academic achievement.

Critical Appraisal: Two levels of schooling were selected to draw the conclusion. It could be more pin-pointed to draw a more focussed conclusion, if the study would have been conducted for only one level of school education or a certain age group could have been targeted.

Mudasir (2012) undertook a case study of higher secondary school students to know about the study habits and academic achievements of science and arts students, both boys and girls. The sample were 80 higher secondary students selected randomly, 40 from science stream and 40 from arts stream. The Study Habit Inventory by Palsane and Sharma was administered. For the academic achievement of the students, the percentage of marks obtained in the previous grade was considered. The data were analysed to reveal that female students had better study habits than the male students. Though, the academic achievements of male students were better than the female students. However, it was observed that students with science background have better study habits and academic achievement than students with humanities background.

Critical Appraisal: The comparison of academic achievement was made between the two streams of education, science and arts. The difference was bound to be there. Instead, two science groups could be compared for physics, chemistry, and mathematics (PCM) and physics, chemistry and biology (PCB) for the study habit.

Bailey and Onwuegbuzie (2010) conducted a study to determine which study habits distinguish successful from unsuccessful foreign language learners. Participants were 219 college students from a variety of disciplinary backgrounds, enrolled in either Spanish, French, German or Japanese classes. A canonical discriminant analysis ($F [6, 117]$, $p < 0.0001$; canonical $R = 0.92$) revealed that, compared to their high-performing counterparts, students with the lowest levels of foreign language performance tended to report that: (a) they frequently include a lot of irrelevant or unimportant information in their notes; (b) when they have difficulty with their assignments, they do not seek help from their instructor; (c) they put their lecture notes away after taking the test and never consult them again; (d) they have to be in the mood before attempting to study; (e) they have a tendency to doodle or daydream when they are trying to study; and (f) they do not look up in a dictionary the meanings of words that they do not understand.

Critical Appraisal: The conclusion could be utilised to understand student behaviour and strategise classroom feedback.

Language Learning and Attitude

This sub-section presents a review of studies on language-learning and attitude. The review has facilitated to understand research trends and concepts in the field of language-learning and attitude.

Colaste (2018) investigated the impact of students' attitude towards the English language on academic achievement. The sample comprised two classes of grade 9, with eighty-eight students from Felisberto Verano National High School, 43 and 45 learners in each class. A Likert scale was used to measure the anxiety level and the attitude of students towards English. It was found that there was a significant relationship between attitude and English language-learning. Findings also revealed that students have a negative attitude towards English as a subject. It was so as they found it difficult to express themselves using the language as a medium of communication.

Critical Appraisal: The study has used the term 'impact' to study the association or relation between attitude and English language-learning. Impact had to be used, had it been a survey; here, it was to study relationship between the two variables.

Khan (2016) explored learners' attitudes towards education in general and learning English in particular. It was aimed to elicit an implicit connection between learners' and teachers' attitudes and achievement in English. The study was descriptive in nature for which data were collected through focus group and questionnaires. The responses of the teachers and students were qualitatively analysed and compared to match with the objectives of the study. The results indicated that the students generally didn't possess positive attitude towards learning. Many reasons could be attributed to this behaviour. It may be concluded that the positive attitude towards learning target language mattered a lot. It was found that there was a positive correlation between attitude towards learning/teaching English and their proficiency in it. It had also been found that in spite of the fact all the necessary equipment and resources were integrated in the pedagogic setting, ultimate language achievement was not up to the expectations of the policy makers and the administrators. Thus, teachers' role was quite crucial in this connection. The findings were likely to be implemented in all those similar institutions that technically as well as academically resemble the sample college.

Critical Appraisal: The data collected could have been triangulated with one more tool besides FGD and questionnaire. Data thus analysed would have supported the conclusion and generalised. But the implementations may not be applicable to other cases.

Nyamubi (2016) explored the role of attitude in secondary school students' performance in the English language. It was explored how learning English was silhouetted by students' utilitarian attitudes and interests to the language. The data was collected from six secondary schools in Morogoro Urban and Mvomero districts in Morogoro Region in Tanzania. Responses were collected from sample students and their teachers of English language. The tools were a questionnaire and an achievement test. It was observed that students did differ in terms of their mastery of English. Though composition was the most poorly scored section, students scored higher in the structure section. In all, students, in both Form One and Form Four, had strong and positive attitudes towards learning English. Particularly, while Form-One students had a more positive interest than their counterparts, Form-Four students displayed more utilitarian attitudes to learn English, as compared to Form-One students. It was emphasised that students' positive attitudes to English should be improved to enhance the learning of the language.

Critical Appraisal: A standardised tool to study attitude could have been used for the study. The tool used had not been described sufficiently to generalise the results. But the positive relationship observed during the study is worth considering.

Ahmed (2015) analysed the results of a survey on 238 undergraduate EFL students at a public university in Malaysia. The survey focussed on their attitudes towards English learning and the causes that might hinder their learning. For data collection, a 19-item questionnaire was designed and administered on 238 students. The objective of this study was to investigate (1) The attitudes of the learners towards the use of English in different areas; (2) Causes that may have influenced the effect of English learning for students (3) Perspectives of English learning among non-major English learners in Malaysia. Results of the qualitative analysis showed that the attitude towards English language learning and using the language in various domains of usage was extremely positive. The data also revealed that most of the students had negative feelings or fear regarding classroom instructions in their learning experience. Students of different fields varied in attitudes towards English language-learning in terms of domains of usage and focus of learning skills, which showed that a single curriculum or teaching methodology was not adequate. Several suggestions have been made regarding teaching methodology, curriculum, teaching materials and the status of English in Malaysia from this point of view.

Critical Appraisal: The study was qualitative in nature and therefore, data could have been triangulated with other sources.

Bhaskar and Soundiraraj (2013) carried out a study to find out if there is any change in the attitude of students towards English Language Learning (ELL) when they come for college education after completing the school education. The changes in the attitudes of students were examined in terms of interest towards understanding the importance of English in securing a job, English language, self- motivation to learn the language, participation in the class and learner-centred language teaching methods that ensure more freedom to the learners. The sample consisted of about 52 first-year Mechanical Engineering students from the Tamil medium stream. The method consisted of administration of an attitude questionnaire and a semi-structured interview. The findings of the study revealed that there was a significant shift in the attitude towards ELL at college level. The change in attitude was observed due to the teaching based on the requirements of employers. The findings showed that there was a positive change in the attitude of sample students towards language-learning. The study suggested that English language teaching in school should undergo some required changes. The examination – oriented approach should be avoided and focus should be more on speaking skill activities, use of audio-visual aids, encouragement for independent learning and use of better innovative teaching methods.

Critical Appraisal: The study did not use any standardized tool to study attitude and also couldn't develop one. Data had not been triangulated which affected the conclusive remarks.

Abidin, Pour-Mohammadi and Alzwari (2012) investigated the attitudes of Libyan secondary school students towards learning English in terms of the behavioural, cognitive and emotional aspects. They also tried to explore if there is a significant difference in the students' attitudes towards the English language based on their demographic profiles of gender, field and year of study. The study was administered on 180 participants in the three study years from three specialisations of Basic Sciences, Life Sciences and Social Sciences with a questionnaire as a measuring instrument. The participants expressed negative attitudes towards learning English regarding the three aspects of attitude i.e., cognitive, behavioural and emotional. It was found that there were statistically significant attitudinal differences in the demographic profiles of gender and field of study but not in the year of study. It was recommended that according to the students' needs and their individual differences, the English curriculum and classroom activities should involve affective aims to build up positive attitudes towards English.

Critical Appraisal: It was a longitudinal study but data was mainly collected only with a questionnaire. Data could have been triangulated with other sources to make the results more reliable over the years.

Mahmoudi, Samad and Razak (2012) investigated the relationship between attitudes toward Computer Assisted English Language Learning (CAELL) and students' performance on English language vocabulary in their study. The attitudes of 30 Iranian postgraduate students at a Malaysian university toward CAELL were assessed via questionnaires and the effects of CALL on their performance were assessed by using vocabulary tests. The data gathered from the vocabulary tests were quantitatively analysed using the Statistical Package for the Social Sciences (SPSS). The results showed that participants possessed positive attitudes towards Computer Assisted English Language Learning (CAELL). Consequently, their attitudes and performance were found to be positively correlated.

Critical Appraisal: The sample size of the study could have been larger for more conclusive findings.

Language-Learning and Motivation

This sub-section presents a review of studies on language-learning and motivation. The review has facilitated an understanding of research trends and concepts in the field of language-learning and motivation.

Rezaei, Keivanpanah and Najibi (2015) attempted to examine the relationship between English as a Foreign Language (EFL) learners' motivational beliefs and their use of learning strategies. The three components, expectancy, value and affective component of motivation were examined in relation to metacognitive, cognitive and effort management strategies. Two hundred and fifty-seven EFL learners representing diverse proficiency levels completed the Persian version of the Motivated Strategies for Learning Questionnaire (MSLQ), consisting of a motivation scale and a learning strategies scale. The analysis depicted a significant effect of proficiency level on test anxiety and extrinsic goal orientation. It suggested that less proficient learners were significantly more anxious and more extrinsically oriented compared to advanced learners of English. It was also observed that intrinsic goal orientation, self-efficacy, control of learning beliefs and task value accounted for 70% of variations in self-regulated learning (SRL) strategies. It was suggested to aid instructors in creating a non-product-oriented approach to learning that promotes foreign language learners' learning outcomes.

Critical Appraisal: The study suggested creating a non-product-oriented approach to learning which countered the learning outcome expectations.

Long, Ming and Chen (2013) discussed the definition of motivation, types of motivation and analysed the role of motivation in English learning. The sample in the work was Gejiu middle school students who were administered a questionnaire on English motivation. The goal of the study was to find out the unfavourable factors affecting motivation. The study presented some suggestions to arouse the students' motivation to learn English and thereby improve the efficiency of English learning and teaching. The suggestions and implication of the study stated that students do need motivation to help them learn English and the right goals should be established to enhance their English learning. Meanwhile, to stimulate students, teachers should pay more attention to communicative learning for effective learning.

Critical Appraisal: The study didn't provide the details of the tool used to study motivation level of the sample. If a standardised tool could have been used, conclusion drawn would have been substantially contributed.

Rotgans and Schmidt (2010) sought to explore the utility of the MSLQ in measuring student motivation and learning strategies related to the general curriculum level rather than the course-specific level. For this purpose, the instrument was slightly modified and administered to newly graduate 1,166 secondary school students in Singapore. The construct and predictive validity of the instrument were resolute using confirmatory factor analysis and by correlating the individual subscales of the instrument with the overall semester grades. Results depicted that the modified MSLQ is a reliable and valid instrument to determine students' motivational beliefs and learning strategies at the general curriculum level.

Critical Appraisal: The modification of MSLQ was an appreciable initiative. The sample size was sufficient to draw conclusions.

Hashwani (2008) attempted to investigate gender-wise students' attitudes, motivation and anxiety towards learning English as a second language in the multilingual context of Karachi, Pakistan. Recognising the significance and multi-dimensional complexities of motivation, attitudes and anxiety, the study adapted Gardner's Attitude Motivation Test Battery to explore attitudes related to English language-learning, anxiety and intrinsic and extrinsic motivation of grade 8th students in a private secondary school. The survey findings of 77 students (40 males and 37 females) depicted that students had affirmative attitudes and high level of enthusiasm towards English language-learning. The findings also illustrated a higher inclination of extrinsic motivational goals attached to the student's language-learning outcomes and future achievements as compared to intrinsic ones, irrespective of the gender. Overall, the results showed girls to have a slightly higher degree of positive attitudes and motivation as compared to the boys. The overall classroom anxiety level demonstrated students' moderate responses with relatively higher standard deviation, highlighting that anxiety levels vary from student to student. The study suggested that teacher training sessions should also assist teachers in understanding the gender perspective in second language-learning and designing the language content according to students' needs. Teachers need to intrinsically motivate students and develop a personal interest for them to value their language-learning endeavours.

Critical Appraisal: The study was conducted to observe gender-wise differences which inclined towards female students being more motivated. Study could have provided suggestions and concern over improvement of male students' motivation.

Language-Learning and Socio-Economic Status

This sub-section presents a review of the studies on language-learning and socio-economic status. The review has facilitated understanding research trends and concepts in the field of language-learning and socio-economic status.

Kukatlapalli, Doyle and Bandyopadhyay (2019) conducted their study on the adjustment and security of international students. The purpose of their study was to examine the English language experiences of Indian students at New Zealand universities. This mixed-method study utilised a questionnaire (n=109) and interviews (n=15). Collectively the participants had high levels of confidence and proficiency in English language and adjusted more rapidly than many international students to the new academic environment. Major differences experienced by the participants between India and New Zealand related to unfamiliar forms of academic writing and tasks and on the role of learning support services. Formal high value assessment was for some the first indication of a problem with writing. While most students adjusted through error-based learning others struggled with argumentation and avoiding plagiarism. These findings had relevance for local and international students. They recommended the use of and research on, early low-stakes assessment of writing and on effective support services for students transitioning into new academic contexts.

Critical Appraisal: The study could have triangulated the data with FGD with the sample students. Number of interviews could have been representative.

Nyamubi (2019) examined how parents' socio-economic status determined students' performance in the English language in Tanzanian secondary schools. Two research questions and two research objectives guided the study. The study was conducted in two randomly selected regions in Tanzania Mainland. It employed a cross-sectional survey design to collect data from 350 students in sixteen secondary schools. Data were collected through a questionnaire and achievement tests and were analysed using both descriptive and inferential statistics to get frequencies, means, percentages, as well as Pearson's correlation and regression coefficients. It was found that students in Tanzanian secondary schools had varying backgrounds in the English language, which was determined by the type of primary school they had attended and the grade at which they started to learn the English language. The regularity of English language usage at home and school enhanced students' performance in the English language together with parents' encouragement as well as material and moral support. It is recommended that parents' socio-economic status should not inhibit learners' exposure to English language-learning. Also, parents, schools and the government should support English language teaching and learning through providing current textbooks as well as providing a favourable environment to learn and use English.

Critical Appraisal: The study didn't provide any details of the questionnaire used to collect the data for socio-economic status. It's not known if thc tool was standardised, was reliable or valid.

Abilasha and Ilankumaran (2018) in their article highlighted the significance of using English as a tool to fulfil the interminably increasing requirements of the competitive corporate world. The tasks before educators in the contemporary day ELT and strategies to overcome were considered in their paper. An analytical survey based on the data collected from the tertiary level students from the regional medium backup and students with English medium backup was taken. The respondents had been selected on the basis of random sampling with varied caste and creed. The method by which the learners could put their knowledge into real daily practice is to fulfil their real-world necessities to gain an expertise over the language was emphasised.

Critical Appraisal: The paper wanted to present an analytical survey but ended up writing an article. Hypothesis section was made but did not justify or test them. Though data were collected from a substantial number of sample but analysis was not presented as per the need.

Murray (2018) argued in the written article that English language teaching takes place in a variety of different contexts around the globe, contexts that are affected by the megatrends of global competition, population mobility and technological interconnectedness. These trends have resulted in an increased demand for English as a tool for advancement individually and nationally. However, because language is a social practice, the introduction of English within existing linguistic, sociocultural and political values and practices could create tensions. Learners' investment in learning English depends on the extent to which they and their communities envision any benefits from English or are positioned by societal forces. Additionally, local educational practices or quality may militate against the learning of English. English may therefore be rejected by communities or may maintain current societal inequities. Teachers, teacher educators and teacher education programs need to be aware that English teaching is not neutral, but a complex educational change.

Critical Appraisal; The paper was mainly an article and not research-based. It presented views and opinion and more of observations rather than any systematic presentation based on primary or secondary data.

Moreno and Callejas (2018) dealt with a crucial variable in CLIL settings: socioeconomic status, which was measured via parents' educational level (high, medium or low). It shed light on the FL, L1 and subject content attainment of 129 bilingual learners in Primary Education and Compulsory Secondary Education schools in Eastern Andalusia (more specifically, in the provinces of Granada and Almería). It provided a detailed comparison of these outcomes with those also obtained from 219 students in traditional EFL streams. Six state and two charter schools participated. Differences in the motivation, verbal intelligence and extramural exposure of these students were also examined, together with their evolution from Primary to Compulsory Secondary Education. All the variables considered were subjected to discriminant analyses in order to determine which of them explained the greatest variance in language attainment and content achievement results.

Critical Appraisal: Number of samples from six state and two charter schools, total eight schools, seemed to be too few for the study.

Kamatchi (2017) argued the notion that impact of globalisation and economic development had made English the 'language of opportunity' and a vital means of improving prospects for well-paid employment. During the last two decades the use of English for communicative purposes had not been confined only to the elite group of the society. The social profile of the students in acquisition of second language pointed to reconsider the focus given to different aspects of language and the methods and techniques adopted in language teaching. Although second language-learning was a complex phenomenon with different variables concerning the psychological factors of the learner and the socio-cultural elements of the contexts, the interactional approach to second language-learning still ensured a successful method, which may make sense in the language classroom. It was suggested to adopt an approach that was sensitive to learners' subjective needs of a social psychological nature, as well.

Critical Appraisal: The paper was mainly theoretical and did not base the arguments on data and analysis. It could have used secondary data to insist and emphasise the observations.

Ariani and Ghafournia (2016) explored the probable relationship between Iranian students' socioeconomic status, general language-learning outcomes and their beliefs about language-learning. To this end, 350 postgraduate students, doing English for specific courses at Islamic Azad University of Neyshabur participated in this study. They were grouped in terms of their socioeconomic status. They answered a questionnaire in which they indicated their beliefs about language-learning in different contexts of language use. Besides, a general language test of proficiency (a Practice test of a TOEFL Test) was administered to all the participants to homogenise them in terms of general language proficiency or general language-learning outcome. The quantitative data were subjected to a set of parametric statistical analyses, including descriptive statistics and factor analysis. The findings manifested a positive relationship between the students' economic status and general language-learning outcome. Besides, the findings manifested a significant relationship between the participants' language-learning outcomes and their beliefs about language-learning. The findings suggest if language instructors are equipped with the necessary information to assist language learners in coping with their negative beliefs, the process of language-learning is not only accelerated, but also probable measurement errors may decrease.

Critical Appraisal: The researchers made a systematic attempt to study the relationship between SES and language-learning.

Khansir, Jafarizadegan and Karampoor (2016) studied the relation between Socio-Economic Status and Motivation of Learners in Learning English as a Foreign Language, in Iran. In their work, investigators selected two hundred and thirty Iranian learners who were studying in third grade high school in Boushehr city. The female and male students in ten high schools participated in order to collect data. The one of instruments of this study was designed based on Garnder's AMTB (1985). The AMTB questionnaire utilised in the study consists of the sections: Integrative component; Motivation component; Orientation component. Another instrument of this paper was designed based on Bourdieu's (1986) in order to collect data from family socio-economic status of students. The finding of this paper indicated that most of the independent variables especially economical capital had appositive relation with motivation in EFL learning. In addition, the results of the study revealed noticeable evidence of the existence of a strong relationship between socio-economic status and motivation in language-learning (English as a FL).

Critical Appraisal: The tools were adopted from a previously standardised tool which seemed to be of 80's. The SES may be studied with immediate factors affecting the variable.

Nimmala, Nowbattula, Mylabattula and Sodadasi (2016) observed in their article a considerable need to enhance the teaching of English-to-English language learners in Andhra Pradesh state. Since the state of Andhra Pradesh had been bifurcated and had become two new states, many companies were being attracted to the development of the state. In this regard, there was an essential need to improve the English language skills of the students who belonged to the bifurcated Andhra Pradesh in promoting employment needs as well as the regional needs. The English language learners of this state had been rigorously locked with their mother tongue because of socio-economic effects in their lives. This paper mainly focussed on socio-economic circumstances and their effects on the English language-learning in Andhra Pradesh region.

Critical Appraisal: Language-learning is a universal phenomenon, may be as a second or foreign language. In the age of globalisation, language is looked at as a primary need of employment, not necessarily due to emergence of a new state.

Kormos and Kiddle (2013) surveyed the English language-learning motivations of 740 secondary school students belonging to different social classes in the capital of Chile, Santiago. They applied multiple analyses of variance to analyse how motivational variables differ depending on students' social class. The results suggested that social class had an overall medium-size effect on motivational factors with self-efficacy beliefs being the most strongly related to socio-economic status. The most important differences in motivation, self-regulation and learner autonomy were found between upper-middle and high social class students on the one hand and low and lower middle-class students on the other hand which researchers explained with reference to the inequality created by the Chilean schooling system.

Critical Appraisal: The tools used for the study were largely adapted from previously standardised tools. The tools were not administered by the researchers themselves, rather handed over to the coordinator. Researchers could have ensured the sound administration of the tools.

Salameh (2012) assessed the impact of social and economic factors on students' English language performance in EFL classrooms in Dubai public secondary schools. The study design exploited in this study is mixed methods research. Two questionnaires were designed to assess the effects of economic and social factors on students' performance in learning the English language. The factors include the parents' occupation, education, and financial status. Students from cycle 3 classes answered the two questionnaires reflecting on the effects perceived of those factors on their performance. Then, their responses were correlated with their grades obtained from their English language instructors and conclusions were drawn. The correlation is measured by Person's correlation coefficient (r = 0.66). The result was significant and a positive correlation between the parents' level of education, income and occupation with pupil's educational performance was observed. Another instrument utilised in this research was interviews. The interviewees were two male and two female teachers of English language, a male principal and a female principal, all of whom were asked about their opinions on the relationship between students' performance in learning the English language and their parents' social and economic status. Overall, teachers and principals observed a relationship between parents' social and economic status and children's performance in learning the English language. Though they justify this relationship differently, the matter of the fact remains that there is a strong correlation between socioeconomic factors and students' performance in the field of English language-learning.

Critical Appraisal: The sample of the study did not belong to the same level of education; students from tenth, eleventh and twelfth grades were selected. The sample could have been selected from a single level or the sample selected from different levels could have been more representative.

Blended Learning

This section presents a review of studies on blended learning. The reviews have helped to understand the research trends in the field of blended learning related to LA.

Hrastinski (2019) discussed the different definitions, models and conceptualisations of blended learning with their implications. Inclusive definitions, models and diverse conceptualisations, meant that essentially all types of education that included some aspect of face-to-face learning and online learning were described as blended learning in the literature. Blended learning had become an umbrella term. Blended learning had also been used to describe other blends, such as combining different instructional methods, pedagogical approaches and technologies. Although these blends were not aligned with influential blended learning definitions. Since blended learning had many meanings, it's important that researchers and practitioners carefully explain initially what blended learning means in their context of study.

Critical Appraisal: The discussion mainly led to widely accepted notion of blended learning and other discussions, in general. The discussion seemed to be for all in.

Arkhipova, Belova, Gavrikova, Lyulyaeva and Shapiro (2017) investigated how blended learning inspired students of different ages to be more motivated in the process of acquiring receptive and productive foreign language skills. The authors analysed the neurobiological and psychological characteristics of various age groups of people learning a foreign language. It was concluded that the age of a student had been a defining factor of the necessity of information technologies used in the learning process. It meant that neglecting a new technology in teaching a foreign language to children, teenagers and young adults had not been an option then. Older students were used to traditional methods of teaching a foreign language and appreciated the use of online resources and tools. The combination of student-centred methods and modern technology was the quintessence of blended learning which served as an effective teaching tool for EFL students.

Critical Appraisal: The study could have provided a model to follow for blended learning for different age groups as per the observations.

Boelens, Wever and Voet (2017) presented the design of blended learning environments with four key challenges: (1) incorporating flexibility, (2) stimulating interaction, (3) facilitating students' learning processes and (4) fostering an affective learning climate. They presented a systematic review attempting to resolve these challenges fragmented across the literature. Approximately 640 sources and 20 studies on the design of blended learning environments were selected through a staged procedure based on the guidelines of the PRISMA statement, using predefined selection criteria. For each study, the instructional activities for dealing with these four challenges were analysed by two coders. The results showed that few studies offered learners control over the realisation of the blend. Social interaction was generally stimulated through introductory face-to-face meetings, while personalisation and monitoring of students' learning progress were commonly organised through online instructional activities. Finally, little attention was paid to instructional activities that foster an affective learning climate.

Critical Appraisal: The study could have delved a little deeper into how these four key challenges were zeroed in and taken up for the study.

Kintu, Zhu and Kagambe (2017) investigated the effectiveness of a blended learning environment through analysing the relationship between student characteristics/background, design features and learning outcomes. It aimed at determining the significant predictors of blended learning effectiveness taking student characteristics/background and design features as independent variables and learning outcomes as dependent variables. The researchers conducted a survey with 238 respondents to gather data on student characteristics/background, design features and learning outcomes. The final semester evaluation results were used as a measure for performance as an outcome. They applied the online self-regulatory learning questionnaire for data on learner self-regulation, the intrinsic motivation inventory for data on intrinsic motivation and other self-developed instruments for measuring the other constructs. Multiple regression analysis results showed that blended learning design features (technology quality, online tools and face-to-face support) and student characteristics (attitudes and self-regulation) predicted student satisfaction as an outcome. The results indicated that some of the student characteristics/backgrounds and design features were significant predictors for student learning outcomes in blended learning.

Critical Appraisal The study could have used standardised tools to validate their data. The data was collected through online mode which raises the concern over administration of the data tool.

Flipped Classroom

This section presents a review of the studies on the flipped classroom. The reviews have helped to understand the research trends in the field of a flipped classroom for language teaching related to LA.

Turan and Akdag-Cimen (2020) examined the trends and main findings of studies concerning the flipped classroom method in the field of English language teaching (ELT). For this purpose, databases including Web of Science, Eric, Taylor & Francis and the Educational full text EBSCO were reviewed and a total of 43 articles were analysed. Systematic review was used as the research methodology. The articles were analysed utilising a content analysis method. The findings of the study revealed that the flipped classroom method in ELT gained popularity among researchers after 2014 and number of the studies in the field rapidly increased in the last two years (2016–2017). In addition, the most commonly used research methods in flipped classroom in ELT studies were found to be mixed and quantitative methods. In the examined studies, speaking and writing abilities were the most commonly studied language skills. Further analysis revealed challenges, as well as benefits related to the use of the flipped classroom method in English as a foreign language (EFL) classrooms. Additionally, in studies reviewed concerning the effectiveness of the flipped classroom methods, the findings mostly pointed to the benefits of the flipped classroom method.

Critical Appraisal: The study was based on content analysis only as methodology. Being a qualitative study, data could have been triangulated.

Vitta and Al-Hoorie (2020) presented a meta-analysis of 56 language-learning reports, which involved 61 unique samples and 4,220 participants. Their results showed that flipped classrooms outperformed traditional classrooms, $g = 0.99$, 95% CI (0.81, 1.17), $z = 10.90$, $p < 0.001$. However, this effect had high heterogeneity (about 86%), while applying the Trim and Fill method for the publication bias made it shrink to $g = 0.58$, 95% CI (0.37, 0.78). Moderator analysis also showed that reports published in non-SSCI-indexed journals tended to find larger effects compared to indexed ones, conference proceedings and university theses. The effect of flipped learning did not seem to vary by age, but it did vary by proficiency level in that the higher proficiency the higher the effects. Flipped learning also had a clear and substantial effect on most language outcomes. In contrast, whether the intervention used videos and whether the platform was interactive did not turn out to be significant moderators. Meta-regression showed that longer interventions resulted in only a slight reduction in the effectiveness of this approach. Researchers also discussed the implications of these findings and recommended that future research move beyond asking whether flipped learning is effective to when and how its effectiveness is maximised.

Critical Appraisal: The study had entirely different results with the Trim and Fill method while considering publication, which itself raises several questions over research and publication approaches.

Kvashnina and Martynko (2019) aimed at contributing to the field of flipped classroom research by briefly examining and analysing the outcomes of the experiment conducted at Tomsk Polytechnic University within the course of English for Engineering. Outlining several challenges, the authors concluded on the significant benefits of the flipped classroom in ESL teaching including an increase in students' overall performance in the course, enhancement of students' motivation and improvement of their autonomous learning skills.

Critical Appraisal: Despite showing the concern over empirical studies on flipped classroom, the paper was mainly theoretical not based on some secondary data or details. Though the paper presented and discussed a model, the work could have used the model for empirical proofs.

Ayçiçek and Yelken (2017) aimed to determine the effect of the flipped classroom model on students' classroom engagement in teaching English. This research was conducted within the English course for a four week period in the Spring term in 2016-2017 school year in a secondary school in the city of Hatay. In the study, pre-test/post-test quasi-experimental design with a control group was applied. The experimental group was lectured with the flipped classroom model whereas the courses were carried out based on the current curriculum in the control group. In the current study, descriptive statistics, Mann Whitney U Test and Wilcoxon Sign Test were used in the analysis of the quantitative data. It was concluded that there was a significant difference between the pre-test and post-test scores of the experimental group whereas there was no significant difference between the pre-test and post-test scores of the control group. Finally, it could be suggested to teachers to use flipped classroom model to enhance classroom engagement.

Critical Appraisal: For the experimental study, the sample size (N = 40) and duration of the experiment could have been improved. Otherwise, it's an empirical study with proper tools and intervention strategy.

Kim, Park, Jang and Nam (2017) investigated the cognitive effects of the flipped classroom approach in a content-based instructional context by comparing second language learners' discourse in flipped vs. traditional classrooms in terms of (1) participation rate, (2) content of comments, (3) reasoning skills and (4) interactional patterns. Learners in two intact classes participated and were taught in either a flipped classroom (n=26) or a traditional classroom (n=25). In the flipped class, the learners listened to an online lecture before class and participated in a small-group discussion in class. In contrast, the learners in the traditional class listened to a teacher-led lecture in class and then immediately participated in a small-group discussion in class. The learners' discussions were audio-recorded. Quantitative and qualitative analyses indicated no difference in participation rates; however, the students in the flipped classroom produced more cognitive comments involving deeper information processing and higher-order reasoning skills. They were able to show more cohesive interactional patterns than did the students in the traditional classroom. These results indicated that flipped classrooms can effectively promote higher-order thinking processes and in-depth, cohesive discussion in the content-based second language.

Critical Appraisal A pre-test and post-test for achievement could have been designed to study the significant difference between the two groups.

5

Learning Analytics Scenario – India vis-a-vis World

Rationale with Literature Review

Global Research Developments related to AbF since Covid-19

Since the Covid-19 pandemic, there has been a sudden rapid shift towards using GenAI in almost all walks of life with education not being left behind. The Learning Analytics and Knowledge (LAK) Conference 2024 was held with a focus on the use of analytics-based feedback in education to provide decision support and feedback, assess student learning, and create personalized and adaptive learning environments. It encouraged to evaluate the effectiveness of feedback systems such as dashboards, early-alert systems, and automated messages. Additionally, studies that focussed on the impact of these systems on learning and teaching processes, and how they inform and support decision-making by educators and students, were highly relevant.

Lim et al. (2023) explored how personalized feedback based on learning analytics can support self-regulated learning in their paper titled 'Personalized Feedback for Self-Regulated Learning'. The study found that tailored feedback can significantly enhance students' ability to manage their learning processes, thereby improving their academic performance.

Cai et al. (2022) explored the integration of mental effort estimation into learning dashboards to provide personalized feedback and presented their research titled 'A Penny for your Thoughts: Personalized Feedback with Mental Effort Estimation in Learning Dashboards.' By analysing mental effort data, their system aimed to offer tailored recommendations and insights to learners, enhancing their self-regulation and engagement in learning activities.

Efrat Vinker and Amir Rubinstein (2022) analyzed code submissions in a MOOC to identify patterns of disengagement and provide feedback to improve retention. By predicting disengagement through submission profiles, the study offers insights into enhancing pedagogical designs and feedback mechanisms in programming courses. Their work was titled as 'Mining Code Submissions to Elucidate Disengagement in a Computer Science MOOC.'

Pozdniakov et al. (2022) proposed a question-driven design approach for learning analytics dashboards to align with teachers' inquiries. The authors developed a tool to monitor students' collaborative activities in real-time, helping teachers make informed decisions and provide timely feedback during synchronous online sessions. The study was titled as 'The Question-driven Dashboard: How Can We Design Analytics Interfaces Aligned to Teachers' Inquiry?'

Rakovic et al. (2022) examined how metacognitive processes during multi-source writing tasks could be supported by learning analytics. The study collected trace data to provide feedback on students' metacognitive monitoring and control, demonstrating the impact of such processes on the quality of their written outputs. Their work was titled as 'Using Learner Trace Data to Understand Metacognitive Processes in Writing from Multiple Sources.'

Gurung, Botelho, and Heffernan (2021) conducted a series of analyses based on response time decomposition (RTD) to explore student help-seeking behaviour in the context of on-demand hints within a computer-based learning platform with particular focus on examining which students appear to be exhibiting effort to learn while engaging with the system. Their findings were centred around examining how the measure of student effort correlates with later student performance measures.

Jensen, Pugh, and D'Mello (2021) published the research titled 'A Deep Transfer Learning Approach to Modeling Teacher Discourse in the Classroom' compared two different machine learning approaches to automatically model seven features of teacher discourse (e.g., use of questions, elaborated evaluations). Researchers compared a traditional open vocabulary approach using n-grams and Random Forest classifiers with a state-of-the-art deep transfer learning approach for natural language processing (BERT). They found a trade-off between data quantity and accuracy, where deep models had an advantage on larger datasets, but not for smaller datasets, particularly for variables with low incidence rates. They also compared the models based on the level of feedback granularity: utterance-level (e.g., whether an utterance is a question or a statement), class session-level proportions by averaging across utterances (e.g., question incidence score of 48%), and session-level ordinal feedback based on pre-determined thresholds (e.g., question asking score is medium [vs. low or high]) and found that BERT generally provided more accurate feedback at all levels of granularity. Thus, BERT appeared to be the most viable approach to providing automatic feedback on teacher discourse provided there is sufficient data to fine tune the model.

Zylich and Lan (2021) presented a paper titled 'Linguistic Skill Modeling for Second Language Acquisition' where the investigators sought to determine whether skill-based models could be combined with memory-based models to improve student modeling and especially retrieval practice performance for SLA. In order to define skills in the context of SLA, they develope methods that could automatically extract multiple types of linguistic features from words.

Using these features as skills, they applied skill-based models to a real-world SLA dataset. They concluded, firstly, that incorporating lexical features to represent individual words as skills in skill-based models outperforms existing memory-based models in terms of recall probability prediction; secondly, incorporating additional morphological and syntactic features of each word via multiple-skill tagging of each word further improves the skill-based models; and lastly, incorporating semantic features, like word embeddings, to model similarities between words in a learner's practice history and their effects on memory also improves the models and appears to be a promising direction for future research.

Research Developments in India related to Learning Analytics

Though gradual development can be observed related to machine learning, EDM and AI with a number of studies in the field of engineering and IT, the education system at the school level is yet to witness a quick-start in research studies and practicing of LA. Now a few papers and works have begun to surface and emerge in the country as mentioned next.

Agrawal and Lalwani (2020) used the tutor Funtoot and presented students working on the topic Addition Word Problems with a subtraction word problem and investigated how they performed in the out-of-context subtraction word problem. Researchers found that students' performance in the topic Addition Word Problems was a strong predictor of their performance in this out-of-context problem. Their results suggested that it was a stronger predictor for higher grades (4*th* and 5*th*) compared to the lower (2*nd* and 3*rd*) grades.

Critical Appraisal: In 2020, the study explored Funtoot as the platform to teach Mathematics but posed out-of-context subtraction and addition word problems at the Primary level of education. The online students who chose to attempt these questions were proportionately less, 2218 students out of 21722. Also, the work did not provide any information on parents' consent or data privacy. Despite all, it was one of the first attempts around LA at the primary level in India and much appreciated.

Kumar, Kinshuk, Somasundaram, Boulanger, Seanosky and Vilela (2015) offered a new perspective on learning and instructional attainments with big data analytics as the underlying framework, discussed approaches to this framework with evidences from the literature and offered a case study that illustrated the need to pursue research directions arising from this new perspective. The study used a combination of software tools to collect data generated from 240 students at the Madras Institute of Technology (Chennai, India) while they completed the course 'Introduction to Programming in C', meant for the study. This case study illustrated for the research the collection of raw data, the transforming the raw data into learning traces, the application of learning analytics techniques on learning traces, the use of results of analytics towards balancing learning and instructional attainment and the measurement of impact of analytics. An open-source Moodle plug-in developed by University of Las Palmas de Gran Canaria called Virtual Programming Lab (VPL)4 was altered to perform a similar data collection task from within Moodle itself for less intensive programming exercises. Further, highly personalised software tutors called MI-LATTE (mixed-initiative learning analytics tutoring and training environment) had also been developed. Each MI-LATTE tutor targets a single assignment problem, where learners were expected to solve the problem by writing 'one line of code' at a time. Finally, learner interaction data with the Eclipse Integrated Development Environment Extension (EIDEE) captured data concerning code design steps, code writing, code debugging, code documenting, code testing, code review/reflection and code optimising. Student interactions with the Moodle content were captured from the Moodle database. Students also completed a built-in survey questionnaire in Moodle to indicate their experience with the Moodle course. The results made a point that students and instructors should be in control of the choice of analyses and the corresponding techniques. Big data analytics enabled students and instructors to proceed further towards regulation opportunities. Competency growth in programming could also be observed at the individual student level, or the course level, or the departmental level, or even at the institutional level.

Critical Appraisal: This study is one of the early attempts to conduct a LA study in India in one of the most prime institutes of engineering. Also, with the then available infrastructure, the study brought forward many implications at the higher education level. Moodle is an open platform and easier to create an LMS for at least 50 participants for free.

Suchithra, Vaidhehi and Iyer (2015) presented a review of literature on learning analytics in the Indian context. The study showed that the usage of learning analytics is very limited to Higher education institutions in India. In many cases, Higher education institutions in India were not aware of the courses needed by the students. Knowledge from the data mining should be brought out to higher education institutions so that courses could be structured based on the need. The literature review showed that the various research activities were concerned mainly on students after joining a particular course. This proved to be detrimental if the student had not selected a course properly. To increase the number of students continuing higher education, the future research work was towards the design of a system for students to choose courses in the Indian universities using Learning Analytics. Course advisory systems were also to help the higher education institutions to plan the education system that is academic curriculum by knowing the demand for each course in an efficient way. This paper provided a detailed review on various Learning Analytics tools, applications and the techniques used to design and develop Learning Analytic systems.

Critical Appraisal: The literature review delved deeper on the usefulness and relevancy plane of course selection in Indian universities. It showed apparently that LA is yet to touch the lines of school education in Indian scenario.

Keshavamurthy and Guruprasad (2014) conducted a survey study that covered several studies revolving around learning analytics – some proposing general framework to be used for learning analytics, one that presented a course management system and its use-cases and several of them that applied and implemented different mining algorithms to establish associations and predictions of student performance. Visualisation of student learning behaviour through learning dashboards with respect to peers and bringing about awareness of student activities can aid in learning process. By studying the learning behaviour, course facilitators can identify students at risk of failure and can take several initiatives such as customising learning materials, providing additional coaching, recommending certain learning resources to help individual students at risk early in the learning process. Also, the survey showed that different experiments had yielded different prediction accuracies and had contradictory comparison results in terms of algorithms used for predictive analysis.

Critical Appraisal: The survey study provided some dos and don'ts of a LA study. Some of the suggestions were contradictory as the studies surveyed provided a contrast view. Therefore, suggestions related to only LA study designs could be taken into consideration. The study could have provided better insights with Indian LA studies and perspective.

Rationale of the Study

The review helped to develop an understanding of LA, language-learning and other associated variables. LA is an emerging field whereas other associated variables of the study have a trail of research for more than two decades or may be longer. Several dimensions in education can be explored with LA as the field has the possibility of growth geographically and technically. Reviews had provided an insight into the current trends and tools required to conduct the study. It had also given the information about the different methodologies that have been adopted to carry out the research in the field. Providing an insight into past trends, reviews are positive for the Feedback studies, in general, where the present study focussed and for the other related variable fields. Analytics-based Feedback (AbF) is also gradually getting popularised among researchers and educators but yet to be empirically established with sufficient numbers of researches. It was observed during review that research studies related to LA in School, especially ESL are few in numbers. Thus, as the present study focussed on the analysis of learning progression of the English subject matter of Higher Secondary students where the efforts were made on Analytics-based Feedback for the participants of the study.

Though the study in 2008 by Leelawong and Biswas with Betty's Brain at the school level education provided quite an insight about the role of feedback but feedback to learners for performance improvement could not somehow gain momentum for more empirical research till 2015–2016. Later, Anjewierden (2012) also worked with Betty's Brain and insisted on the significance of feedback's role with actionable insights. Berland et al. (2014) also observed the significance of feedback in a quantitative study with EDM in a constructionist learning environment. Papamitsiou and Economides (2014) emphasized the role of personalisation of feedback whereas Ebner and Schön (2013) highlighted the importance of feedback in their study related to maths education and also provided suggestions for language education. Lately, Cavalcanti et al. (2020), Iraj et al. (2020), Wang and Eberhard (2020), Mori et al. (2019), Vigentini et al. (2019), Jørnø and Gynther (2018), and Shum et al. (2017) also presented their researches accentuating the role of feedback to improve learners' performance. All the reviews incline towards positive outcomes related to feedback for learners' performance improvement. It is also to be noticed that only a handful of studies are at the school level education with a research gap in second language education.

At the school level of education, a number of studies have been conducted related to Mathematics and Science pedagogy to explore avenues to understand the teaching-learning of the subject. Crossley et al. (2020) worked to gain insights into non-cognitive constructs of Maths; Zheng et al. (2019) worked on predictive modelling in the mathematics subject; Lang (2014) used Inverse Bayesian estimation to summarise and make predictions about students' behaviour in an adaptive educational setting to math problems; and Pardos et al. (2014) used ASSISTments for the same subject. Rodríguez-Triana et al. (2016) also promoted STEM (Science, Technology, Engineering and Mathematics) education with Go-Lab European project. Liu et al. (2019) improved Science knowledge engaging learners in PBL learning for disadvantaged middle school at risk students; Liu et al. (2018) assessed the learning trajectory with Virtual Lab tutoring system of ChemVLab; and Segedy et al. (2015) used Betty's Brain in different contexts to teach Science for their students to perform better. Lewis et al. (2020) attempted to maximise high school students' sense of choice while selecting elective subjects. Ahmad Khanlari et al. (2019) engaged elementary school students in knowledge building, whereas Holstein et al. (2019) tuned analytics to evaluate in real-world contexts with methodological recommendations. Wei et al. (2019) studied tertiary instructors' degree of familiarity with LA using LA tools in various contexts; whereas, Divjak and Vondra (2016) studied specific challenges of ethics and privacy issues of LA in pre-tertiary and primary education as compared to higher education. Cejnar and Kao (2018) described a novel real-time LA tool providing teachers and educators feedback on actual computer usage to improve teaching and policies. Ferguson (2018), Ferguson et al. (2016), and Baker (2013) drew action principles and guidelines for Australian and European policymakers. These studies related to pedagogical aspects of Mathematics and Science education provided a supporting outcome with LA.

In researches related to LA for Language teaching, a number of studies favoured but one due to orientation of the participants of the study. Friedl et al. (2020) in their very positive feedback from learners focussed on the development of a prototype of a mobile application for Android and iOS for language acquisition; Lecailliez et al. (2020) supported EFL teachers in identifying possible problems that arose through dictionary use while reading; Hilliard (2019) used learner corpus in an advanced ESL writing course with continual cycle of evaluation and implementation for more successful student outcomes; Reinders (2018) concluded that LA, both in its synchronous and its asynchronous forms, offers genuinely exciting opportunities for insights into the language-learning process that were previously unattainable; Rienties et al. (2018) found 55% of variance in weekly online engagement by the way language teachers designed activities; Peng (2017) facilitated students' learning English more actively along with reliable data and results that made teachers and students more convinced about LA; Tan et al. (2017) provided empirical evidence with WiREAD, one of the first LA-focused learning environments on how the promise and perils of LA dashboards and visual analytics, also reminding of the restrictive effects of one-sized-fits-all approaches to assessment; Volk et al. (2015) observed the strong influence of the factor time, the time and activity structure of a school year on usage behaviour; Dowell and Graesser (2014) highlighted the advantages of using theoretically grounded automated linguistics tools to identify pedagogically valuable discourse features; Tran and Duong (2013) revealed that significant differences existed between academic achievements with English anxiety, organisation, and environmental management strategy usage; Swalander and Taube (2007) studied how reading attitude and family reading background relates to reading ability. All these studies have a similar perspective for LA but Admiraal and Bulterman-Bos (2017) concluded that students were generally not very satisfied with an individual approach of their teacher during the lessons. Neither the poor performing students nor the high performing students evaluated an individual teaching approach positively as they felt that they get too much attention making them conscious in a group. The study also accepted that they lack on orienting the participants of the study.

A handful of studies were found which have produced empirical evidences for the relationship between LA and motivation. Wang and Zhan (2020) suggested that stronger learner beliefs of self-efficacy and the perceived value of English learning promoted learning motivation and self-regulation; Nagy (2016) suggested the need to create high-quality data-driven conversations between students, teachers and parents for improving student motivation; Ali et al. (2014) presented empirical support for building new models and reuse of precious and previous datasets collected for some other primary purposes; Jahedi (2012) observed significant correlation between motivational beliefs components and self-regulated learning components of the students which also influenced the academic achievement of students; and Turingan and Yang (2009) used Motivated Strategies Learning Questionnaire (MSLQ) to assess the self-regulation of learning skills and the motivational orientation of students.

Cho et al. (2018) observed a moderately positive effect of using mobile devices on language acquisition and language-learning achievement; Cummins (2017) and Khatib and Taie (2016) presented their work on BICS and CALP; Harsono (2015) described a teaching-learning materials development for English for Specific Purposes (ESP); and, Heritage and Bailey (2014) addressed the theoretical and empirical issues related to the development and evaluation of language-learning progressions.

Islam (2020) suggested that students with different learning styles had different reading comprehension scores; Pawlak (2020) postulated on the previous cognitive-interactionists approach and investigated the impact of English learners' proficiency, gender and learning style on the occurrence; Wong (2015) also observed EAP classrooms with multiple learning style preferences; Gülbahar and Ilgaz (2014) chose Moodle LMS an e-learning environment where instructional materials could be offered based on students' learning styles; Karthigeyan and Nirmala (2013) observed that the primary and secondary learning styles of the language students were visual and auditory learning style; Yassin (2012) concluded that ESL Arab Gulf students' learning styles were affected by their cultural backgrounds and their gender as well; Chen (2009) cautioned as it's critical for classroom teachers to be more aware of the differences in their students learning styles; and, O'Brien (1989) developed 'The Learning Channel Preference Checklist' (O'Brien, 1988), a questionnaire designed to identify the learning styles of learners.

Vyas and Choudhary (2016), Nadeem et al. (2014), Yazdani and Godbole (2014), Mudasir (2012) used Palsane and Sharma's Study Habits Inventory (PSSHI) by M. N. Palsane (1989) to collect data. Kumari and Chamundeswari (2015) and Siahi, Maiyo (2015) and Yazdani and Godbole (2014) observed significantly positive correlation between achievement, study habits and performance of students. Pandey and Singh (2015) also observed significant difference between study habits as well as the academic achievements of rural and urban first-generation learners and subsequent generation learners. Bailey and Onwuegbuzie (2010) observed study habits to distinguish successful from unsuccessful foreign language learners.

Colaste (2018), Khan (2016), Nyamubi (2016), Ahmed (2015), Bhaskar and Soundiraraj (2013), Abidin et al. (2012), and Mahmoudi et al. (2012) observed a positive correlation between English language teaching learning, attitude and academic achievement in the subject.

Rezaei et al. (2015) and Rotgans and Schmidt (2010) used Motivated Strategies Learning Questionnaire (MSLQ) to study the motivation and academic achievement whereas, Hashwani (2008) used Gardner's Attitude Motivation Test Battery for the same purpose. Long et al. (2013) observed positive correlation between motivation and academic achievement in ESL.

Kukatlapalli et al. (2019) examined the adjustment and security with respect to English language experiences of Indian students; Nyamubi (2019), Murray (2018), Moreno and Callejas (2018), Ariani and Ghafournia (2016), Nimmala et al. (2016) of Andhra Pradesh state, India, Kormos and Kiddle (2013), Salameh (2012), also, Gömleksiz (2010) observed the positive relationship between socio-economic status determining students' performance in the English language. They implied that socio-economic status should not inhibit learners' exposure to English language-learning. Abilasha and Ilankumaran (2018) highlighted the significance of using English as a tool to fulfil the interminably increasing requirements of the competitive corporate world whereas, Kamatchi (2017) argued the notion that impact of globalisation and economic development had made English the 'language of opportunity'. Khansir et al. (2016) and Gayton (2010) studied an association between socio-economic status and language-learning motivation for English as a Foreign Language.

Hrastinski (2019), Arkhipova, et al. (2017), and Boelens et al. (2017) presented mainly theoretical understandings, discussions and deliberations on blended learning whereas Kintu et al. (2017) deliberated on empirical evidences supporting the blended learning environment for students. Turan and Akdag-Cimen (2020), Kvashnina and Martynko (2019), Ayçiçek and Yelken (2017), and Kim et al. (2017) presented their theoretical and mostly empirical works on the flipped classroom supporting the usage of the method. However, Vitta and Al-Hoorie (2020) have raised concern over the quality of publications and research.

Harrak et al. (2019) established their work around using feedback as a substantial tool of LA. Yang et al. (2020) observed the correlation of the students' concentration degree with the course topics, analysing audio features. Ferguson (2019) and Ferguson and Shum (2012) provided a framework for essential work for ethics and privacy in learning analytics and later reviewed some of the 'tectonic forces' reshaping the learning landscape. Liu et al. (2019), Dvorak and Jia (2016), Gašević et al. (2015), Andergassen et al. (2014), Gilmore (2014), and Hecking et al. (2014) based their works on LMSs and CMSs on MOODLE and Massive Open Online Course (MOOC) and thereby analysing the data generated. Saint (2019), Brooks et al. (2013), Nguyen et al. (2018), and Kovanović et al. (2015) recognised the potential of temporal processes traced from data and essentials of time-on task and thus exploring more on students online learning behaviour. Atapattu and Falkner (2018) explored the association between video interactions and non-visual (i.e., verbal) content focusing on language and discourse features of lecture video contents. Viberg et al. (2018) interrogated past LA works of 252 research papers by posing four questions, whether learning analytics i) improve learning outcomes, ii) support learning and teaching, iii) are deployed widely, and iv) were used ethically. The results demonstrated that overall, there was little evidence that showed improvements in students' learning outcomes (9%) as well as learning support and teaching (35%). Similarly, little evidence was found for the third (6%) and the fourth (18%) proposition. Aguiar et al. (2014), Gray et al. (2014), Gunnarsson and Alterman (2014), and Jayaprakash et al. (2014) presented substantial contribution towards predictive modelling using different tools of e-portfolios, blogosphere, Open Academic Analytics Initiative (OAAI) and much more. Buerck and Mudigonda (2014), Ye and Biswas (2014), and Lauría et al. (2007) worked for improving student performance and retention by using analytics to identify under-performing students early and dropout worries. Chiu and Fujita (2014) described an application of learning analytics for synchronous and asynchronous data offering huge and exciting opportunities for analysing how people influence and effect one another through their interactions. Dunbar et al. (2014) described how data from institutional, learning, and what we call 'developmental' analytics can be incorporated into course and curricular design by using a purposefully built analysis tool that permits the exploration of data relevant to course/curriculum design. Kovanović and Gašević (2014) and Kruse and Pongsajapan (2012) developed a LA framework by building on the Community of Inquiry model (CoI) and proposed a student-centric, inquiry-based model of analytics that puts the tools and premises of analytics into the hands of students, empowering them as metacognitive agents of their learning and understanding, respectively; Monroy et al. (2014) presented a scalable approach for integrating learning analytics into an online K-12 science curriculum mixed methods strategy; and Scheffel et al. (2014) brought forward a five-dimensional framework of quality indicators for learning analytics to aid standardise the evaluation of LA tools. A study by Worsley and Blikstein (2014) uncovered novel insights and served to advance the field's understanding of engineering design patterns using machine learning and developed a fine-grained representation. Dimopoulos et al. (2013) presented an assessment tool, called Learning Analytics Enriched Rubric (LAe-R) based on the popular assessment technique of rubrics.

Lately, LA studies have surfaced in India with a handful studies like literature review by Suchithra et al. (2015) and a survey study by Keshavamurthy and Guruprasad (2014). Kumar et al. (2015) at Madras Institute of Technology (Chennai, India) also offered a new perspective on learning and instructional attainments with big data analytics whereas Agrawal and Lalwani (2020) used tutor Funtoot for Addition and Subtraction Word Problems at the Primary Level but yet a start for adopting LA in India.

Summary and Conclusion

During a thorough review of the literature on LA, it was observed that most of the research work was revolving around establishing theories and definition till 2020-21 and gradually a paradigm shift has been observed to bring forward implicative studies by 2024. Since 2021 there is a rise of studies around AbF and a definition indeed needed. The present book is also a result of a pragmatic and experimental trial of LA at school level education and defines AbF as provided earlier in the book. Reviews helped to identify the gap and advances in the field and thereby formulating research questions, objectives and hypothesize the chances.

6

The Study Essentials

Usually, any research is structured with problem statement, research questions, objectives and thereby formulated hypothesis, delimitations in the beginning only. Yet, the book presents a wide literature review of the field followed by the empirical study essentials. The earlier chapters in the book present the introduction and reviews as rationale of the study. The current chapter presents problem statement, operational definitions, research questions, objectives, hypothesis and delimitations, the empirical study essentials.

Statement of the Problem

The purpose of the investigation was to analyse English language-learning progression using Analytics-based Feedback for Higher Secondary students. Accordingly, progress was analysed, recorded, tested, assessed, reported, and interpreted to arrive at educational implications of the study.

Research Questions

The study had six research questions to inquire. The research questions were worded as below:

1: What are the descriptive statistics in terms of effectiveness for the Analytics-based feedback during the English language learning progression of higher secondary students of Madhya Pradesh in terms of BICS, CALP and overall achievement scores?

2: How is the trend of progression for the effect of Analytics-based feedback on BICS, CALP and Overall Achievement in English language of higher secondary students of Madhya Pradesh?

3: What is the relationship between Analytics-based feedback (Treatment) with gender, learning style, and socio-economic status and BICS, CALP and overall achievement scores in English language through the progression?

4: What is the effect of the Analytics-based feedback and the interactive of AbF and gender on the selected variables (study habits, motivation, attitudes towards English language)?

5: How have teachers, principal and parents opined about Analytics-based feedback as stakeholders of the study?

6: What are the issues and challenges related to conducting Learning Analytics study in India?

Objectives

In line with the focus on the research questions of the study, the objectives of the study are given below.

1. To study the effectiveness of Analytics-based Feedback in English Language for Higher Secondary Students in terms of:
   a. Achievement of students in English Language with BICS Scores;
   b. Achievement of students in English Language with CALP Scores;
   c. Achievement of Students in English Language with Overall Scores.
2. To study the trend of the effect of the Treatment on the BICS component of Achievement in English language progression of Class XI students.
3. To study the trend of the effect of the Treatment on the CALP component of Achievement in English language progression of Class XI students.
4. To study the trend of the effect of the Treatment on Overall Achievement in English language progression of Class XI students.
5. To study the relationship between the BICS component of Achievement in English language progression and the Treatment, Gender, Socio-economic status, and Learning style of Class XI students.
6. To study the relationship between the CALP component of Achievement in English language progression and the Treatment, Gender, Socio-economic status, and Learning style of Class XI students.
7. To study the relationship between Overall Achievement in English language progression and the Treatment, Gender, Socio-economic status, and Learning style of Class XI students.
8. To study the interactive effect of Treatment and Gender on Study Habits of Class XI students by taking the Pre-test scores of Study Habits of students as a covariate.
9. To study the interactive effect of Treatment and Gender on the Attitude towards English Language of Class XI students by taking the Pre-test scores of Attitudes towards English Language as a covariate.
10. To study the interactive effect of Treatment and Gender on the Motivation Level of Class XI students when measured with MSLQ by taking the Pre-test scores of MSLQ of the students as a covariate.
11. To study the effectiveness of Analytics-based Feedback in English Language for Higher Secondary Students in terms of:
    a. Opinion of Teacher towards Analytics-based Feedback;
    b. Opinion of Principal towards Analytics-based Feedback; and
    c. Opinion of Parents towards Analytics-based Feedback.
12. To study the issues and challenges related to conducting Learning Analytics studies in India.

Hypotheses

The following hypotheses were formulated for the study.

1. There is no significant change in the learning progression in terms of the BICS component of Achievement in the English language in the successive trials of Class XI learners.
2. There is no significant change in the learning progression in terms of the CALP component of Achievement in the English language in the successive trials of Class XI learners.
3. There is no significant change in the learning progression in terms of the Overall Achievement in the English language in the successive trials of Class XI learners.
4. There is no significant relationship between the BICS component of Achievement in the English language progression and the Treatment, Gender, Socio-economic status, and Learning style of Class XI students.
5. There is no significant relationship between the CALP component of Achievement in the English language progression and the Treatment, Gender, Socio-economic status, and Learning style of Class XI students.
6. There is no significant relationship between Overall Achievement in the English language progression and the Treatment, Gender, Socio-economic status, and Learning style of Class XI students.
7. There is no significant interactive effect of Treatment and Gender on Study Habits of Class XI students when their Pre-test scores of Study Habits were taken as a covariate.
8. There is no significant interactive effect of Treatment and Gender on the Attitude towards the English Language of Class XI students by taking the Pre-test scores of Attitudes towards the English Language as a covariate.
9. There is no significant interactive effect of Treatment and Gender on the Motivation Level of Class XI students when measured with MSLQ by taking the Pre-test scores of MSLQ of the students as a covariate.

Delimitations

The study was conducted under the following constraints:

1. It was limited to students of Higher Secondary of CBSE studying in Central Schools of Madhya Pradesh District.
2. It was limited to Bhopal city of Madhya Pradesh only.
3. The contents of English textbooks published by NCERT were taken in to consideration for developing the E-course.
4. It was limited only to Class XI at the Higher Secondary level.
5. Analytics-based Feedback was used as a sophisticated strategy of LA.

7

Methodology and Approach

The present chapter of the book presents the Methodology of the study. It deals with the methodology, design of the experiment, sample, tools, instructional materials, and statistical techniques for the analysis of data. These are presented under separate captions, below.

Methodology

The study was conducted to study the progression of English as a second language by providing Analytics-based Feedback (AbF). it was experimental in nature with a mixed method approach; therefore, an Experimental Method was employed for the study.

Design of the Study

A quasi-experimental design was used for the study. The study used two groups: the Experimental group with the benefits of Analytics-based Feedback and the Control group. The Experimental group was taught by providing various feedback about them and their performance whereas the Control group was provided none and was taught through the traditional method of teaching.

As the study measured the Overall Achievement in English Language of the class XI students, therefore, the researcher employed the *Non-equivalent Control Group Design* and the schematic representation of the experiment is shown in the Table 1.

Table 1: Schematic Representation of the Experiment

Sl. No.	*Name of the Activity*	*Experimental Group*	*Control Group*	*Time*
1.	Administration of All the Tools for Pre-score	✓	✓	Day 1
2.	Analytics-based Feedback and further Counselling	✓	✗	For the entire intervention duration
3.	Second Achievement Test	✓	✓	At the End of the First Month
4.	Third Achievement Test	✓	✓	At the End of the Second Month
5.	Administration of All the Tools for Post-score	✓	✓	At the End of the Experiment

The design may be diagrammatically presented as, below:

$$\frac{O \quad X \quad O}{O \qquad\quad O}$$

Sample of the Study

The study was conducted in Bhopal city in Madhya Pradesh, India. The sample was selected at the first level through a lottery method randomly from the CBSE Govt. schools. Thus, K.V. No. 1 of Bhopal city at Maida Mill Road was selected. The sample comprised 81 students of Class XI. The sample selection has been presented in Figure 10 below.

The students of one section were designated as the Experimental group and another section was designated as the Control group based on the drawing of chits for sections to maintain randomisation. The Experimental group was provided Analytics-based Feedback as a sophisticated strategy of LA whereas the Control group was not provided any. Likewise, a semester term, approximately three months treatment was given to both the sample groups in the respective methods. There were 39 students in the Experimental Group with 11 Females and 28 Males whereas the Control Group had 42 students with 22 Females and 20 Males of Class XI of Kendriya Vidyalaya No. 1. Thus, there were 81 students selected as the sample.

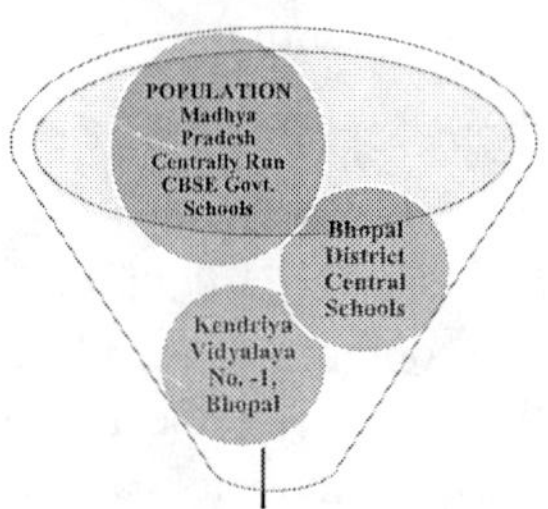

Figure 10: Sample Selection for the Study

Development of E-Content and LMS on MOODLE

For the purpose of conducting LA study, the most indispensable need was an online Learning Management System (LMS) or Content Management System (CMS) for Class XI English Language Core course of NCERT for CBSE students. The study was possible only with the needed course and e-content. But both were unavailable for the purpose in the country.

Moodle as Learning Management System Platform

The first need of the study was a platform where the E-content could be made available for the participants of the study. As most of the LMSs and CMSs are heavily cost-ridden, it would be difficult for academic institutions and teachers to invest such a sum. Therefore, it was covertly planned to conduct the study with least expenses. Thus, a platform was required which was available relatively cheaper and readily available. It was reviewed that Liu et al (2019), Kovanovi´c et al (2015), Kumar et al (2015), Gülbahar & Ilgaz (2014) and Dimopoulos et al (2013) based their works on the Moodle platform. Up to a certain extent, Moodle is free and open-source LMS. It is widely used by the schools, universities and other work places for blended learning, distance education, e-learning or online education and other purposes.

Figure 11: Moodle Logo and the Platform Used for the Study

The platform offered free space for fifty students and data up to 1 GB in version 3.6.1 where the course was created at learningenglish11@moodlecloud.com as My Learning Class (MLC). The platform was found to be appropriate as per the need of the study. The platform had several in-built analytics for various purposes. It was easy to use and simple to design. A pilot study was essential with the platform before the main study to rectify the shortcomings.

Development of E-Content

The second need of the study was E-content for the Class XI English Core course of NCERT for CBSE on an LMS platform. But neither the course nor any content was readily available for the study on any platform. For developing the E-content, the target subject-areas were finalised. For, teaching BICS, some E-content was required on communication skills where Assessment for Speaking and Listening introduced by CBSE in 2014 as skill testing for speaking and listening was kept in mind for E-content. For CALP, the content was required for the first three lessons of the Hornbill Textbook and Snapshot Supplementary Reader by NCERT, Reading Comprehension, Creative-writing and Letter Writing.

Thus, to conduct the study, not only the course but e-content was also developed for Class XI English language NCERT textbook for CBSE with the help of subject experts. To develop the content, a studio setting was required which was met at the study centre Regional Institute of Education, a constituent unit of NCERT, Bhopal. To develop the E-content, the scripts of these subject areas were written and finalised by subject-experts. The contents were recorded and edited as per the need of the E-course designed.

Initial Try-out: After creating the course on Moodle, it was initially tried out in an experimental set-up of school. The students were asked to navigate through the course on their own after the orientation on the course. During the feedback session on the online course, it was observed that students needed support on vocabulary too. Therefore, an additional section was added to the course at the start of it.

Final Try-out: For a final try-out before the main study, a pilot study was conducted successfully with all the tools' administration and running the e-course in Jawahar Navodaya Vidyalaya, Ratibad, Bhopal.

Tools Used

The study used tools related to English language Achievement Assessment, Learning Styles, Motivation, Study Habits, Attitude, Socio-economic Status, Interview Schedule, Observation Schedule and Questionnaires. Tool-wise description has been given below.

Achievement Test for English Language

An achievement test was developed by the researcher to assess the participants at regular intervals. Expert suggestions were sought to finalise the test items for BICS and CALP. The objective of the test was to assess Knowledge, Understanding, Application and Skills. The test was designed according to the objectives of assessing BICS and CALP abilities. Accordingly, the types of questions, course content and levels of difficulty were finalised.

As BICS is mainly about inter-personal communication abilities, i.e. listening and speaking, a format provided by CBSE as Assessment of Speaking and Listening (ASL) test was adopted. This test has a sub-test as Listening Test where an audio is played and students are to mark the answers

Table 2: Design of the Achievement Test – Part 1 Weightage

Subject: English Language				Class/ Level: XI
1. Weightage to Instructional Learning Outcomes				
S.N.	*Objectives*	*Marks*	*Percentage of Marks*	
1.	Knowledge	10	20	
2.	Understanding	10	20	
3.	Application	10	20	
4.	Skill	20	40	
Total		50	100	
2. Weightage to Content				
1.	BICS (Listening and Speaking)		20 Marks	
2.	CALP (Reading and Writing)		30 Marks	
3. Weightage to Types of Questions				
S.N.	*Forms of Questions*	*Marks*	*No. of Questions*	**Total**
1	Long answer	5 & 4 Marks	5x2, 4x2	16
2	Short Answer	5 & 2 Marks	5x2, 2x1	12
3	MCQs / Objective Type	1 Mark	1x22	22
4. Expected Length (No. of Words and Expected Time for Each Question)				
S.N.	*Forms of Questions*	*Marks*	*Expected Length*	*Expected Time*
1	Long answer	16	20-30 Words	12-15 Min.
2	Short Answer	12	One-Five Words	8-10 Min.
3	MCQs	22	One Word to Tick	30-35 Min.
Difficulty level: Moderate	*Duration: 60 minutes*			

Table 3: Blue-print of the Achievement Test

BLUE PRINT OF THE ACHIEVEMENT TEST

Name of the Test: Achievement Test

Subject: English **Class:** XI

Units: BICS and CALP

Maximum Marks: 50 **Time:** 1 Hour

Objectives	*Knowledge*			*Understanding*			*Application*			*Skill*			*Total*		
Forms of Questions/LSRW	*LA**	*SA***	*MCQ****	*LA*	*SA*	*MCQ*	*LA*	*SA*	*MCQ*	*LA*	*SA*	*MCQ*	*LA*	*SA*	*MCQ*
BICS – Listening	-	-	2.5	-	-	2.5	-	-	2.5	-	-	2.5	-	-	10
BICS – Speaking	-	2.5	-	-	2.5	-	-	2.5	-	-	2.5	-	-	10	
CALP – Reading	-	-	2	-	-	2	-	1	2	-	1	2	-	2	8
CALP – Writing	4	-	1	4	-	1	4	-	1	4	-	1	16	-	4
Total	4	2.5	5.5	4	2.5	5.5	4	3.5	5.5	4	3.5	-	16	12	22

No. of Sections – Two (BICS with Listening and Speaking and CALP with Reading and Writing)

*LA – Long Answer

**SA – Short Answer

***MCQ – Multiple-choice Questions

Table 4: The Classification of Item Discriminating Power

Discrimination Index	*Quality*
0.00 – 0.20	Poor
0.21 – 0.40	Satisfactory
0.41 – 0.70	Good
0.71 – 1.00	Excellent

Table 5: The Classification of Item Difficulty Level

P	*Interpretation*
0.00 – 0.30	Difficult
0.31 – 0.70	Moderate
0.71 – 1.00	Easy

of Multiple-Choice Questions (MCQs) in their assessment sheets. Speaking test also had Interaction, Pronunciation, Fluency & Coherence and Vocabulary and Grammar as assessing criteria. Thus, for the BICS section, ASL format was followed and items were finalised accordingly after the discussion with the experts. CALP involved reading and writing abilities of students which was assessed through a reading test, reading comprehension, and writing section. Consequently, the Achievement test was designed with due emphasis on knowledge with 10 marks, understanding with 10 marks, application with 10 marks and skills with 20 marks. A moderate difficulty level was maintained for all the students. The duration of the test was an hour. Duration of the MCQs was 30-35 minutes as it required playing of two audio clips twice each. Thus, the test was designed with utmost care and due consideration was given to several aspects of the achievement test. Thus, the test design for the assessment of BICS and CALP has been presented in the Table 2. The blue-print of the test designed has been presented in the Table 3.

The Achievement Test items for BICS and CALP were finalised with the Discriminating Power 0.61 and Difficulty Index of 0.70 calculated using Ebel's (1972) approach as shown in the Table 4 and 5. Based on the marks obtained by a sample of 240 students, scores were rearranged in descending order of magnitude, which was from highest to lowest. Then, the first 27 per cent and the last 27 per cent scores were used for item analysis, difficulty index and discriminating power using the formulas. Items with 'Poor' and 'Satisfactory' quality of discrimination were removed to finalise the items for the test.

Thus, the Achievement Test was found to be 'Good' as per Item Discrimination Power and 'Moderate' as per Item Difficulty Level. The tool was used to study Achievement in English language as a dependent variable. The Achievement scores were studied as BICS, CALP and Overall scores.

Table 6: Reliability Estimates, Confidence Intervals for Alpha (95%), Scale Means for Scores on the Learning Channel Preference Checklist and Scale Standard Deviations

Scale	*Cronbach's α*	*95% Confidence Intervals for Cronbach's α*	*Scale M*	*SD for Scale*
Visual	0.52	0.43 – 0.60	42.69	5.02
Auditory	0.42	0.31 – 0.52	38.66	4.79
Haptic	0.51	0.42 – 0.60	36.32	5.45

Learning Style Inventory

Learning Style was an important aspect of the study as Analytics-based Feedback could be provided in a better manner if the learning style of the learner was known to improve the outcome. For this study, a simple learning style assessment tool was needed. O'Brien (1988) developed The Learning Channel Preference Checklist (LCPC), a questionnaire designed to develop this awareness. Teachers can administer the Learning Channel Preference Checklist and follow it up with an interpretive discussion. There are a total of thirty items, with ten items for each sub-category of Visual, Auditory or Kinaesthetic. The tool was appropriate for school level education. Students were asked to rank each statement according to how it generally relates to them. There were no right or wrong answers. Students' final cluster scores indicates what is their learning style, i.e. Visual, Auditory or Kinesthetics. Reliability Estimates for Scores on the LCPC Reliability estimates (Cronbach's α) for scores on the LCPC are presented in Table 6 with the scale means.

The instrument is self-administered for intermediate students. For each item, the student must indicate how often the sentence applies to her/him, according to the scale. It is a three-point scale with responses 'Never applies to me' for 1 score, 'Sometimes applies to me' for 2 score and 'Often applies to me' for 3. The maximum score in every section is 30 and the minimum score is 10. The total maximum score is 90 and the minimum is 30. The modality type with the highest score indicates your preferred learning channel. The higher the score, the stronger the preference. If a student has relatively high scores in two or more sections, he/she probably has more than one strength. If the scores in the sections are roughly equal, the student probably does not have a preferred learning channel but is a multi-sensory learner. The Learning Style was studies as an independent variable in the study.

Motivation Scale

Several studies used Motivated Strategies Learning Questionnaire (MSLQ) by Pintrich and De Groot published by National Center for Research to Improve Postsecondary Teaching and Learning. Ann Arbor, MI. Rezaei et al (2015), Rotgans and Schmidt (2010) and Turingan and Yang (2009) used MSLQ to assess the motivational orientation of students and further related to achievement of students. The tool was found to be appropriate to collect data for Motivation level of students.

The tool used has seven-point Likert Scale with forty-four items. The scale consisted of three Motivational scale items viz. Self-efficacy, Intrinsic Value and Test Anxiety whereas two Cognitive scale items viz. Cognitive Strategy Use and Self-regulation. The item's scale Self-Efficacy (Nine items numbered 2, 6, 8, 9, 11, 13, 16,18, 19), Intrinsic Value (Nine items numbered 1, 4, 5, 7, 10, 14, 15, 17, 21), Test Anxiety (Four items numbered 3, 12, 20, 22), Cognitive Strategy Use (Thirteen items numbered 23, 24, 26, 28, 29, 30, 31, 34, 36, 39, 41, 42, 44) and Self-Regulation (Nine items numbered 25, 27, 32, 33, 35, 37, 38, 40, 43). The item numbered 26, 27, 37 and 38 are reversed ones. The assessment scale for motivation ranges on a 7-point scale where score ranges 1 is not at all true of me to 7 is very true of me. The scores had to be calculated 1 to 7 for straight items whereas 7 to 1 for reversed items.

The Self-efficacy scale ($\alpha = 0.89$) consisted of nine items regarding perceived competence and confidence in the performance of class work (e.g. 'I expect to do very well in this class', 'I am sure that I can do an excellent job on the problems and tasks assigned for this class', 'I know that I will be able to learn the material for this class'; cf. Eccles, 1983; Schunk, 1981). The Intrinsic Value scale ($\alpha = 0.87$) was constructed by taking the mean score of the student's response to nine items concerning intrinsic interest in ('I think what we are learning in this Science class is interesting') and perceived importance of course work ('It is important for me to learn what is being taught in this English class'; cf., Eccles, 1983) as well as preference for challenge and mastery goals ('I prefer class work that is challenging so I can learn new things'; cf., Harter, 1981). Four items (e.g. 'I am so nervous during a test that I cannot remember facts I have learned,' 'When I take a test, I think about how poorly I am doing'; cf., Liebert & Morris, 1967) concerning worry about and cognitive interference on tests were used in the Test Anxiety scale ($\alpha = 0.75$).

On the basis of the results of the factor analysis, two cognitive scales were constructed: cognitive strategy use and self-regulation. The Cognitive Strategy Use scale ($\alpha = 0.83$) consisted of 13 items pertaining to the use of rehearsal strategies (e.g. 'When I read material for science class, I say the words over and over to myself to help me remember'), elaboration strategies such as summarising and paraphrasing (e.g. 'When I study for this English class, I put important ideas into my own words'), and organisational strategies (e.g. 'I outline the chapters in my book to help me study', cf., Weinstein et al., 1987).

Although metacognitive and effort management strategies were intended to be separate scales originally, factor analysis of the items did not support the construction of two different scales. One scale, labelled Self-Regulation ($\alpha = 0.74$) was constructed from metacognitive and effort management items. The items on metacognitive strategies, such as planning, skimming and comprehension monitoring (e.g. 'I ask myself questions to make sure I know the material I have been studying', 'I find that when the teacher is talking I think of other things and don't really listen to what is being said' and 'I often find that I have been reading for class but don't known what it is all about', with the latter two items reflected before scale construction) were adapted from Weinstein et al. (1987) and Zimmerman and Pons (1986). The variable was studied as dependent one for the present study.

Study Habits Inventory

Palsane & Sharma's Study Habits Inventory (PSSHI) by M. N. Palsane (1989) to collect data on research study habits was found to be appropriate tool for administration to collect data on study habits of students at Higher Secondary level. This is a three-point scale with 45 items. Every item has three points like 'Always', 'Sometimes' and 'Never'. In this inventory the overall scores give a measure of study habits.

The study habits of the individual cover the Budgeting Time (Five items numbered 1, 2, 3, 4, 32), Physical Conditions for Study (Six items numbered 5, 6, 7, 8, 9, 43), Reading Ability (Eight items numbered 10, 13, 14, 15, 16, 17, 22, 28), Note Taking (Three items numbered 11, 18, 19), Factors in Learning Motivation (Six items numbered 20, 21, 23, 24, 25, 40), Memory (Four items numbered 12, 26, 27, 37), Taking Examination with Preparation for Examination and Use of Examination Results (Ten items numbered 29, 30, 31, 33, 34, 35, 36, 38, 39, 42) and Health (Three items numbered 41, 44, 45). The inventory is self-administering for Intermediate to Postgraduate levels.

The procedure of scoring is simple. For 'Always' response, score of 2 is awarded, whereas 1 and 0 scores are to be given for 'Sometimes' and 'Never' response, respectively. The item numbers 6, 9, 13, 15, 24, 26, 34, 36, 37, 41 and 42 are reversed items. The maximum obtainable score is 90. Higher score indicates good study habits.

The reliability of the inventory was determined by two methods.

1. The reliability coefficient was found to be 0.88 by test-retest method (with an interval of 4 weeks) on a sample of 200 male students of undergraduate classes.
2. The reliability coefficient was found to be 0.67 with an interval of 3 months on samples of 60 girls studying in intermediate classes.
3. Using slip half techniques on 150 boys of intermediate and undergraduate classes, the coefficient of correlation was found to be 0.56 between odd and even items.

The inventory, besides having high face validity, has the other validity coefficients which are given in Table 7 and Table 8:

(A) With external criterion (similar type of study habit inventories)

Table 7: Validity with External Criterion (Similar Type of Study Habit Inventories)

Sl. No.	*Name of Other Tests*	*Validity Coefficients*
1.	Study Habit Inventory Mukhopadhyaya and Sansanwal (1963)	0.69
2.	Test of Study Habits and Attitudes Mathur (2002)	0.67
3.	Study Habit Inventory – Patel (1976)	0.74
4.	Study Involvement Inventory – Bhatnagar (1982)	0.83

(B) With other variable measures

Table 8: Validity of Study Habits Inventory with Other Variable Measures

Sl. No.	*Name of Other Tests*	*Validity Coefficients*
1.	Verbal Achievement Motivation Test Bhargava (2009)	0.46
2.	Scholastic Achievement (Total Marks in Annual Examination)	0.42
3.	Level of Aspiration - Shah and Bhargava (1971)	0.58
4.	Projective Test of Achievement Motivation - Deo (1986)	0.53
5.	Reading Comprehension Test - Ahuja & Ahuja (1991)	0.76

The above validity coefficients indicate that the inventory has sufficiently high validity with other similar inventories and allied measures by other authors and have significant relationship with other variables which influence the study habits and academic performances. For research purposes, the inventory can be safely recommended for use with the sample for which it has been prepared. Thus, Study Habits Inventory by Palsane and Sharma was used to observe the study habits as a dependent variable in the study post feedback.

English Language Learning Attitude Scale

Questionnaire of Students' Attitude towards Learning English was used to assess attitude towards English language learning before and after the study. The questionnaire had fifteen items with five-point Likert scale. The scale ranged from Strongly Agree to Strongly Disagree. There were four reversed items numbered at 4, 7, 8, 9 and 13. The content validity was established by 10 language specialists. The referees were invited to validate the content of the questionnaire and their suitability to research questions and objectives. The remarks of the referees, notes and suggestions were taken into consideration for the final draft. In order to establish the reliability of the questionnaire, a pilot study was conducted in a group of 15 students, who were randomly chosen from the population of the study. The questionnaire was distributed to the same group to check the reliability after two weeks. It was taken to ensure that questionnaire directions, content, form and time were stable. Cronbach's alpha was used to measure internal consistency and calculated. It was found to be 0.88, which is considered very high from statistical point of view for the purposes of this study. Students' Attitude towards Learning English has been studied as a dependent variable in the study.

Socio-Economic Scale

Socio-economic status (SES) is a person's or family's economic and social position in reference to different community members. Sometimes financial gain, education and occupation are taken into consideration to work out socioeconomic status. Socio-economic scales are captivated with analysis of financial gain and need to be updated with dynamical consumer index. The present study has used Kuppuswamy Scale for the year 2018 to collect the data from the participants of the study. According to the scale, a score between 26 to 29 was Upper, score between 16 to 25 was Upper Middle, score between 11 to 15 was Lower Middle, score 5 to 10 was Upper Lower and score below 5 was Lower Class. It will be studied as an independent variable for the present work.

Questionnaire for Teacher

A researcher-made questionnaire was prepared for the feedback from the teacher who had observed the entire intervention and process of Analytics-based Feedback. The questionnaire contained twenty items on a five-point scale from Strongly Disagree to Strongly Agree with an open-ended item for suggestions. It was to elicit response and reflections of the teacher who had experienced the first -hand observation of the entire process.

Interview Schedule for Principal

A structured interview was scheduled post intervention with the Principal of Kendriya Vidyalaya No. 1, Bhopal. As infrastructure plays an essential role in the study and the management also has to be involved regarding data-ethics, privacy and permission, the Principal's feedback regarding the study was indispensable. Five questions were scheduled for the Principal of the school to elicit response and reflections who had got the first-hand observation of the entire process as administration.

Questionnaire for Parents

A five-item questionnaire was prepared by the researcher for the parents of the participants to elicit responses and experiences of the parent as they were significant stakeholders of the study. As the study was conducted with the consent of the parents and they were updated periodically, it was essential to seek feedback from them. A few parents were also interviewed with a semi-structured schedule post intervention.

Procedure of Data Collection

The study was conducted in two phases for data collection.

Phase-I: The first phase involved developing the content materials, strategies and conducting Pilot Study. The pilot study was conducted to test the design of the final Study, which if needed, was be adjusted. The Quasi-experimental research was conducted to study the progression of English language of Class XI students with the intervention. The E-content was developed and the CMS at Moodle were prepared for the intervention. E-content development took approximately a year with script finalisation to execution at studio. After the development of E-content, the E-course was designed. As Moodle provided only 1 GB data at the platform in the 3.6.1, You Tube links were used to insert the videos at the platform. As the You Tube linked account was for the sole purpose, it facilitated with video analytics with the view and usage time. Google forms were used for analytics and assessment of the taught content. The feedback provided were based on these assessments.

The E-course so developed was tested and improved through a pilot study in a randomly selected CBSE school. The pilot study was conducted at Jawahar Navodaya Vidyalaya, Ratibad, in Bhopal District at Bhopal, M.P. A permission was sought from the Principal of the school. All the tools, Observation schedules and check list for class-room observation, recording and reporting were checked, updated and prepared while completing the pilot study. During the study, it was observed that residential schools have limitations for the access to the E-course besides the school. So, for the main study, sample had to have access to the E-course after the school also. Tools were easy to administrate and no hassles were observed while administrating them. The pilot study paved the way for the main study.

Phase-II: For the main study, a lottery was drawn among all the Central schools (Kendriya Vidyalaya) in Bhopal. It was needed that students must have access to the E-content after the school also. Thus, Kendriya Vidyalaya No. 1, Maida Mill Road, Bhopal was selected for the main study. Intervention was to be given and observed for three months. Permission was sought from K.V. Commissioner from the Regional Office of Bhopal to conduct the main study. Before the study could be set off, a consent letter was sent to all the parents to inform them with the details of the study and data to be collected about their wards. It was to ensure ethics, data privacy and security for the data which were to be collected. Parents were provided with the complete knowledge of the study. All the parents provided the permission but one. So, one student was dropped from the sample. The Control Group and Experimental Group were selected by drawing the chits. The Class XI B with 39 students (Forty students except one with 'No Permission' thus 39) was assigned as Experimental Group and the Class XI C with 42 students was the Control Group. Lesson plans were prepared. The data were collected by administrating the Achievement Test, LCPC, MSLQ, Habits Inventory, English Language Learning Attitude Scale and Socio-economic Scale.

After the first administration of LCPC and Habits Inventory, students were counselled about their Learning Style and Study Habits to improve the learning outcomes of English as second language. Their written and communication language were observed and feedback were provided. They were advised to work on their language skills errors and mistake consciously. During the study, parents were met at the PTM and feedback were sought from them about changes in their behaviour. Parents were kept updated on their performance through a WhatsApp group created for the sole purpose. Achievement Test was administered at a regular interval of thirty days. Thus, Achievement scores were at four points of intervention. At the end of three months, Teachers, Principal and Parents were interviewed. The teacher involved during the intervention also filled up a questionnaire prepared for the sole purpose. Principal held a lengthy discussion and feedback session with the Experimental Group before the interview. Data thus collected were analysed quantitatively as well as qualitatively.

Statistical Techniques Used for Data Analysis

The statistical techniques used for analysing the data are given here objective-wise.

1. In order to study the effectiveness of Analytics-based Feedback in English Language of Higher Secondary Students in terms of:
   a. Achievement of students in English Language with BICS Scores was analysed by computing percentiles, mean, S.D. and Coefficient of variation;
   b. Achievement of students in English Language with CALP Scores was analysed by computing percentiles, mean, S.D. and Coefficient of variation;
   c. Achievement of Students in English Language with Overall Scores was analysed by computing percentiles, mean, S.D. and Coefficient of variation;

   d. Opinion of teacher towards Analytics-based Feedback was analysed by examining the questionnaire and interview;
   e. Opinion of Principal towards Analytics-based Feedback was studied by analysing interview; and
   f. Opinion of Parents towards Analytics-based Feedback was analysed by examining the questionnaire and interview.
2. In order to study the trend of the effect of the Treatment on BICS, CALP and Overall Achievement Scores of Class XI students in English language, trend analysis of the Overall Achievement was studied.
3. In order to study the relationship between BICS, CALP and Overall Achievement in English language progression and the Treatment, Gender, Socio-economic status, and Learning style of Class XI students, Multiple Regression analysis was used.
8. In order to study the interactive effect of Treatment and Gender on Study Habits, Attitude towards English Language and Motivation Level of Class XI students by taking their Pre-test scores as covariate, ANCOVA was employed.

8

Data Analysis, Results and Findings

The chapter is dedicated to the presentation of data analysis, patterns observed during the study, actionable insights, meaningful results, and their interpretation. This has been done objectives-wise under separate captions.

Objective 1: Effectiveness of Analytics-Based Feedback in Terms of Descriptive Analysis

The first objective of the investigation was to study the effectiveness of the Analytics-based Feedback in terms of Achievement in English Language with BICS Scores, CALP Scores, and Overall Scores with descriptive statistics. The results and interpretations related to each of these indicators are presented below.

a. Effectiveness of Analytics-based Feedback in Terms of Achievement in English Language with BICS Scores

The effectiveness in terms of students' Achievement in English Language with BICS Scores was studied by administering the Achievement test in BICS of English language developed by the investigator. The data were analysed with the help of mean, standard deviation, percentiles, and coefficient of variation. The results are presented in Table 9 given below.

Table 9: Mean, SD, CV and Percentiles for Achievement in BICS of English Language

Mean	*Std. Deviation*	*Variance*	*Range*	*Minimum*	*Maximum*
16	1.64	2.68	6	13	19

Percentiles	10	20	30	40	50	60	70	80	90	95
Scores	14	14	15	16	16	16	16.6	18	18	18.1

Table 10 shows that the mean of Achievement scores in BICS of English language is 16 out of 20 marks. Average score of BICS Achievement in English language is above I division as shown in figure 12. The coefficient of variation of BICS Achievement is 10.25. The 10th percentile is 14. It shows that only 10 percent students scored 70 percent marks or below that. For the I division, 70 Percent is near to the 75% which is the distinction benchmark. This kind of achievement is not observed in the traditional method of teaching. Thus, it

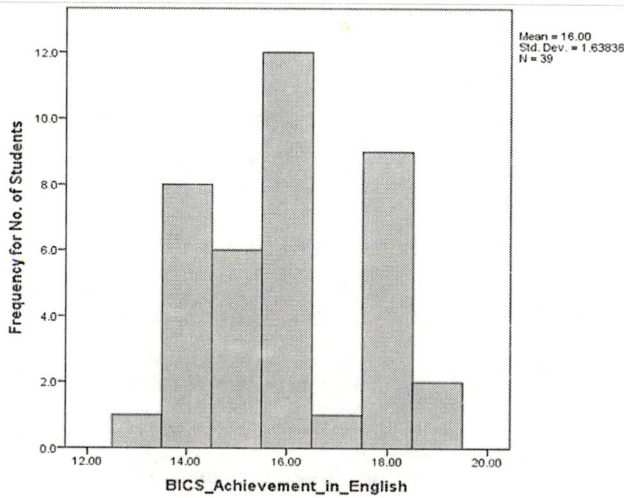

Figure 12: Spread of Scores of the Experimental Group for BICS Scores

appears that the students were benefitted by the Analytics-based Feedback. In other words, Analytics-based Feedback was effective in terms of BICS Achievement in English language and the spread of scores may be observed in Figure 12.

b. Effectiveness of Analytics-based Feedback in Terms of Achievement in English Language with CALP Scores

The effectiveness in terms of the students' Achievement in English Language with CALP Scores was studied by administering the Achievement test in CALP of English language developed by the investigator, after three months of Treatment. The data were analysed with the help of mean, standard deviation, percentiles, and coefficient of variation. The results are presented in Table 10 below.

Table 10: Mean, SD, CV, and Percentiles for Achievement in CALP of English Language

Mean	*Std. Deviation*	*Variance*	*Range*	*Minimum*	*Maximum*
24.38	2.99	8.93	12	17	29

Percentiles	10	20	30	40	50	60	70	80	90	95
Scores	20.8	22.6	23	24.2	25	25	26	27	28	28.1

Table 10 shows that the mean of Achievement scores in CALP of English language is 24.38. Average score of CALP Achievement in English language is above I division as shown in the figure 13. The coefficient of variation of CALP Achievement is 12.26. The 10th percentile is 20.8. It shows that only 10

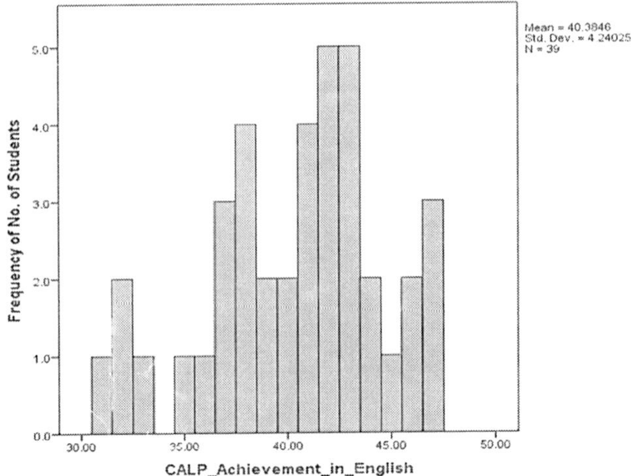

Figure 13: Spread of Scores of the Experimental Group for CALP Scores

percent students scored 20.8 percent marks or below that. For the I division, 50 percent is near to the 83.33%. This kind of achievement is not observed in the traditional method of teaching. Thus, it appears that the students were benefitted by the Analytics-based Feedback. In other words, Analytics-based Feedback was effective in terms of CALP Achievement in English language and spread of the scores may be observed in the figure 13.

c. Effectiveness of Analytics-based Feedback in Terms of Achievement in English Language with overall Scores

The effectiveness in terms of the students' achievement in English Language with Overall Scores was studied by administering the achievement test in Overall English language developed by the investigator, after three months of Treatment. The data were analysed with the help of mean, standard deviation, percentiles, and coefficient of variation. The results are presented in Table 11 below.

Table 11: Mean, SD, CV, and Percentiles for Achievement in Overall Scores of English Language

Mean	*Std. Deviation*	*Variance*	*Range*	*Minimum*	*Maximum*
40.38	4.24	17.98	16	31	47

Percentiles	10	20	30	40	50	60	70	80	90	95
Scores	34.6	37	38	40	41	42	43	43.4	46	47

Table 11 shows that the mean of Achievement scores in Overall scores of English language is 40.38. Average score of Overall Achievement in English

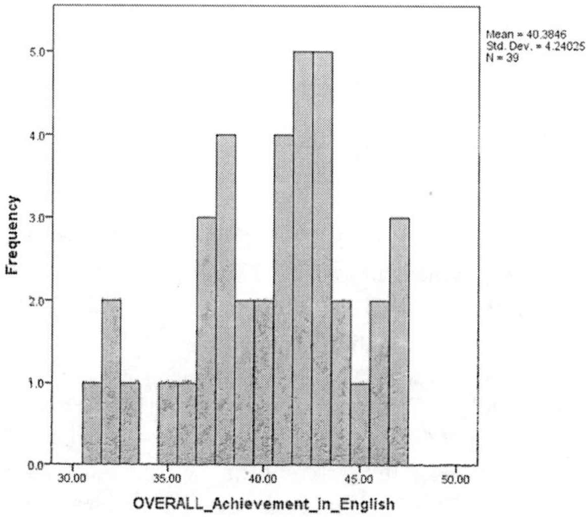

Figure 14: Spread of Scores of the Experimental Group for Overall Scores

language is above I division as shown in figure 14. The coefficient of variation of Overall Achievement is 10.50. The 10th percentile is 34.6. It shows that only 10 percent students scored 34.6 percent marks or below that. For the I division, 50 percent is near to the 82%. This kind of achievement is not observed in the traditional method of teaching. Thus, it appears that the students were benefitted by the Analytics-based Feedback. In other words, Analytics-based Feedback was effective in terms of Overall Achievement in English language and spread of the scores may be observed in the figure 14.

Objective 2: Trend of Effect of the Treatment on BICS Component of Achievement in English Language

The second objective was to study trend of effect of the treatment on BICS component of Achievement in English language of Class XI students. It was to study the progression of BICS component of English language of Class XI students. In order to study the trend of effect of the treatment on BICS Component of achievement, four achievement tests were conducted over a period of three months at an interval of a month each. The treatment had two levels, namely, Analytics based Feedback and Traditional Method. Analytics based Feedback is the Experimental Group and Traditional Method is the Control Group. Thus, the data were analysed with the help of Trend analysis, repeated measures. The results, interpretations and findings related to the above components are presented below in Table 12 and 13.

Table 12: Summary of Trend Analysis Repeated Measures for BICS Scores

Effect		*Value*	*F*	*Hypothesis df*	*Error df*	*Remark*
Factor-BICS	**Wilks' Lambda**	0.12	183.43	3	76	p<0.01*

* Significant at 0.01 Level

From Table 12, the results for BICS component of Achievement indicate a significant time effect, Wilks' Lambda is 0.12 and F value of 183.43 is significant at 0.01 level with df equal to 3/79. Thus, it can be said that the alternative hypothesis namely, 'there is a significant change in the learning progression in terms of the BICS component of Achievement in English language in the successive trials of Class XI learners,' is not rejected. The results show that the F-Value is significant for the BICS component of English language. So, it can be said that the scores in the different trials were not normally distributed. Follow-up comparisons indicate that each pairwise difference was significant, p< 0.01. There was a significant increase in scores over the time, suggesting that participation in the intervention for ESL, increased the learning outcomes level of BICS component.

Finding: There is a significant change in the learning progression in terms of BICS component of Achievement in English language in the successive trials of Class XI students when Analytics-based personalised feedback is provided based on previous performance.

Table 13: Mean and SD of Achievement in BICS Component of Achievement in English Language for the Four Successive Tests

Descriptive Statistics for the Two Groups of Experiment				
Tests	*Groups*	*Mean*	*SD*	*N*
	Experimental Group	11.28	1.95	39
BICST1	Control Group	11.33	2.62	42
	Total	11.31	2.31	81
	Experimental Group	12.59	1.50	39
BICST2	Control Group	12.05	2.25	42
	Total	12.31	1.93	81
	Experimental Group	14.79	1.59	39
BICST3	Control Group	12.90	2.21	42
	Total	13.81	2.15	81
	Experimental Group	16.00	1.64	39
BICST4	Control Group	13.83	2.25	42
	Total	14.88	2.25	81

Further from Table 13, the mean and SD of the Experimental group is 11.28 and 1.95, respectively in the first BICS component of the Achievement test which progressed to 12.59 and 1.50 in the second test, further to 14.79 and 1.59

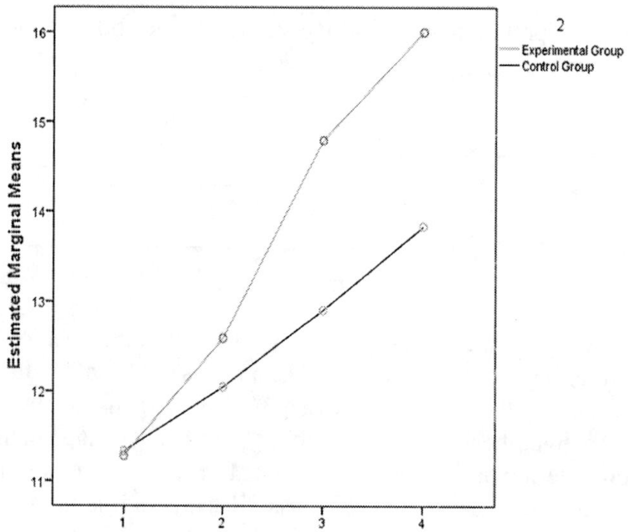

Figure 15: Estimated Marginal Means of BICS Component of ESL Progression in the Successive Trials of the Two Groups

in the third and lastly to 16 and 1.59, respectively in the fourth Achievement test. The mean and SD of the Control group are 11.33 and 2.62, respectively in the first BICS component of the Achievement test which could progress only to 12.05 and 2.25 in the second test, further to 12.90 and 2.21 in the third and lastly to 13.83 and 2.25, respectively in the fourth Achievement test. It can be inferred that the feedback provided to the learners brought a significantly positive and better effect on their learning outcomes of BICS component of ESL. In figure 15, the graph presents estimated marginal means of BICS scores over the four tests out of 20 marks each for both the groups. The first test scores of the Achievement test have been used as the base for the comparison and map the progression over the period of three months.

Objective 3: Trend of Effect of the Treatment on CALP Component of Achievement in English Language

The third objective was to study trend of effect of the treatment on CALP component of Achievement of students in English language. It was to study the progression of CALP component in English language of Class XI students. In order to study trend of effect of the treatment on CALP component of achievement, four achievement tests were conducted over a period of three months at an interval of a month each. The treatment had two levels, namely, Analytics based Feedback and Traditional Method. Analytics based Feedback is the Experimental Group and Traditional Method is the Control Group. Thus, the data were analysed with the help of Trend analysis, repeated measures.

The results, interpretations and findings related to the above components are presented below.

Table 14: Summary of Trend Analysis Repeated Measures for Overall Scores

Effect		*Value*	*F*	*Hypothesis df*	*Error df*	*Remark*
Factor-CALP	Wilks' Lambda	0.08	283.46	3	76	p<0.01*

* Significant at 0.01 Level

From Table 14, the results for the CALP component of Achievement indicate a significant time effect, Wilks' Lambda is 0.08 and F value of 283.46 is significant at the 0.01 level with df equal to 3/79. Thus, it can be said that the alternative hypothesis namely, 'there is a significant change in the learning progression in terms of the CALP component of Achievement in the English language in the successive trials of Class XI learners.', is not rejected. The results show that the F-Value is significant for the CALP component's scores. So, it can be said that the scores in the different trials were not normally distributed. Follow-up comparisons indicate that each pairwise difference was significant, p< 0.01. There was a significant increase in scores over time, suggesting that participation in the intervention for ESL, increased the learning outcomes level of the CALP component.

Finding: There is a significant change in the learning progression in terms of the achievement in CALP component scores in the successive trials of Class XI learners when Analytics-based personalised feedback is provided on the basis of previous performance.

Table 15: Mean and SD of Achievement in CALP Component of Achievement in English Language for the Four Successive Tests

	Descriptive Statistics for the Two Groups of Experiment			
Tests	*Groups*	*Mean*	*SD*	*N*
	Experimental Group	15.82	2.20	39
CALPT1	Control Group	15.17	2.28	42
	Total	15.48	2.25	81
	Experimental Group	19.31	2.47	39
CALPT2	Control Group	16.81	2.24	42
	Total	18.01	2.66	81
	Experimental Group	22.33	3.22	39
CALPT3	Control Group	18.55	2.13	42
	Total	20.37	3.30	81
	Experimental Group	24.38	2.99	39
CALPT4	Control Group	19.86	2.41	42
	Total	22.04	3.52	81

Further from Table 15, the mean and SD of the Experimental group are 15.82 and 2.20, respectively in the first Overall Achievement test which progressed to 19.31 and 2.47 in the second test, further to 22.33 and 3.22 in the third and lastly to 24.38 and 2.99, respectively in the fourth Achievement test. The mean and SD of the Control group are 15.17 and 2.28, respectively in the first Overall Achievement test which could progress only to 16.81 and 2.24 in the second test, further to 18.55 and 2.13 in the third and lastly to 19.86 and 2.41, respectively in the fourth Achievement test. It can be inferred that the feedback provided to the learners brought a significantly positive effect on their learning outcomes of ESL. In figure 16, the graph presents estimated marginal means of CALP scores over the four tests out of 30 marks each for both the groups. The first test scores of the Achievement test have been used as the base for comparison and map the progression over the period of three months.

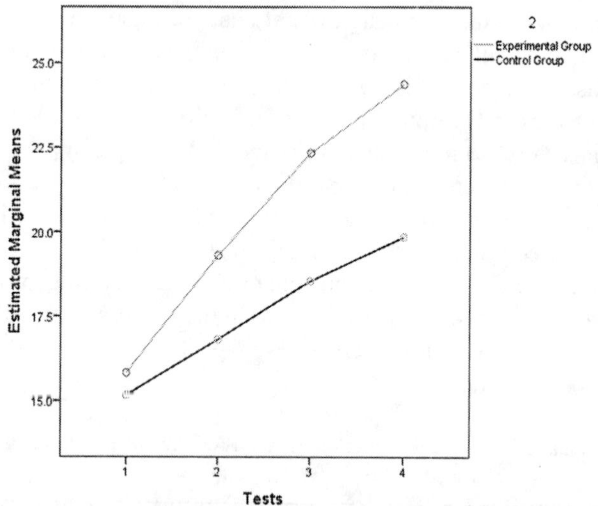

Figure 16: Estimated Marginal Means of CALP Component of ESL Progression in the Successive Trials of the Two Groups

Objective 4: Trend of Effect of the Treatment on Overall Achievement in English Language

The fourth objective was to study the trend in the successive trials during the treatment on Overall Achievement in the English language of Class XI students. It was to study the progression in the English language skills of Class XI students. To study the trend, four achievement tests were conducted over a period of three months at an interval of a month each. The treatment had two levels, namely, Analytics based Feedback and Traditional Method. Analytics based Feedback is the Experimental Group and Traditional Method is the Control Group. Thus, the data were analysed with the help of Trend analysis, repeated measures. The results, interpretations and findings related to the above components are presented below.

Table 16: Summary of Trend Analysis Repeated Measures for Overall Scores

Effect		*Value*	*F*	*Hypothesis df*	*Error df*	*Remark*
Factor-Overall	Wilks' Lambda	0.41	36.08	3	76	p<0.01*

* Significant at 0.01 Level

From Table 16, the results for Overall Achievement indicate a significant time effect, Wilks' Lambda is 0.41 and F value of 36.08 is significant at the 0.01 level with df equal to 3/79. Thus, it can be said that the alternative hypothesis namely, 'there is a significant change in the learning progression in terms of the Overall Achievement in the English language in the successive trials of Class XI learners', is not rejected. The results show that the F-Value is significant for the Overall scores. So, it can be said that the scores in the different trials were not normally distributed. Follow-up comparisons indicate that each pairwise difference was significant, $p < 0.01$. There was a significant increase in scores over time, suggesting that participation in the intervention for ESL, increased the learning outcomes level of Overall.

Finding: There is a significant change in the learning progression in terms of the achievement in Overall scores in the successive trials of Class XI learners when Analytics-based personalised feedback is provided on the basis of previous performance.

Table 17: Mean and SD of Achievement in Overall Achievement in English Language for the Four Successive Tests

Descriptive Statistics				
	Group	*Mean*	*SD*	N
Overall T1	Experimental Group	27.10	3.48	39
	Control Group	26.50	4.32	42
	Total	26.79	3.92	81
Overall T2	Experimental Group	31.90	3.57	39
	Control Group	28.86	3.95	42
	Total	30.32	4.05	81
Overall T3	Experimental Group	37.13	4.23	39
	Control Group	31.45	3.93	42
	Total	34.19	4.95	81
Overall T4	Experimental Group	40.38	4.24	39
	Control Group	33.69	4.09	42
	Total	36.91	5.33	81

Further, from Table 17, the mean and SD of the Experimental group are 27.10 and 3.48, respectively in the first Overall Achievement test which progressed to 31.90 and 3.57 in the second test, further to 37.13 and 4.23 in the third and lastly to 40.38 and 4.24, respectively in the fourth Achievement test. The mean and SD of the Control group are 26.50 and 4.32, respectively in the first Overall Achievement test which could progress only to 28.86 and 3.95 in the second test, further to 31.45 and 3.93 in the third and lastly to 33.69 and 4.09, respectively in the fourth Achievement test. It can be inferred that the feedback provided to the learners brought a significantly positive effect on their learning outcomes of ESL. In figure 17, the graph presents estimated marginal means of Overall scores over the four tests out of 50 marks each for both the groups. The first test scores of the Achievement test have been used as the base for comparison and map the progression over the period of three months.

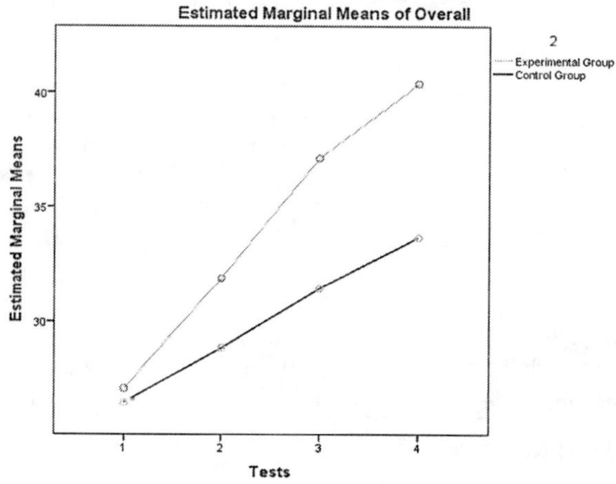

Figure 17: Estimated Marginal Means of Overall ESL Progression in the Successive Trials of the Two Groups

Objective 5: Relationship between BICS Component of Achievement in English Language Progression and the Treatment, Gender, Socio-economic Status and Learning Style

The fifth objective was to study the relationship between BICS Component of achievement in English Language Progression and the Treatment, Gender, Socio-economic Status and Learning Style of Class XI Students. To study the relationship, BICS was the dependent variable and Treatment, Gender, Socio-economic Status and Learning Style were the independent variables. The relationship was to be observed collectively for the change in the dependent variable due to changes in the independent variables. Thus, the data were analysed with the help of multiple regression analysis, and coefficients and regression equation were observed. The results, interpretations and findings related to the above components are presented below.

Table 18 shows coefficient values for the two Treatments, AbF (Treatment 1) and Traditional (Treatment 2) and their respective P-values with standard error. The coefficients with the P-values of 0.000 for the predictor variables indicate they are all statistically significant. Thus, Treatments and Genders are coefficient with significant effect on the outcome variable but not Categories and Learning Styles. Standard Error measures the variability of the coefficient estimate suggesting a moderate level of precision.

Table 18: Summary of Multiple Regression for BICS Component as Dependent Variable and Treatment, Gender, Socio-economic Status and Learning Style as Independent Variables

Predictor Variable	*Coefficients*	*P-value**	*Std Error*
Intercept	7.01	0.00	0.42
Treatment 1	4.53	0.00	0.33
Treatment 2	2.48	0.00	0.33
Gender Female	3.54	0.00	0.30
Gender Male	3.46	0.00	0.37
Category 1	0	0	0
Category 2	0	0	0
Category 3	0	0	0
Category 4	0	0	0
Visual Learning Style	0	0	0
Auditory Learning Style	0	0	0
Kinaesthetic Learning Style	0	0	0

* Significance Level Reference 0.05

The highest coefficient is for Treatment 1 with 4.53, statistically significant, indicating that AbF is associated with an increase of 4.53 units in the outcome variable compared to the reference category which is likely teaching. Additionally, Category and Learning Styles have coefficients and p-values of 0, which suggests that they may not have a significant effect on the outcome variable.

Table 19: R-squared, Adj. R-squared and Regression Equation for BICS

R-squared	*Adj. R-squared*
0.30	0.28

Coefficients of the Multiple Linear Regression for BICS

BICS ~ (7.01) * Intercept + (4.53) * Treatment_1 + (2.48) * Treatment_2 + (3.54) * Gender_F + (3.46) * Gender_M + (0.0) * category_1 + (0.0) * category_2 + (0.0) * category_3 + (0.0) * category_4 + (0.0) * LS_1 + (0.0) * LS_2 + (0.0) * LS_3 +

Table 19 shows R-squared and Adj. R-squared values explaining approximately 30% of the variance in the outcome variable. This indicates that the predictor variables included in the model collectively account for 30% of the variability observed in the outcome variable. The adjusted R-squared value considers the number of predictors in the model and provides a more conservative estimate of the model's explanatory power, suggesting that about 28% of the variability in the outcome variable can be attributed to the predictors while adjusting for the degrees of freedom. The regression equation explains that when Treatment 1 increases by 1 unit, BICS score increases by 4.53 units, keeping all other predictors constant whereas when Treatment 2 increases by 1 unit, CALP increases by only 2.48 units, keeping all other predictors constant.

Thus, the null hypothesis, namely, 'There is no significant relationship between BICS component of Achievement in English language progression and the Treatment, Gender, Socio-economic status, and Learning style of Class XI students' is summarily rejected.

Finding: BICS component of Achievement in English language progression as an output variable significantly varies with predictor variables, most notably with AbF as the treatment.

Objective 6: Relationship between CALP Component of Achievement in English Language Progression and the Treatment, Gender, Socio-economic Status and Learning Style

The sixth objective was to study the relationship between CALP Component of achievement in English Language Progression and the Treatment, Gender, Socio-economic Status and Learning Style of Class XI Students. To study the relationship, CALP was the dependent variable and Treatment, Gender, Socio-economic Status and Learning Style were the independent variables. The relationship was to be observed collectively for the change in the dependent variable due to changes in the independent variables. Thus, the data were analysed with the help of multiple regression analysis, and coefficients and regression equation were observed. The results, interpretations and findings related to the above components are presented below.

Table 20: Summary of Multiple Regression for CALP Component as Dependent Variable and Treatment, Gender, Socio-economic Status and Learning Style as Independent Variables

Predictor Variable	*Coefficients*	*P-value**	*Std Error*
Intercept	10.23	0.00	0.54
Treatment 1	7.64	0.00	0.42
Treatment 2	2.59	0.00	0.43
Gender Female	5.49	0.00	0.39
Gender Male	4.73	0.00	0.48

Predictor Variable	*Coefficients*	*P-value**	*Std Error*
Category 1	0	0	0
Category 2	0	0	0
Category 3	0	0	0
Category 4	0	0	0
Visual Learning Style	0	0	0
Auditory Learning Style	0	0	0
Kinaesthetic Learning Style	0	0	0

* Significance Level Reference 0.05

Table 20 shows coefficient values for the two Treatments, AbF (Treatment 1) and Traditional (Treatment 2) and their respective P-values with standard error. The coefficients with the P-values of 0.000 for the predictor variables indicate that they are all statistically significant. Thus, Treatments and Genders are coefficient with significant effect on the outcome variable but not Categories and Learning Styles. Standard Error measures the variability of the coefficient estimate suggesting a moderate level of precision.

The highest coefficient is for Treatment 1 with 7.64, statistically significant, indicating that AbF is associated with an increase of 7.64 units in the outcome variable compared to the reference category which is likely teaching. Additionally, Category and Learning Styles have coefficients and p-values of 0, which suggests that they may not have a significant effect on the outcome variable.

Table 21: R-squared, Adj. R-squared and Regression Equation for CALP

R-squared	*Adj. R-squared*
0.53	0.49
Coefficients of the Multiple Linear Regression for CALP	
CALP ~ (10.23) * Intercept + (7.64) * Treatment_1 + (2.59) * Treatment_2 + (5.49) * Gender_F + (4.74) * Gender_M + (0.0) * category_1 + (0.0) * category_2 + (0.0) * category_3 + (0.0) * category_4 + (0.0) * LS_1 + (0.0) * LS_2 + (0.0) * LS_3 +	

Table 21 shows R-squared and Adj. R-squared values explaining approximately 53% of the variance in the outcome variable. This indicates that the predictor variables included in the model collectively account for 53% of the variability observed in the outcome variable. The adjusted R-squared value considers the number of predictors in the model and provides a more conservative estimate of the model's explanatory power, suggesting that about 49% of the variability in the outcome variable can be attributed to the predictors while adjusting for the degrees of freedom. The regression equation explains that when Treatment 1 increases by 1 unit, BICS score increases by 7.64 units, keeping all other predictors constant whereas when Treatment 2 increases by 1 unit, CALP increases by only 2.59 units, keeping all other predictors constant.

Thus, the null hypothesis, namely, 'There is no significant relationship between CALP component of Achievement in English language progression and the Treatment, Gender, Socio-economic status, and Learning style of Class XI students' is summarily rejected.

Finding: CALP component of Achievement in English language progression as an output variable significantly varies with predictor variables and most with AbF as the treatment.

Objective 7: Relationship between Overall Achievement in English Language Progression and the Treatment, Gender, Socio-economic Status and Learning Style

The seventh objective was to study the relationship between Overall achievement in English Language Progression and the Treatment, Gender, Socio-economic Status and Learning Style of Class XI Students. To study the relationship, BICS was the dependent variable and Treatment, Gender, Socio-economic Status and Learning Style were the independent variables. The relationship was to be observed collectively for the change in the dependent variable due to changes in the independent variables. Thus, the data were analysed with the help of multiple regression analysis, and coefficients and regression equation were observed. The results, interpretations and findings related to the above components are presented below.

Table 22 shows coefficient values for the two Treatments, AbF (Treatment 1) and Traditional (Treatment 2) and their respective P-values with standard error. The coefficients with the P-values of 0.000 for the predictor

Table 22: Summary of Multiple Regression for Overall Achievement as Dependent Variable and Treatment, Gender, Socio-economic Status and Learning Style as Independent Variables

Predictor Variable	*Coefficients*	*P-value**	*Std Error*
Intercept	17.24	0.00	0.87
Treatment 1	12.17	0.00	0.68
Treatment 2	5.07	0.00	0.69
Gender Female	9.04	0.00	0.76
Gender Male	8.20	0.00	0.62
Category 1	0	0	0
Category 2	0	0	0
Category 3	0	0	0
Category 4	0	0	0
Visual Learning Style	0	0	0
Auditory Learning Style	0	0	0
Kinaesthetic Learning Style	0	0	0

* Significance Level Reference 0.05

variables indicate they are all statistically significant. Thus, Treatments and Genders are coefficient with significant effect on the outcome variable but not Categories and Learning Styles. Standard Error measures the variability of the coefficient estimate suggesting a moderate level of precision.

The highest coefficient is for Treatment 1 at 12.17, which is statistically significant, indicating that AbF is associated with an increase of 12.17 units in the outcome variable compared to the reference category which is likely teaching. Additionally, Category and Learning Styles have coefficients and p-values of 0, which suggests that they may not have a significant effect on the outcome variable.

Table 23: R-squared, Adj. R-squared and Regression Equation for Overall Scores

R-squared	*Adj. R-squared*
0.48	0.43
Coefficients of the Multiple Linear Regression for Overall Score	
Overall Scores ~ (17.24) * Intercept + (12.17) * Treatment_1 + (5.07) * Treatment_2 + (9.04) * Gender_F + (8.2) * Gender_M + (0.0) * category_1 + (0.0) * category_2 + (0.0) * category_3 + (0.0) * category_4 + (0.0) * LS_1 + (0.0) * LS_2 + (0.0) * LS_3 +	

Table 23 shows R-squared and Adj. R-squared values explaining approximately 48% of the variance in the outcome variable. This indicates that the predictor variables included in the model collectively account for 48% of the variability observed in the outcome variable. The adjusted R-squared value considers the number of predictors in the model and provides a more conservative estimate of the model's explanatory power, suggesting that about 43% of the variability in the outcome variable can be attributed to the predictors while adjusting for the degrees of freedom. The regression equation explains that when Treatment 1 increases by 1 unit, BICS score increases by 12.17 units, keeping all other predictors constant whereas when Treatment 2 increases by 1 unit, CALP increases by only 5.07 units, keeping all other predictors constant.

Thus, the null hypothesis, namely, 'There is no significant relationship between Overall Achievement in English language progression and the Treatment, Gender, Socio-economic status, and Learning style of Class XI students' is summarily rejected.

Finding: Overall Achievement in English language progression as an output variable significantly varies with predictor variables and most with AbF as the treatment.

Objective 8: Effect of Treatment and Interactive Effect of the Treatment and Gender on Study Habits by Taking the Pre-Test Scores of Study Habit as a Covariate

The eighth objective was to study the effect of Treatment and the interactive effect of Treatment and Gender on Study Habits of students by taking their

Pre-test Scores of Study Habits as a covariate. Treatment and Gender were two independent variables. Treatment had two levels, namely, Analytics-based Feedback and Traditional Method. Gender has two levels, namely, Male and Female. Pre-test Scores of Study Habits have been taken as a covariate. Thus, the data were analysed with the help of 2 X 2 Factorial Design ANCOVA. The results, interpretations and findings related to each of these above components are presented below.

Effect of Treatment on Study Habits Students When Their Pre-test Scores of Study Habits Taken as Covariate

In Table 24, the adjusted F-Value for Treatment was 89.83 which was significant at the 0.01 level with degrees of freedom equal to 1/79. It indicates that the adjusted mean scores of Study Habits belonging to Analytics-based Feedback and the Traditional Method differ significantly when their pre-test scores of Study Habits are taken as a covariate.

Table 24: Summary of 2 X 2 Factorial Design ANCOVA for Study Habits of Students by Taking Pre-test Scores of Study Habits as a Covariate

Source of Variance	*Df*	$SS_{y.x}$	$MSS_{y.x}$	$F_{y.x}$ - *Value*	*Remark*
Treatment (A)	1	762.75	762.75	89.83	p<0.01*
Gender (B)	2	3.44	3.44	0.41	
A X B	2	3.25	3.25	0.38	
Error	74	645.28	8.49		
Total	80				

* Significant at 0.01 Level

So, there was a significant effect of Treatment on Study Habits of students by taking Pre-test Scores of Study Habits taken as covariate. Thus, the null hypothesis namely, 'there is no significant effect of Treatment on Study Habits of students when their Pre-test Scores of Study Habits taken as a covariate,' is rejected.

Table 25: Gender-wise Mean and SD for Study Habits

Descriptive Statistics				
Dependent Variable: Habit Post				
Groups	*Gender*	*Mean*	*Std. Deviation*	*N*
Experimental Group	Female	69.64	6.55	11
	Male	68.18	8.14	28
	Total	68.59	7.67	39
Control Group	Female	64.14	5.91	22
	Male	60.30	8.71	20
	Total	62.31	7.54	42

Further, Table 25 indicates that the mean score and SD of Study Habits of the Feedback with Analytics Group are 68.59 and 7.67, respectively. The mean score and the SD of Study Habits of the group taught through the Traditional Method are 62.31 and 7.54, respectively. It is evident from the table that the mean score of Study Habits of the Experimental Group was higher than the Traditional group. The SD show that the SD of the Experimental group was slightly higher than the Traditional group. But it was negligent. It may be concluded that the Analytics-based Feedback is superior to the Traditional Method in terms of improving Study the Habits of Class XI students.

Finding: There is a significant effect of Treatment (Analytics-based Feedback) on the Study Habits of Class XI students compared to the Traditional method.

Interactive Effect of Treatment and Gender on Study Habits of Students When Their Pre-Test Scores of Study Habits Taken as a Covariate

The adjusted F-value for interaction between the Treatment and Gender is 0.38 which is not significant. It indicates that the adjusted mean scores of Study Habits of Female and Male students treated through Analytics-based Feedback and Traditional Method did not differ significantly. So, there was no significant effect of interaction between Treatment and Gender on Study Habits of students when their Pre-test Scores of Study Habits is taken as a covariate. Thus, the null hypothesis, namely, 'there is no significant effect of interaction between Treatment and Gender on Study Habits of students when their Pre-test Scores of Study Habits taken as a covariate', is not rejected. It indicates that the interaction between Treatment and Gender did not produce a significant differential effect on Study Habits of students as shown in Figure 18.

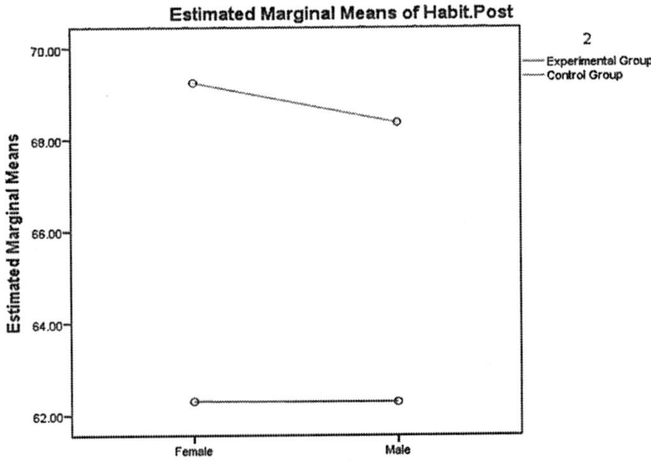

Figure 18: Interactional Effect of Treatment and Gender on Study Habits

It may, therefore, be said that Study Habits were found to be independent of Gender of students when their Pre-test Scores of Study Habits were taken as a covariate.

Finding: There is no significant effect of interaction between Treatment and Gender on Study Habits of the Class XI students.

Objective 9: Effect of Treatment and Interactive Effect of Treatment and Gender on the Attitude towards English Language of Students by Taking the Pre-Test Scores of Attitudes Towards English Language as a Covariate

The ninth objective was to study the effect of Treatment and interactive effect of Treatment and Gender on the Attitude towards English language of students by taking their Pre-test Scores of Attitudes as a covariate. Treatment and Gender were two independent variables. Treatment had two levels, namely, Analytics-based Feedback and Traditional Method. Gender has two levels, namely, Female and Male. Pre-test Scores of Attitudes towards English language has been taken as a covariate. Thus, the data were analysed with the help of 2 X 2 Factorial Design ANCOVA.

From Table 26, it can be seen that the adjusted F-Value for Treatment is 71 which is significant at 0.01 level with df equal to 1/79. It indicates that the adjusted mean scores of Attitude towards English language of students belonging to Analytics-based Feedback and Traditional Method differ significantly when their pre-test scores of Attitude towards the English language of students taken as a covariate.

Table 26: Summary of 2 X 2 Factorial Design ANCOVA for Attitude towards English Language of Students by Taking Pre-test Scores of Attitudes as a Covariate

Source of Variance	*Df*	$SS_{y.x}$	$MSS_{y.x}$	$F_{y.x}$ *- Value*	*Remark*
Treatment (A)	1	659.01	659.01	71	p<0.01*
Gender (B)	2	2.75	2.75	0.30	
A X B	2	3.52	3.52	0.38	
Error	74	705.41	9.28		
Total	80				

* Significant at 0.01 Level

So, there was a significant effect of Treatment on Attitude towards the English language of students by taking Pre-test Scores of Attitudes towards the English language taken as a covariate. Thus, the null hypothesis namely, 'there is no significant effect of Treatment on Attitude towards the English language of students when their Pre-test Scores of Attitudes towards the English language are taken as a covariate,' is rejected.

Table 27: Gender-wise Mean and SD for Attitude towards English Language

Descriptive Statistics				
Dependent Variable: Attitude Post				
Groups	*Gender*	*Mean*	*SD*	*N*
Experimental Group	Female	70.73	6.18	11
	Male	69.21	8.09	28
	Total	69.64	7.55	39
Control Group	Female	65.45	5.45	22
	Male	61.85	8.14	20
	Total	63.74	7.02	42

Further, Table 27 indicates that the mean score and SD of Attitude towards the English language of Feedback with Analytics Group is 69.64 and 7.55, respectively. The mean score and the SD of Attitude towards the English language of the group taught through the Traditional Method is 63.74 and 7.02, respectively. It is evident from the table that the mean score of Attitude towards the English language of Experimental Group was higher than the Traditional group. The SD show that the SD of Experimental group was slightly higher than the Traditional group. But it was negligent. It may be concluded that Analytics-based Feedback is superior to the Traditional Method in terms of improving the Attitude towards the English language of Class XI students.

Finding: There is a significant effect of Treatment (Analytics-based Feedback) on attitude towards the English language of Class XI students as compared to the Traditional method.

Interactive Effect of Treatment and Gender on Attitude towards English Language of Students When Their Pre-Test Scores of Study Habits are Taken as a Covariate

The adjusted F-value for the interaction between treatment and gender is 0.38 which is not significant (Vide Table 4.25). It indicates that the adjusted mean scores of attitude towards the English language of Female and Male students treated through Analytics-based Feedback and Traditional Method did not differ significantly. So, there was no significant effect of interaction between Treatment and Gender on Attitude towards English language of students when their Pre-test Scores of Attitude towards English language is taken as a covariate. Thus, the null hypothesis, namely, 'there is no significant effect of interaction between Treatment and Gender on Attitude towards English language of students when their Pre-test Scores of Attitude towards English language taken as a covariate', is not rejected. It indicates that the interaction between Treatment and Gender did not produce a significant differential effect on attitude towards the English language of students as shown in Figure 19. It may, therefore, be said that attitude towards the English language was found to

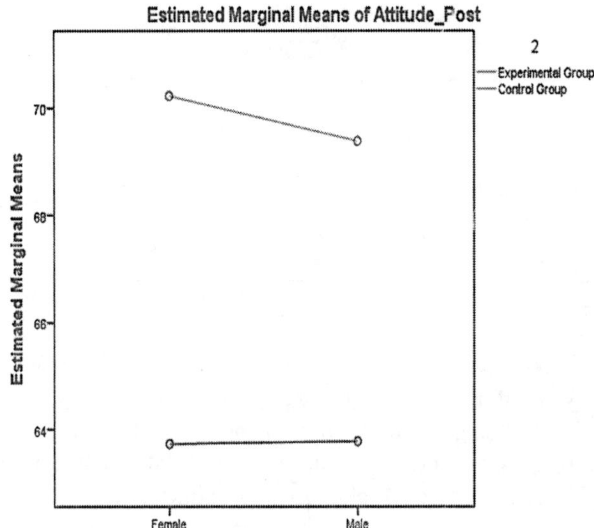

Figure 19: Interactional Effect of Treatment and Gender on Attitude towards English language

be independent of the gender of students when their Pre-test Scores of Attitude towards the English language were taken as a covariate.

Finding: There is no significant effect of interaction between Treatment and Gender on Attitude towards the English language of the Class XI students.

Objective 10: Effect of Treatment and Interactive Effect of Treatment and Gender on the Motivation Level of Students When Measured with MSLQ by Taking the Pre-Test Scores of MSLQ as a Covariate

The tenth objective was to study the effect of Treatment and interactive effect of Treatment and Gender on the Motivation Level of students when measured with MSLQ by taking their Pre-test Scores of MSLQ of the students as a covariate. Treatment and Gender were two independent variables. Treatment had two levels, namely, Analytics-based Feedback and Traditional Method. Gender has two levels, namely, Male and Female. Pre-test Scores of MSLQ has been taken as covariate. Thus, the data were analysed with the help of 2 X 2 Factorial Design ANCOVA.

From the Table 28, the adjusted F-Value for Treatment is 92.38 which is significant at 0.01 level with df equal to 1/79. It indicates that the adjusted mean scores of Motivation Level when measured with MSLQ, belonging to Analytics-based Feedback and Traditional Method differ significantly when their pre-test scores of Motivation Level taken as a covariate. So, there was a

Table 28: Summary of 2 X 2 Factorial Design ANCOVA for Motivation of Students by Taking Pre-test Scores of Motivations as a Covariate

Source of Variance	*Df*	$SS_{y.x}$	$MSS_{y.x}$	$F_{y.x}$ - *Value*	*Remark*
Treatment (A)	1	1240.58	1240.58	92.38	p<0.01*
Gender (B)	1	5.82	5.82	0.43	
A X B	1	38.79	38.79	2.89	
Error	76	1020.61	1020.61		
Total	80				

* Significant at 0.01 Level

significant effect of Treatment on Motivation Level of students when measured with MSLQ by taking Pre-test Scores of Motivation Level taken as a covariate. Thus, the null hypothesis, namely, 'there is no significant effect of Treatment on Motivation Level of students when measured with MSLQ by taking Pre-test Scores of Motivation Level taken as a covariate,' is rejected.

Table 29: Gender-wise Mean and SD for Motivation Level

Descriptive Statistics				
Dependent Variable: Motivation				
Group	*Gender*	*Mean*	*SD*	*N*
Experimental Group	Female	256.18	19.43	11
	Male	238.36	19.74	28
	Total	243.38	21.03	39
Control Group	Female	237.77	24.58	22
	Male	234.75	30.22	20
	Total	236.33	27.11	42

Further, Table 29 indicates that the mean score and SD of Motivation Level of Feedback with Analytics Group is 243.38 and 21.03, respectively. The mean score and the SD of Motivation level of the group taught through the Traditional Method is 236.33 and 27.11, respectively. It is evident from the table that the mean score of Motivation level of Experimental Group was higher than the Traditional group. The SD show that the SD of Traditional was higher than the Experimental group. It may be concluded that the Analytics-based Feedback is superior to Traditional Method in terms of improving Motivation level of Class XI students.

Finding: There is a significant effect of Treatment (Analytics-based Feedback) on Motivation level of Class XI students as compared to Traditional method.

Effect of Interaction Between Treatment and Gender on Motivation Level of Students When Measured with MSLQ and Their Pre-Test Scores of Motivation Level Taken as a Covariate

The adjusted F-value for interaction between the Treatment and Gender is 2.89 which is not significant (Vide Table 29). It indicates that the adjusted mean scores of Motivation Level of Female and Male students treated through Analytics-based Feedback and Traditional Method did not differ significantly. So, there was no significant effect of interaction between Treatment and Gender on Motivation Level of students when measured with MSLQ and their Pre-test Scores of Motivation Level is taken as a covariate. Thus, the null hypothesis, namely, 'there is no significant effect of Gender on Motivation Level of students when measured with MSLQ and their Pre-test Scores of Motivation Level taken as a covariate,' is not rejected. It indicates that the interaction between Treatment and Gender did not produce a significant differential effect on Motivation level of students as shown in figure 20. It may, therefore, be said that Motivation level was found to be independent of Treatment and Gender of students when their Pre-test Scores of Motivation level measured with MSLQ was taken as a covariate.

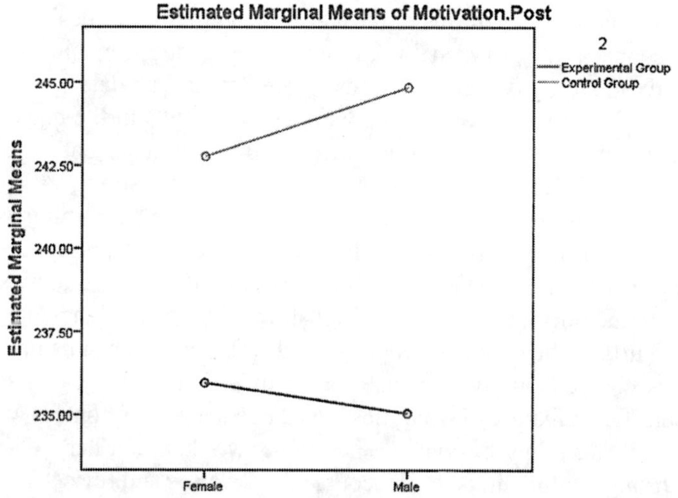

Figure 20: Interactional Effect of Treatment and Gender on Motivation Level

Finding: There is no significant effect of interaction between Treatment and Gender on Motivation level of the Class XI students.

Objective 11: Effectiveness of Analytics-based Feedback in Terms of Qualitative Aspect

The eleventh objective of the investigation was to study the effectiveness of Analytics-based Feedback in terms of the opinions of teachers, principals, and parents towards Analytics-based Feedback. The results and interpretations related to each of these indicators are presented below.

a. Effectiveness of Analytics-based Feedback in Terms of Opinion of the Teacher towards the Method

The effectiveness of Analytics-based Feedback was studied in terms of teacher's observations. The course was developed for teaching BICS and CALP components of the English language along the lines of Analytics-based Feedback. As indicated in the previous chapter, the researcher taught the students of the experimental group by using the blended mode of teaching. Thus, the course developed on the Moodle platform was supported by in-class discussions and feedbacks based on the online performances. This kind of teaching-learning was a novel experience for the students, teacher, and parents alike. Quite a preparation was needed to teach in this mode of instructions. The regular teacher attended and became a part of the entire intervention and her observations were also sought through the above questionnaire.

The effectiveness in terms of the teacher's opinion towards the Analytics-based Feedback was studied by administrating a questionnaire, developed by the investigator, after three months of Treatment. The data were collected using five-point Likert scale. There were 20 statements in the questionnaire. The statements were related to the different dimensions of entire process of Analytics-based Feedback.

It was strongly agreed upon that learning through Learning Analytics helped students in learning English and improve. Students enjoyed using Learning Analytics to learn English. Learning through Analytics helped students to memorise and retain an English vocabulary and language in better manner. Further, the course teacher assisted sufficiently when using Learning Analytics course. Timely feedback was provided during the course, which was a significant feature of Analytics-based Feedback. The content was taught clearly while teaching the course. The teacher would prefer her students to be taught through online mode of the course to save time and revise. The teacher agreed that in order to use Learning Analytics, knowledge of computer skills is required. The use of Learning Analytics made learning English easier and faster. She felt the degree of efficiency and effectiveness of Learning Analytics was a high means of the quality of learning English. Students started to like learning English through Learning Analytics course. By using Learning Analytics for the course, it had encouraged students to continue their learning with curiosity. The Learning Analytics for English course is easy and clear to use for its' users. In her opinion using Learning Analytics course had helped to solve problems in learning a second language. It was encouraging to her observation that the attitude towards teaching the English language can be changed through analytics. There was neutrality in the observation of the teacher though it was disagreed that the traditional way of teaching was better than the online- and off-line mode of instruction for learning using analytics. The teacher disagreed if students felt bored while learning through Learning Analytics and the use of Learning Analytics was useless in learning. She also disagreed that the role of a teacher was not needed when using a computer-based language learning course and students wasted their time by using Learning Analytics course. Thus, the opinion speaks of positive influence of the treatment in the teaching-learning process. Therefore, on the basis of above favourable opinion of the English language teacher of the class, it may be said that Analytics-based Feedback was effective and useful for the students and teachers alike.

During the interview, further suggestions were sought to promote the Analytics-based Feedback. The provided response has been quoted below.

'Such courses should be launched at a central level. Trainings to teachers should be provided to conduct these courses independently. We should be oriented and trained for such new innovative ways of teaching where technology can be used with its full potential. MHRD should take further initiatives to develop E-content for X and XI Class also.'

b. Effectiveness of Analytics-based Feedback in Terms of Opinion of the Principal towards the Method

The effectiveness towards the Analytics-based Feedback in terms of the principal's opinion was studied with an interview, questions lined up with an interview schedule developed by the investigator, after three months of Treatment. The data collected through interview has been presented below.

The first question was on the line of requirement of infrastructure, to which the Principal replied –

'For such teaching-learning, infrastructure is very important. The school has all the facilities as we have smart classes. Classroom has projectors with screens and audio system and the school campus is wi-fi enabled that made the study possible.'

The second question was about the changing role of teacher, to which the reply was -

'Today the role of teacher is more of a facilitator. In this particular study, teacher has set up a rapport with each student that led to a comfort level for everyone in the classroom transaction. They've participated more and, therefore, it has definitely benefitted the students.'

The third question was about the difference between available online material and present course. It was replied as under -

'Though there are lot of online material available, with so many apps but there are hardly any chances of getting the feedback individually. The problems of the students were resolved quickly and were delighted to receive the feedbacks on the issues and problems that were there for many years.'

The fourth question was regarding the utility of Analytics-based Feedback. It was answered as under -

'We know that learning is a continuous process and if someone can assist you in finding your mistake and assess the present learning level, then you can improve the competency and learning level by following the standard expected level which is desired output. It is possible before the final learning. It has helped students to a great extent.'

The Principal had a session about the entire intervention and their varied experiences. Students' feedback according to the Principal was as under -

'Whenever students were given anything to do online, they were happy to do it as they received prompt reply from the course coordinator.' He quoted students. *'the moment they've submitted their assignments online, prompt respond was received from their course coordinator which was very helpful for them. They also mentioned that when they submitted their assignments online and received replies and next day it was discussed in the classroom and realised through the feedback that the same errors, they went on repeating for years. They were also happy that their problems were being heard and shared, problems are discussed and suggestions are passed on to them.'*

The last question was regarding suggestions and issues, if any. It was replied as under -

'This experiment was conducted on a very small level. If we need to think for a larger perspective, then there might be different sorts of constraints over there. Then, we would need different planning and premises. A teacher is taking 6 classes out of 8 classes conducted in the school. Teacher has no time for proper planning, there is no such training on such type of teaching, motivational factor. Infrastructure is one the greatest constraints with internet facilities and other requirements.'

Thus, according to the interview, the Principal's opinion speaks of positive influence of the treatment in the teaching-learning process. Therefore, on the basis of above favourable opinion of the Principal of the school, it may be said that Analytics-based Feedback was effective and useful for the students and teachers alike. Though the suggestions and issues are on larger perspectives of implementations of Analytics-based Feedback but it would require planning and execution on national level.

c. Effectiveness of Analytics-based Feedback in Terms of Opinion of the Parents towards the Method

The effectiveness of Analytics-based Feedback was studied in terms of parents' observations and opinions. The parents' consent was sought for the enrolment of students in the online course. A consent letter was signed by parents for their approval. A WhatsApp group was created for the parents for the regular update about their wards and any inquiry. At the end of three months, a questionnaire was filled up by the parents.

The effectiveness towards the Analytics-based Feedback in terms of the Parents' opinion was studied with, questions lined up with a questionnaire and interview schedule developed by the investigator, after three months of Treatment. During the intervention, 97.44% parents got to know the learning style of their child. All the parents reported that they support the study habits of their child. There were 94.87% parents who had observed some changes in the study habits of their child whereas 5.13% parents didn't feel so. There were 97.44% parents who motivated their child to learn English language through the Analytics-based Feedback approach. It was observed that 97.44% parents updated themselves with their child's progress through the WhatsApp group created for this very purpose. All the parents found Analytics-based Feedback system useful for their ward's studies. In one of the interviews of the parents, the feedback on the intervention was received which is as under –

'I have observed two important changes in my ward. Number one is, now he knows what is his problems in terms of literature and language of English. Number two, he has learnt how to redress these short-comings. So, these are two important changes that I have observed during last three months. As my ward is kinaesthetic learner, he would not sit for longer durations of studies. Little changes could be seen in this aspect but now he knows it. Though I could not understand the entire process but the changes that we observed were encouraging as we did not know that this was possible.'

Thus, the parents' observations and opinions speak of positive influence of the treatment in the teaching-learning process. Gradual and little changes were observed. Parents had a novel experience of Analytics-based Feedback of which they were unaware. Therefore, on the basis of above favourable opinion of the parents of the students, it may be said that Analytics-based Feedback was effective and useful for the students.

Objective 12: Issues and Challenges Related to Conducting Learning Analytics Study in India

The twelfth objective was to study issues and challenges related to conducting LA work in India. It was studied with students' feedback, Principal's feedback, teacher's feedback, parents' feedback and researcher's observations. These are listed below pointwise.

Students' Feedback

The issues and challenges faced by the students during the study are mentioned below:

1. During the pilot study at Jawahar Navodaya Vidyalaya, Ratibad, Bhopal, some of the students did not have a Gmail account. Gmail accounts had to be created for 75% of the students. They reported that though they had

written emails in the format in their copies, they had never used Gmail before.

2. During the main study, students did not own any gadgets except their phones which they mainly used while going through the course as reported by 76.92% of students. They depended upon their parents' gadgets to complete their assignments and submissions.
3. While seeking parental permissions, it was observed that one parent refused to permit due to previous experiences with their child. Due to the online course, internet usage was involved which were restraint from parents' end. The student reported so.
4. As students were provided individual feedbacks, students always wanted to compare their feedbacks due to their old habit-patterns which they found it missing here.
5. Some of the students faced issues related to data usage which was resolved by making the ICT room available to them.

Principal's Feedback

The issues and challenges discussed by the Principal of the school during the study have been mentioned below.

1. Infrastructural issues were presented as one of the key challenges.
2. Training of teachers and their motivation to conduct classes with AbF would be a huge challenge and task. They may be oriented about AbF but it needs dedication to teach with technological advances.
3. Teachers are already burdened with several classes throughout the day. Student-teacher ratio is not yet balanced in the country. Transforming education without addressing these issues would not be possible.
4. Parents' involvement and convincing them regarding their child's online security would be a challenge.
5. Data ethics and privacy would be a matter of great concern as it would be the school which would be answerable in every situation.

Teacher's Feedback

The issues and challenges discussed by the teacher of the class during the study have been mentioned below.

1. Teacher responded that they were unaware of the term Learning Analytics and its other associated sophisticated strategies. Thus, awareness is a serious issue and challenge for Indian education system considering the growth of LA across the world.
2. With technological advances, they've been provided basic trainings but they would need a readily available course and training to teach in a similar way.

3. As they are assigned several classes, managing blended mode of learning would be a difficult task for them. They found personalised learning difficult to manage with a high student-teacher ratio.
4. Personalised learning needs support and mutual understanding among all the teachers as it is about understanding learners first. A shared and known portfolio of every learner should be made available to the teachers who are dealing with those learners.
5. Completion of the syllabus remains a greater concern and pressure for teachers. With the academic calendar rush and co-curricular activities throughout the year, online material would be a help but providing AbF would be demanding.

Parents' Feedback

The issues and challenges discussed by parents of the learners during the study have been mentioned below.

1. Children use technology for a number of purposes including social media and networking websites which leads to a lot of screen time. It is difficult to differentiate the purpose of using internet services.
2. When permission was sought from the parents through 'Consent Letter', it was observed that one of the parents reported that they were apprehensive about the right usage of internet facility due to their past experiences with their ward.
3. Parents also showed concern about data privacy and its further usage. They were conveyed and convinced about its privacy and the purpose of the research.
4. Parents understood little about personalised learning with the learning style and other counselled aspects of the AbF.
5. Parents knew about their wards learning style but did not know how they could support them with this piece of information with respect to other subjects.

Researcher's Observation

The issues and challenges as observed during the entire study have been mentioned below.

1. Sufficient infrastructural facilities and courses are not available to conduct LA study in India. A course had to be developed to carry out a study which took a lot of time with respect to finalising scripts and content. Developing a course for blended mode learning was challenging without formal training.
2. Developing online course needed financial assistance which was not possible at the stage of course development, immediately. The study had

also covertly aimed for cost-effective solutions. Conducting LA study can heavily demand on financial assistance and be greatly cost-ridden.

3. It was difficult to seek permission from institutes for conducting such study as infrastructural necessities had to be identified first. During the pilot study, it was difficult to avail the facilities to students as it was residential school. Students had to be taken to the information technology lab (IT Lab) as no projector was available in the classroom.
4. School authorities and parents had to be convinced regarding data privacy and ethics as students were involved. Proper orientation was needed to create general awareness and information about LA.
5. Course coordinator had to be technically very sound, experienced and well-oriented to conduct the LA study. As Moodle provided only 50 enrolments and 1 GB data for free, creating the course with such limited dimensions was challenging.
6. While conducting main study, a few students could have access to the course only through mobiles phones of their parents. This led to another dimension of understanding the usage of gadgets during course access.
7. While teaching CALP aspects, a categorised set of mistakes were repeated which were grouped together for AbF. Some of the mistakes could have been eliminated at a lower level for better learning outcomes.
8. The Indian classroom set-ups do not offer infrastructural facility of systems in the classroom itself. Though the smart-class had projector in the classroom, but it has long way to go. Only projector was available in the classroom during the main study, but IT lab had to be used to allow access to all the students some times.
9. As the study was conducted in K.V. No. 1, it was a regular school. Besides the target content, the investigator had to also focus on syllabus completion for the semester exams.
10. The portfolios of students were not readily available which could have guided better about student's profile and background.

9

Research Discussions, Implications and Suggestions

The discussion of results and implications is presented in the current chapter based on the previous chapter. Objective-wise interpretation of results and the related discussions are presented below under different headings in this chapter. Summary, implications, and suggestions for further studies are also part of this chapter.

The study was conducted with sixteen objectives. Findings of these objectives were observed in the previous chapter under different sub-headings. Objective-wise findings and interpretation of results with discussions have been presented in this section under different sub-headings. Let us first observe objective-wise findings given below.

Objective-wise Major Findings

The following objective-wise findings flow from the interpretation of data presented in the previous chapter.

1. For the first objective, Analytics-based Feedback was found to be effective.. The experimental group students were observed to score higher on average than the control group students.
2. For the second objective, firstly, there was a significant increase in scores over time observed over the four successive trial and trend, suggesting that participation in the intervention for ESL, increased the learning outcomes level of the BICS component. There was a significant change in the learning progression in terms of the achievement in the BICS component of the English language in the successive trials of Class XI learners when Analytics-based personalised feedback is provided on the basis of previous performance.
3. For the third objective, there was a significant increase in scores over time observed over the four successive trial and trend, suggesting that participation in the intervention for ESL, increased the learning outcomes level of the CALP component. There was a significant change in the learning progression in terms of the achievement in CALP component scores in the successive trials.
4. For the fourth objective, there was a significant increase in scores over the time observed over the four successive trials and trends, suggesting

that participation in the intervention for ESL, increased the learning outcomes level of Overall Achievement. There was a significant change in the learning progression in terms of the Overall Achievement in the successive trials.

5. For the fifth objective, a relationship was observed between the BICS component and the predictor variables, viz, analytics-based feedback, traditional approach, student category, gender and learning style. Any outcome variable should never be studied in isolation. Regression allowed to observe AbF's relationship with BICS in comparison to the other and AbF was found to be most coefficient of all for BICS component of Achievement.
6. For the sixth objective, a relationship was observed between the CALP component and the predictor variables, viz, analytics-based feedback, traditional approach, student category, gender and learning style. Regression allowed to observe AbF's relationship with CALP in comparison to the other and AbF was found to be most coefficient of all for CALP component of Achievement.
7. For the seventh objective, a relationship was observed between the Overall achievement and the predictor variables, viz, analytics-based feedback, traditional approach, student category, gender and learning style. Regression allowed to observe AbF's relationship with Overall achievement in comparison to the other and AbF was found to be most coefficient of all for Overall Achievement.
8. For the eighth objective, firstly, there was a significant effect of Treatment (Analytics-based Feedback) on Study Habits of Class XI students as compared to Traditional method. Secondly, there was no significant interactive effect of Treatment and Gender on study habits. It signifies that AbF does not discriminate between the study habits of male or female students.
9. For the ninth objective, firstly, there was a significant effect of Treatment (Analytics-based Feedback) on the attitude towards the English language of Class XI students compared to the Traditional method. Secondly, there was no significant effect of the interaction between Treatment and Gender on Attitude towards English language. It signifies that AbF does not discriminate between the attitudes towards the English language of male or female students.
10. For the tenth objective, firstly, there was a significant effect of Treatment (Analytics-based Feedback) on the Motivation level of students compared to the Traditional method. Secondly, there was no significant effect of the interaction between Treatment and Gender on the Motivation level. It signifies that AbF does not discriminate between the motivation levels of male or female students.

11. For the eleventh objective, the opinions of the concerned teacher, principal and parents state positively about the AbF approach used to map the progression of the Class XI students with the English language.
12. For the twelfth objective, issues and challenges were studied according to the stakeholders involved in the research. Questionnaires, interviews, and observation schedules were used to elicit data from students, teachers, principals, parents, and the investigator. These issues and challenges were mainly around financial constraints while developing the course, course availability and development, data ethics and privacy, infrastructure, unawareness, stakeholders' preparedness, student-teacher ratio, syllabus completion and portfolio management.

Interpretation of Results and Discussion

The interpretation of results and discussions related to each objective have been presented below.

Objective 1: Effectiveness of Analytics-based Feedback

a. Achievement of Students in English Language with BICS Scores

The Analytics-based Feedback was found to be effective in terms of the achievement of students in the English language with BICS scores. Cavalcanti et al. (2020) indicated a positive contribution of feedback for the improvement of learning but with a condition of the relevance and quality of such feedback. Wang and Eberhard (2020) noticed a big improvement in the English as a second language of the class as students were more engaged. They could potentially feel more valued, as the feedback they received was generated according to their own personal assessments. During the intervention, students were encouraged to use the target language and motivated to speak with friends and teachers. They were made aware and cautioned about the significance of the language career-wise. As mentioned in Chapter I, habits were gradually developed over a period of three months with several strategies. They were advised to record themselves, mirror-talk, express and participate in everyday conversation with the target language. With the developed content, they were taught the pointers to improve the conversational language. They were constantly reminded of the significance of communication skills. Some were lacking fluency, coherence or pronunciation and others struggled with vocabulary, grammar or content. Each student was guided according to the problem areas. The results of the present investigation are an outcome of the constant feedback that students received. Consequently, it may be concluded that Analytics-based Feedback along with its guided measures and sophisticated strategies led to the results observed in this study. The elements of novelty (new and different approach) or the 'orienting effect' might have contributed towards the present result.

b. Achievement of Students in English Language with CALP Scores

The Analytics-based Feedback was found to be effective in terms of Achievement of students in English language with CALP scores. Cavalcanti et al. (2020) indicated positive contribution of feedback for the improvement of learning but with a condition of the relevance and quality of such feedback. Wang and Eberhard (2020) noticed a big improvement in the English as second language of the class as students were more engaged. Mori et al. (2019) confirmed that the collected information affected students learning activities. Rienties et al. (2018) supported the assumption of correlation between observation errors and predictors with the way language teachers designed weekly learning design activities. Ebner and Schön (2013) showed that automated precise testing and feedback can be seen as an individual assistance and an effort to an effective learning process. During the intervention, students were informed about their respective learning styles and were informed about their errors and mistakes committed in the first test and online assessments through Google forms where online feedback was provided. As the problem-areas were identified in the online performance assessment with Google forms, it was

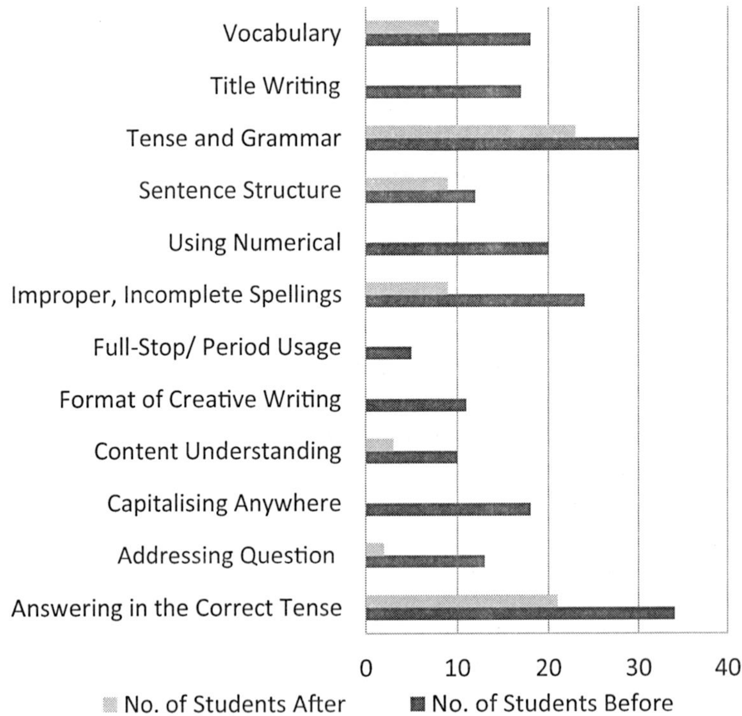

Figure 21: Identified Problem-Areas for CALP and No. of Students Before and After the Analytics-based Feedback

easier to guide the learners with AbF in their respective problem areas. There were twelve problem-areas identified in the performance, according to the online assessment of the performance for CALP competencies. These twelve problem-area components were the focus for feedback. For instance, a few students were writing the titles incorrectly and using numerical while writing English language. In another instance, while writing the closure of formal letter, 'Yours' was spelt incorrectly by many learners along with the incorrect format in the creative-writing. After providing them the AbF, a constant deliberation to improve the identified problem-areas were worked upon by the teacher and learner. Likewise, all the identified problem areas presented in figure 21 were dealt using AbF. The results of the present investigation are an outcome of the constant feedback that students received.

Consequently, it may be concluded that Analytics-based Feedback along with its guided measures and sophisticated strategies led to the results observed in this study.

c. Achievement of Students in English Language for Overall Scores

The Analytics-based Feedback was found to be effective in terms of the Achievement of students in English language for Overall scores. Admiraal and Bulterman-Bos (2017) observed that neither the poor performing students nor the high performing students evaluated an individual teaching approach positively as they felt that they get too much attention making them conscious in a group. Cavalcanti et al. (2020) indicated positive contribution of feedback for the improvement of learning but with a condition of the relevance and quality of such feedback. Iraj et al. (2020) revealed that early engagement with the feedback was associated with higher chances of succeeding in the course. Wang and Eberhard (2020) noticed a big improvement in the English as second language of the class as students were more engaged. Jørnø and Gynther (2018) also emphasised and focussed on the importance of the feedback loop between action capabilities, data and end goals in relation to actionable insights. Peng (2017) also confirmed evidently that all the data-based activities facilitated students to learn English more actively and the reliable data and results made teachers and students more convincing about LA in their study. Tan et al. (2017) also significantly presented on how students made sense of and accounted for the promise and perils of LA dashboards and analytics with awareness of the restrictive effects of one-sized-fits-all approaches to assessment. Berland et al. (2014) supported constructionist traditions with learning analytics methods reinforcing the provision of automated feedback to learners. Ebner and Schön (2013) summarised that LA is an important step to give learners precise feedback. In Anjewierden's study (2012), students used the feedback from the agents based on the quality of the models they created. Leelawong and Biswas (2008) indicated that self-regulated learning feedback better prepared students to learn in new domains. The above-mentioned works also support the significant role of feedback for better learning outcomes. The study has focussed on AbF as a sophisticated tool of LA with other assisted aspects of learning. The Overall scores of achievements in the English language are the scores of BICS and CALP combined. The positive results of the present investigation are an outcome of the constant feedback that students received. Consequently, it may be concluded that Analytics-based Feedback along with its guided measures and sophisticated strategies led to the results observed in this study. The elements of novelty (new and different approach) or the 'orienting effect' might have contributed towards the present result. The other aspects like feedback on the learning style, study habits and motivation may have contributed towards the present results of Overall Achievement. AbF emphasises proper and timely feedback understanding the context and pattern, mainly scaffolding the learning. Thus, AbF was found to be effective in terms of Overall Achievement in the English language of Class XI students.

Objective 2: Trend of Effect of the Treatment on BICS Achievement Scores of Class XI Students in English Language

The progression was studied through the trend of the effect due to the Treatment in the BICS component of Achievement scores of students in English language. A positive significant change was observed in the learning progression in terms of the achievement in the BICS component of Achievement of scores in the successive trials of Class XI learners when Analytics-based personalised feedback is provided on the basis of previous performance. Turan and Akdag-Cimen (2020) and Papamitsiou and Economides (2014) support this finding. Turan and Akdag-Cimen (2020) had also observed positive trends and main findings of the studies concerning the flipped classroom method in the field of English language teaching (ELT). Papamitsiou and Economides (2014) had highlighted a detected trend that Total Time to Answer Correct (TTAC) and Total Time to Answer Wrong (TTAW) had a significant direct positive and negative effect on Actual Performance (AP), respectively. In the present study, there were four successive trials with a gap of one month each. The trend of these trial showed a significant difference in the mean scores of the BICS component of Achievement of the two groups. Both the trends were positive but the Experimental group had the higher slope due to higher mean score than the Control group mean scores over the successive trials. Consequently, there was a significant change in the learning progression in terms of the achievement in the BICS component of Achievement in the successive trials of Class XI learners when Analytics-based personalised feedback is provided on the basis of previous performance.

Objective 3: Trend of Effect of the Treatment on CALP Achievement Scores of Class XI Students in English Language

The progression was studied through the trend of effect of the Treatment on CALP component of Achievement scores of students in English language.

A positive significant change was observed in the learning progression in terms of the achievement in CALP component of Achievement of scores in the successive trials of Class XI learners when Analytics-based personalised feedback is provided on the basis of previous performance. Turan and Akdag-Cimen (2020) and Papamitsiou and Economides (2014) support this finding. Turan and Akdag-Cimen (2020) had also observed positive trends and main findings of the studies concerning the flipped classroom method in the field of English language teaching (ELT). Papamitsiou and Economides (2014) had highlighted a detected trend that Total Time to Answer Correct (TTAC) and Total Time to Answer Wrong (TTAW) had a significant direct positive and negative effect on Actual Performance (AP), respectively. In the present study, there were four successive trials with a gap of one month each. The trend of these trial showed a significant difference in the mean scores of CALP component of Achievement of the two groups. Both the trends were positive but the Experimental group had the higher slope due to higher mean score than the Control group mean scores over the successive trials. Consequently, there was a significant change in the learning progression in terms of the achievement in CALP component of Achievement in the successive trials of Class XI learners when Analytics-based personalised feedback is provided on the basis of previous performance.

Objective 4: Trend of Effect of the Treatment on Overall Achievement Scores of Students in English Language

The progression was studied through the trend of the effect of the Treatment on Overall Achievement scores of students in the English language. A positive significant change was observed in the learning progression in terms of the achievement in Overall scores in the successive trials of Class XI learners when Analytics-based personalised feedback is provided on the basis of previous performance. Turan and Akdag-Cimen (2020) had also observed positive trends and main findings of the studies concerning the flipped classroom method in the field of English language teaching (ELT). Papamitsiou and Economides (2014) had highlighted a detected trend that Total Time to Answer Correct (TTAC) and Total Time to Answer Wrong (TTAW) had a significant direct positive and negative effect on Actual Performance (AP), respectively. In the present study, there were four successive trials with a gap of one month each. The trend of these trials showed a significant difference in the mean scores of Overall Achievement of the two groups. Both the trends were positive but the Experimental group had a higher slope due to a higher mean score than the Control group mean scores over the successive trials. Consequently, there was a significant change in the learning progression in terms of the achievement in Overall scores in the successive trials of Class XI learners when Analytics-based personalised feedback is provided on the basis of previous performance.

Objective 5: Regression Equation for Predicting BICS Achievement of Class XI Students on the Basis of Relationship between BICS and Treatments, Gender, Categories and Learning Styles

The multiple regression equation for establishing the relationship of the BICS component of Achievement of students on the basis of Treatment (Analytics-based Feedback and Traditional method), Gender, Socio-economic status, and Learning Style was established. Vitta and Al-Hoorie (2020), Zheng et al. (2019), Nyamubi (2019) Kintu et al. (2017) Kovanović et al. (2015) Ali et al. (2014), Aguiar et al. (2014), Gray et al. (2014), Jayaprakash et al. (2014) and Yazdani and Godbole (2014) had also established regression equations for their studies. They suggested predictive modelling considering the demographic variables through their regression analysis. For the outcome of the BICS component of Achievement represented by Y, the other two independent variables were $X_{1,}$ the Treatment (Analytics-based Feedback) and $X_{2,}$ male and female genders, four soci0-economic categories, and learning style of students with some error. The equation established for the present study is, BICS ~ (7.01) * Intercept + (4.53) * Treatment_1 + (2.48) * Treatment_2 + (3.54) * Gender_F + (3.46) * Gender_M + (0.0) * category_1 + (0.0) * category_2 + (0.0) * category_3 + (0.0) * category_4 + (0.0) * LS_1 + (0.0) * LS_2 + (0.0) * LS_3 + which may be used to predict outcomes for some other studies with similar demographic variables.

Objective 6: Regression Equation for Predicting CALP Achievement of Class XI Students on the Basis of Relationship between CALP and Treatments, Gender, Categories and Learning Styles

The multiple regression equation for establishing the relationship of the CALP component of Achievement of students on the basis of Treatment (Analytics-based Feedback and Traditional method), Gender, Socio-economic status, and Learning Style was established. Vitta and Al-Hoorie (2020), Zheng et al. (2019), Nyamubi (2019) Kintu et al. (2017) Kovanović et al. (2015) Ali et al. (2014), Aguiar et al. (2014), Gray et al. (2014), Jayaprakash et al. (2014) and Yazdani and Godbole (2014) had also established regression equations for their studies. They suggested predictive modelling considering the demographic variables through their regression analysis. For the outcome of the BICS component of Achievement represented by Y, the other two independent variables were $X_{1,}$ the Treatment (Analytics-based Feedback) and $X_{2,}$ male and female genders, four soci0-economic categories, and learning style of students with some error. The equation established for the present study is, CALP ~ (10.23) * Intercept + (7.64) * Treatment_1 + (2.59) * Treatment_2 + (4.74) * Gender_F + (5.49) * Gender_M + (0.62) * category_1 + (0.0) * category_2 + (0.0) * category_3 +

(0.0) * category_4 + (1.43) * LS_1 + (0.0) * LS_2 + (1.24) * LS_3 + which may be used to predict outcomes for some other studies with similar demographic variables.

Objective 7: Regression Equation for Predicting Overall Achievement of Class XI Students on the Basis of Relationship between Overall achievement and Treatments, Gender, Categories and Learning Styles

The multiple regression equation for establishing the relationship of Overall Achievement of students on the basis of Treatment (Analytics-based Feedback and Traditional method), Gender, Socio-economic status, and Learning Style was established. Vitta and Al-Hoorie (2020), Zheng et al. (2019), Nyamubi (2019) Kintu et al. (2017) Kovanović et al. (2015) Ali et al. (2014), Aguiar et al. (2014), Gray et al. (2014), Jayaprakash et al. (2014) and Yazdani and Godbole (2014) had also established regression equations for their studies. They suggested predictive modelling considering the demographic variables through their regression analysis. For the outcome of Overall Achievement represented by Y, the other two independent variables were $X_{1,}$ the Treatment (Analytics-based Feedback) and $X_{2,}$ male and female genders, four soci0-economic categories, and learning style of students with some error. The equation established for the present study is, Overall ~ (17.24) * Intercept + (12.17) * Treatment_1 + (5.07) * Treatment_2 + (8.2) * Gender_F + (9.04) * Gender_M + (1.84) * category_1 + (0.0) * category_2 + (0.0) * category_3 + (0.0) * category_4 + (1.63) * LS_1 + (0.0) * LS_2 + (1.44) * LS_3 + which may be used to predict outcomes for some other studies with similar demographic variables.

Objective 8: Effect of Treatment and Interactive Effect of Treatment and Gender on Study Habits of Class XI Students by Taking the Pre-Test Scores of Study Habit as a Covariate

The effect of Treatment (Analytics-based Feedback) was found to be significant on the Study Habits of Class XI students as compared to the Traditional method. For the second part, the effect of Gender was not significant on the Study Habits. Vyas and Choudhary (2016) no significant difference observed in study habits of male and female adolescent students. Iraj et al. (2020) Siahi and Maiyo (2015) Nadeem et al. (2014) Yazdani and Godbole (2014) Mudasir (2012) Bailey and Onwuegbuzie (2010) support the finding of the present study. Iraj et al. (2020) revealed that early engagement with the feedback was associated with higher chances of succeeding in the course leading to better study habits. Likewise, previous engagement with feedback was highly predictive of students' engagement in the future and also that certain student sub-populations, (e.g., female students), were more likely to engage than others.

Siahi and Maiyo (2015) also showed a positive correlation between study habits and academic achievement. Nadeem et al. (2014) had also confirmed that there was a significant mean difference observed between the two groups under observation about their study habits and academic achievements. Yazdani and Godbole (2014) had concluded that study habits had proved to be positively correlated with academic performance of students. Though Mudasir (2012) had analysed to reveal that female students had better study habits than the male students which was not observed in the present study. Further, the effect of interaction between Treatment and Gender on Study Habits of the Class XI students was not found significant. During the study, after assessing the pre-test of Study Habits, students were counselled about the significance of study habits and how to improve them. They were guided with the support of their parents for an improvement in their study habits over a period of three months. Conscious efforts were made by the students with the support of teachers and parents. After three months, AbF showed significant effect on the Study Habits of Class XI students.

Objective 9: Effect of Treatment and Interactive Effect of Treatment and Gender on Attitude towards English Language of Class XI Students by Taking the Pre-Test Scores of Study Habit as a Covariate

The effect of Treatment (Analytics-based Feedback) was significant on the Attitude towards the English language of Class XI students compared to the Traditional method. The effect of Gender was not significant on the Attitude towards the English language. Colaste (2018) found that there was a significant relationship between attitude and English language-learning. Khan (2016) found that there was a positive correlation between attitude towards learning/teaching English and their proficiency in it. Nyamubi (2016) emphasised that students' positive attitudes to English should be improved to enhance the learning of the language. Ahmed (2015) showed that the attitude towards English language learning and using the language in various domains of usage was extremely positive. Tran and Duong (2013) observed that the academic achievements and attitudes towards ELL were positively correlated to SRL, yet only attitudes towards ELL were predictors of SRL. Abidin et al. (2012) found that there were statistically significant attitudinal differences in the demographic profiles of gender and field of study. Mahmoudi et al. (2012) found that participants possessed positive attitudes towards Computer Assisted English Language Learning (CAELL). Consequently, their attitudes and performance were found to be positively related. Hashwani (2008) depicted that students had affirmative attitudes and high level of enthusiasm towards English language-learning. During the study, students were informed about the significance of language in the near future with respect to career and job-opportunities. They were guided when they came up with their queries. As a result, it was found that AbF had a significant effect on the Attitude towards the English language after the study. Gender had no significant effect possibly due to equal guidance to all students. The effect of the interaction between Treatment and Gender on the Attitude towards the English language of the Class XI students was not significant.

Objective 10: Effect of Treatment and Interactive Effect of Treatment and Gender on Study Habits of Class XI Students by Taking the Pre-Test Scores of Study Habit as a Covariate

The effect of Treatment (Analytics-based Feedback) was significant on the Motivation level of Class XI students compared to the Traditional method. The effect of Gender was not significant on the Motivation level. Wang and Zhan (2020) had suggested that stronger learner beliefs of self-efficacy and perceived value of English learning promoted learning motivation and self-regulation. Kvashnina and Martynko (2019) had concluded on the significant benefits of the flipped classroom in ESL teaching including an increase in students' overall performance on the course, enhancement of students' motivation and improvement of their autonomous learning skills. Kintu et al. (2017) indicated that motivation as the students' characteristics/backgrounds and design features were significant predictors for student learning outcomes in blended learning. Tan et al. (2017) in their empirical study revealed positive benefits to learning in terms of fostering greater self-awareness and self-regulatory learning natures, improved learning motivation and engagement and nurturing connective literacy among students. Khansir et al. (2016) had revealed noticeable evidence of the existence of a strong relationship between socio-economic status and motivation in language-learning (English as a FL). Nagy (2016) had observed to improve student motivation for learning in all cohorts, creating high-quality data-driven conversations between students, teachers and parents. Kumari and Chamundeswari (2015) had observed a significant difference between students of different categories and gender of the sample pertaining to achievement motivation, study habits and academic achievement. Rezaei et al. (2015) had depicted a significant effect of proficiency level on test anxiety and extrinsic goal orientation for motivation in English language learning. Ali et al. (2014) had suggested that the MSLQ datasets could reveal mastery approach, mastery avoidance and performance approach goal orientations for the achievement goal orientations of students. Yazdani and Godbole (2014) had showed that there was a significant positive relationship between achievement motivation and study habits to academic performance. Kormos and Kiddle (2013) had suggested that social class had an overall medium-size effect on motivational factors with self-efficacy beliefs being the most strongly related to socio-economic status. Long et al. (2013)

had presented some suggestions to arouse the students' motivation to learn English and thereby improve the efficiency of English learning and teaching. Jahedi (2012) had showed that there was significant correlation between motivational beliefs components and self-regulated learning components of the students. Rotgans and Schmidt (2010) had depicted that the modified MSLQ is a reliable and valid instrument to determine students' motivational beliefs and learning strategies at the general curriculum level. Hashwani (2008) had illustrated a higher inclination of extrinsic motivational goals attached to the student's language-learning outcomes and future achievements as compared to intrinsic ones, irrespective of the gender. The sample consisted of students with the background of science stream. Their entire focus is on the subjects like physics, chemistry or mathematics. English was considered to be a subject to be studied solely for the examination purpose. This attitude towards language was difficult to change without proper motivation and guidance. During the study, all the students were motivated to consider English language as a medium of communication in their near future with some examples. They were shown how language proficiency is helpful in studying other subjects too. As a result, it was found that AbF had a significant effect on the Motivation level of the students after the study. Gender had no significant effect possibly due to equal guidance to all the students. The effect of the interaction between Treatment and Gender on the Motivation level of the Class XI students was not significant.

Objective 11: Effectiveness of Analytics-based Feedback in English Language of Higher Secondary Students in terms of Opinions

a. Opinion of Teacher towards Analytics-based Feedback

The Analytics-based Feedback was found to be effective in terms of opinion of teacher towards Analytics-based Feedback. Admiraal and Bulterman-Bos (2017) presented the observation that without proper orientation, LA study may not succeed. Yang et al. (2020) helped teachers to explore find the effective teaching characteristics to better improve students' concentration degree better. Holstein et al. (2019) delved on the notion that involving stakeholders such as teachers throughout the creation of new educational technologies can help ensure their usefulness and usability in real-world contexts. Wei et al. (2019) revealed tertiary instructors' degree of familiarity with LA and their attitudes to, interest in and concerns about using LA tools in various contexts which were limited also observed in the present study. Findings of Rienties et al. (2018) indicated that 55% of variance of weekly online engagement in these four modules was explained by the way language teachers designed weekly learning design activities. Nagy (2016) insisted that the engagement and continuing professional development of teachers was also critical to embed and sustain the project. It was also pointed out by the involved teacher in the present study. Real-time awareness tools by Rodríguez-Triana et al. (2016) were well received by the teachers both in terms of usability and applicability. Teachers in their study stated that the tools helped them to monitor the progress of the students in the classroom but they could be also useful in order to have evidence of the work done at home. Wong (2015) explored the nature of teaching styles and the possible variables, including students' English language proficiency and their learning styles, influencing their teaching styles in English for Academic Purposes (EAP) classrooms. Heritage and Bailey (2014) in their article had reiterated learning progressions, in contrast with standards, that can show incremental growth and were placed to support teachers' formative assessment practices with K-12 students who are acquiring English as an additional language. Baker (2013) had suggested that teachers using the system review student homework before class and were able to change the focus of classroom activities based on student understanding and providing feedback. Ebner and Schön (2013) had also suggested after their work in Mathematics to measure the reading competences of school children with some simple partial competences which could be observed, measured and perhaps trained without appreciable investments – and without additional stresses and strains for the teachers. During the present study, the involved English language teacher actively participated and attended the entire intervention. Her feedback was positive for AbF and pointed out in a similar manner to the other literature reviews. AbF was found to be effective in terms of teacher's opinion.

b. Opinion of Principal towards Analytics-based Feedback

The Analytics-based Feedback was found to be effective in terms of opinion of teacher towards Analytics-based Feedback. This finding was supported by Crossley et al. (2020), Ferguson (2019), Liu et al. (2019), Zheng et al. (2019), Cejnar and Kao (2018), Ferguson (2018), Liu et al. (2018), Peng (2017), Divjak and Vondra (2016), Ferguson et al. (2016), Kumar et al. (2015), Volk et al. (2015), Aguiar et al. (2014), Dunbar et al. (2014), Gray et al. (2014), Pardos et al. (2014), Baker (2013) and Anjewierden (2012). Studies by Crossley et al. (2020), Liu et al. (2019), Zheng et al. (2019), Peng (2017), Kumar et al. (2015), Pardos et al. (2014) and Anjewierden (2012) had presented, emphasised and discussed the infrastructural necessities to conduct LA studies. Ferguson (2019) had presented challenges that could be clustered under six headings: duty to act, informed consent, safeguarding, equality and justice, data ownership and protection and privacy and integrity of self. Cejnar and Kao (2018) had discussed that Australian K-12 classrooms had adopted 1:1 computer use, however, academic results had been inconsistent arguably due to a lack of ICT skills and distraction. Ferguson (2018) identified a diverse set of contexts including ethics, legislation, teaching and learning, decision-making and planning in addition to the data sources and stakeholders producing and consuming data. Liu et al. (2018) presented the learning trajectory visualisations to assess the work served as illustrative examples of how this generalisable approach can assist to handle large volumes of rich data at multiple levels of granularity. Divjak and Vondra (2016) examined the specific challenges of ethics and privacy issues of LA in pre-tertiary education, the most useful data sources about learners in pre-tertiary education and to integrate data from face-to-face classroom with data from LMS and other e-sources. Ferguson at al. (2016) presented a policy document to help European policymakers for high-quality, innovative ways of learning and teaching through LA. Volk et al. (2015) also confirmed that the usage behaviour is strongly influenced by the factor time and the time and activity structure of a school year in an e-learning environment. Aguiar et al. (2014) derived measurements of engagement from students' electronic portfolios and show how these features can be used effectively to augment the quality of predictions. Dunbar et al. (2014) described how data from institutional, learning and what we call 'developmental' analytics can be incorporated into course and curricular design by using a purposefully built analysis tool that permits the exploration of data relevant to course/curriculum design. Gray et al. (2014) also had reviewed factors that could be used to predict academic performance, but which were currently not systematically measured in tertiary education. Baker (2013) had also proposed some action principles for schools, local education agencies (LEAs) and state education agencies (SEAs). During the present study, the Principal of K.V. No. 1 carried out an in-depth discussion and had a dialogue with the sample students regarding the entire intervention and experience. The interview was entirely based on the experience from seeking permission to completing the study. It was conveyed that infrastructure and data privacy were two significant concerns earlier. Post-study, the feedback was positive for AbF from students and classes were silently observed during the intervention without the information of the investigator. The two concerns were also pointed out in a similar manner to the other literature reviews. AbF was found to be effective in terms of the Principal's opinion.

c. Opinion of Parents towards Analytics-based Feedback

The Analytics-based Feedback was found to be effective in terms of opinion of Parents towards Analytics-based Feedback. This finding was supported by Ferguson (2019), Divjak and Vondra (2016), Nagy (2016), Rodríguez-Triana et al. (2016), Scheffel et al. (2014), Baker (2013) and Turingan and Yang (2009). These studies also expressed their concern over data privacy, ethics and issues related to them. Parents had expressed their concern over data privacy and therefore, they were informed and assured about the process through the consent letter. In a post study questionnaire, every parent responded to be found satisfied with Analytics-based Feedback system. They also observed AbF to be useful for their ward's studies. AbF was found to be effective in terms of Patents' opinion.

Objective 12: Issues and Challenges Related to Conducting Learning Analytics Study in India

Issues and challenges related to conducting LA work in India were studied with students' feedback, Principal's feedback, teacher's feedback, parents' feedback and researcher's observations. The interpretations and discussion are listed below pointwise.

1. Issues and Challenges According to Students' Feedback

During the pilot study, 75% students did not have their mail ID which is a grave issue with respect to technological advancements. It also depicts diverse and heterogeneous situations across population. Fair usage of facilities among the young minds is also seemed to be one of the issues which should be addressed with counselling and guidance. Breaking the old habit-patterns like comparison was also a challenge and therefore, individual learning is needed to be promoted. Transformation from the cognitive models to constructivist model of learning seemed novel to them but gradually it is yet to be adopted in the process. During the main study, it was observed that students used mobile phones instead of some system to access the content and take up the assignments. It was observed thorough YouTube analytics that mobile phones were used for 94.9% views whereas computers were used for 2.9% views as shown in the figure 22 on the next page. It points out towards rise in the

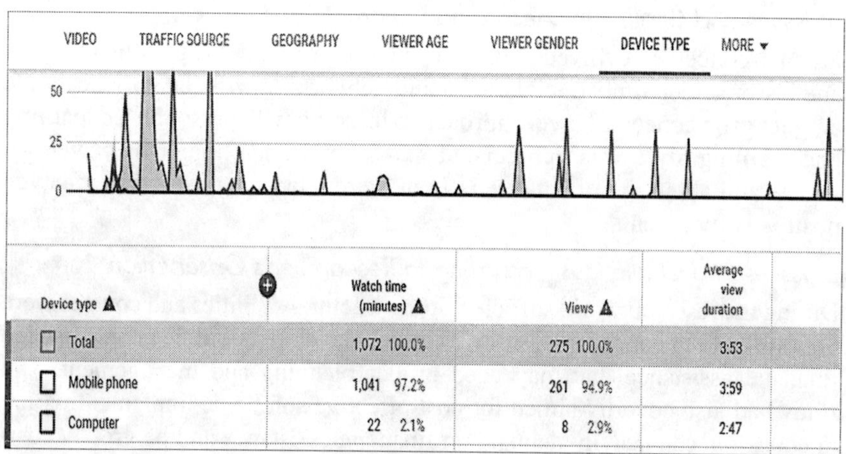

Device type ▲	Watch time (minutes) ▲	Views ▲	Average view duration
Total	1,072 100.0%	275 100.0%	3:53
Mobile phone	1,041 97.2%	261 94.9%	3:59
Computer	22 2.1%	8 2.9%	2:47

Figure 22: Analytics of You Tube Views through MYLEARNINGCLASS Course at Moodle Platform for Class XI

(Mobile-assisted Language Learning) MALL rather than (Computer-assisted Language Learning) CALL.

2. Issues and Challenges According to Principal's Feedback

The focal issues and challenges discussed by the principal of the school revolved around infrastructure, training of teachers and their motivation to conduct classes with AbF, over-burdened teachers with an imbalanced student-teacher ratio, parents' involvement and data ethics and privacy. With the New Education Policy being implemented soon in the country, these issues should be addressed for education to be transformed through technology. Though the Right to Education has provided guidelines regarding student-teacher ratio, it may be further improved. Data privacy is a global issue and a major breakthrough is needed in this regard. Parents may be oriented towards novel approaches to teaching learning processes.

3. Issues and Challenges According to Teacher's Feedback

The issues and challenges discussed by the teacher of the class were mainly about the unawareness of Learning Analytics and its associated sophisticated strategies in Indian scenario. It was rightly pointed out that they would need a readily available course but they may be involved in creation and development of such online courses and learning designs. Student-teacher ratio and portfolio management was another concern for personalised learning. Concrete steps should be taken in this regard within the system. Syllabus completion is yet another task that concerns and pressurise teachers throughout the academic calendar. New Education Policy may address these issues and challenges by offering solutions and practices in the upcoming years.

4. Issues and Challenges According to Parents' Feedback

Parents concerns revolved around right usage of infrastructural facilities and lesser screen time. Social media and networking with data privacy were another grim concern. Novel approach to learning with personalised learning and learning style was appreciated and supported. Though they were to understand about their own role in their ward's learning, AbF was received positively by parents.

5. Issues and Challenges According to Researcher's Observation

During the research work, sufficient infrastructural facilities and courses were not available to conduct LA study in India. Developing online course needed financial assistance that may need proper planning and management. The study had also covertly aimed for cost-effective solutions. Implementing LA in education can heavily demand on financial assistance and be greatly cost-ridden. Administration and institutes need to be prepared with infrastructural facilities and human resources to implement LA in India. Along with institutes and management, parents also need an orientation towards it being the

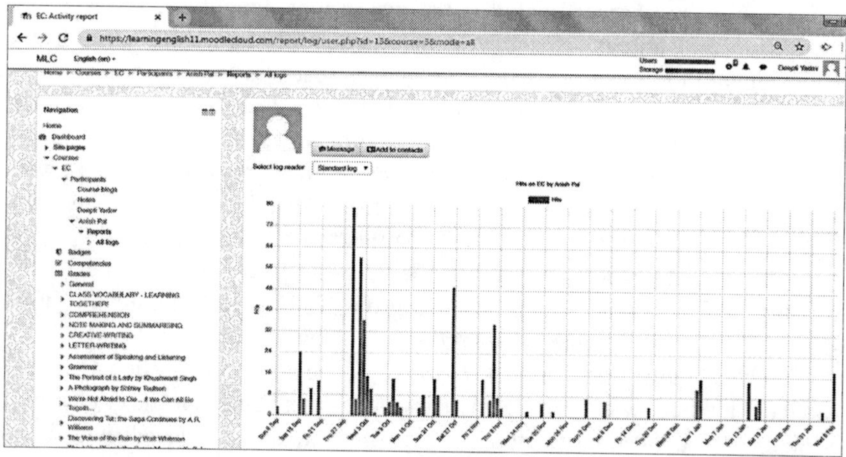

Figure 23: Analytics of Log Views of Student through MLC Course at Moodle Platform for Class XI

stakeholder of such works. Educationists, teachers and researchers also need to me made aware of LA and its other associated sophisticated aspects. Students have been mainly using mobile phones to access the content and submit their assignments. This had led to rise in MALL instead of CALL. Students were more tech-savvy than the teachers and parents that signify towards a technological update needed for teachers. A need for syllabus and curriculum upgradation was also observed during content development and delivery.

An academic pressure to complete the syllabus would also make a difference to promote personalised learning. Technical training would be a dire need if LA is to be used to transform education through technology. While using the Moodle platform, it is important to learn how to check the progress of learners individually. It has to be checked for every learner as shown in Figure 23 for an exemplar. Thus, LA is certainly technology oriented which demands a sound knowledge of running the online course even if used in a blended mode or with a flipped classroom.

Implications of the Study

Learning Analytics and its sophisticated approach with Analytics-based Feedback are mainly technologically-driven. The study observed positive and significant results with the sample selected. It primarily focussed on feedback based on analytics to improve the learning outcomes. The feedback procedure helped students gradually to break old study habit patterns, know their learning styles, better motivation level and a change in the attitude towards learning English as a second language. The findings have imperative ramifications for planning English as a second language learning. Definite differences were observed between the two groups, taught through AbF and the customary strategy. Hence, AbF in the school classroom can enhance achievement in English as a second language. Teachers and educators require effective instructional material with apt feedback based on analytics to get hold of this methodology and teaching approach. It is, therefore, proposed that language module architects and curriculum designers should find a way to integrate the AbF model in the classroom. The stakeholders of the study are students, teachers, parents and school administration. The course and syllabus are planned and developed on a national basis and further researches in the LA field is a dire need for this area to grow. The implications for different stakeholders and others have been presented below.

Teachers: Digital education holds the key to the future of education. Learning Analytics has been widely accepted mainly for higher education and gradually, it is taking up school education too. Teachers need to update themselves with the latest technology and models available to teach. They need to consider the current world issues and scenarios around pandemic that will lead to dynamic changes in future education. Education had been on infusing stage before pandemic but sudden need of the hour catapulted the entire education into transformation stage without proper orientation and training. Teachers of the country somehow dealt with the situation and continued classes within a very short span of time. Data are available to them but using it to its full potential would need some training. Therefore, they need to adjust to the technological advancements and be vigilant of such changes. They also need not to depend on a central system for orientation or training and rather attend some available training programmes wherever and whenever possible.

Students: Since in the present study, Analytics-based Feedback has been discovered to be more effective than the traditional strategy for instructing in enhancing Achievement and understanding of the students towards their own learning and subject of the examination, they may utilize technology in a better manner and means. The model provides feedback which facilitates improvement if considered consciously and diligently. In the 21st century, students are more technology-friendly and appreciate its blended mode. They may further deepen their insights and knowledge on the model and use it for their own benefits and improvements. They may be more receiving towards the feedbacks received on the errors or mistakes and continue to make improvements for further assistance.

Parents: Substantially more exertion on the part of parental control in the model may be observed. Usually, parents are not much participative in other available models of learning. But the proposed model in the study emphasises on the parental involvement and support due to online learning and data privacy. Besides, students are in the school for a limited period of time and major learning takes place in a combination of school and home environment. Continuous monitoring of learners will certainly lead to needed changes in the modes and manners of learning. Consequently, parents need to be involved and kept updated of technological advances and novel approaches to learning. It is also due to age limits of students to maintain data ethics and privacy.

Administrators: The heads of institutes should endeavour to improve around infrastructure, materials, planning and management to implement novel ideas to improve the standard of education and learning. They hold the key to empower teachers to utilise innovative and inventive strategies for better transactions in the classroom. They may offer ideas and opportunities encouraging and inviting more from others.

Teacher Educators: Teacher educators initiate the understanding of the learning process. A noteworthy pivotal point of instruction at this level is encouraging critical, logical, and reasoning capacities in young teachers with an aim to empower them with technology and resources to further take strong decisions for the education system. Educators deeply understand this cycle of transferring methodologies and strategies to additionally invigorate the thinking capacity. Learning Analytics has grown substantially across the globe over the last decade mainly for higher education. School education has recently begun to experience its benefits and usage. Teacher educators play significantly dominant role in popularising and familiarising the concept in school education. Thus, they not only need to develop an understanding on the subject but gain a command to transfer the knowledge and application to future teachers.

Curriculum Designers and Planners: The architects of educational programs and courses organize the substance and components of a subject. It is not merely the designing and planning of the curriculum but the entire education system and its deliberation revolve around it. The curriculum features the expansive standards of subject matters and methodologies for future to come. They develop educational modules to be instructed by teacher educators and teachers for conventional teaching in the classroom. As per the present study findings and reviews, Learning Analytics and AbF need some emphasising space in the curriculum at teacher education level and school level, both, considering the need of the hour with technological advances and concerns. The curriculum plan for LA inculcation in teacher education should in consistency with school education. It requires a deeper understanding of the field's strategies, models and methods. Course and educational modules' designers need to plan the standards and highlights of the AbF model in different types of instructional material for teacher educators, teachers and students.

Researchers and Understudies: Curiosity and ideas are the building squares of learning and invention. The instructional material created during the study is an accomplishment for the work. Subject specialists may develop similar or better instructional material researching the field and carry-on research around it to further develop it. It was developed for class XI. Similarly, it may be developed for other levels and subjects. As LA needs more empirical evidences, some researches may be conducted gathering proofs and findings. Theoretical guidelines are also needed considering Indian scenarios and conditions as developed and provided by other countries for their local set-ups. Since theoretical and empirical guidance are the need of the hour for the field to grow, researches may be further taken up. The present study has defined Analytics-based Feedback (AbF) as follows -

. . . *any information about a person's performance of a task resulting from the systematic analysis of data with the help of statistics which provides meaningful patterns that can be further used as a basis for improvement in performance.*

Suggestions for Further Studies

Learning Analytics has gained immense popularity worldwide in just one decade of its existence. Technology has given desired boost and support to its various theoretical and empirical dimensions of growth and developments. There is much more promising with LA besides AbF which the present empirical study explored in the Indian scenario. The field has been constantly explored and experimented worldwide in higher education and to some extent in school education. The field had not even a handful of studies, theoretical or empirical, on an Indian platform in higher education or school education. The present study explored the emerging field in Indian conditions with available resources and created some in its attempt for empirical findings. During the research work, several points and subjects were noted for the new field that may be explored in further works of investigations. These observations have been listed below.

1. The instructional material of on the lines of Analytics-based Feedback may be produced for other study subjects and levels and its adequacy and effect may be examined.
2. Analytics-based Feedback may be implemented with different strategies for instructing with some other model like inquiry-based or problem-based learning. The effect of AbF with these models may be further investigated.
3. The effect of AbF may be studied for an inclusive set up exclusively considering various dimensions of the field.
4. Another significant dimension of Learning Analytics is time-on-task researches popular worldwide. A study may be conducted focusing on time as a significant variable for learning outcomes.
5. The present study used a blended learning model to study the learning progression. Further studies may be conducted with an entirely online mode of instructions to study learning outcomes.
6. The present study observed an inclination towards MALL instead of CALL. A similar study with AbF may be designed with the creation of

some Application-based instructional material where students may be taught with the help of app-based features.

7. 'Betty's Brain' is an exemplar with higher education and school level education brought together to create learning resources. If higher education institutions may be involved to create the learning resources and the impact may be measured.
8. Longitudinal and cross-sectional studies may be conducted with AbF and several other dimensions of Learning Analytics.

Conclusion

1. Analytics-based Feedback was found to be effective for English Language of Higher Secondary Students in terms of Achievement of students in English Language with BICS Scores.
2. Analytics-based Feedback was found to be effective for English Language of Higher Secondary Students in terms of Achievement of students in English Language with CALP Scores.
3. Analytics-based Feedback was found to be effective for English Language of Higher Secondary Students in terms of Achievement of Students in English Language with Overall Scores.
4. A positive trend was observed as there was an increase and change in the learning progression in terms of the BICS component of achievement in the successive trials of Class XI learners when Analytics-based personalised feedback is provided on the basis of previous performance as compared to traditional method.
5. A positive trend was observed as there was an increase and change in the learning progression in terms of the CALP component of achievement in the successive trials of Class XI learners when Analytics-based personalised feedback is provided on the basis of previous performance as compared to traditional method.
6. A positive trend was observed as there was an increase and change in the learning progression in terms of the achievement in Overall scores in the successive trials of Class XI learners when Analytics-based personalised feedback is provided on the basis of previous performance as compared to traditional method.
7. Analytics-based Feedback was better coefficient in terms of BICS component of Achievement in English Language of Class XI students as compared to traditional method when the BICS component was observed in terms of relationship with the two methods, gender, socio-economic status, and learning styles.
8. Analytics-based Feedback was better coefficient in terms of the CALP component of Achievement in English Language of Class XI students as compared to traditional method when the CALP component was observed

in terms of relationship with the two methods, gender, socio-economic status, and learning styles.

9. Analytics-based Feedback was better coefficient in terms of Overall Achievement in English Language of Class XI students as compared to traditional method when the Overall achievement was observed in terms of relationship with the two methods, gender, socio-economic status, and learning styles.
10. Gender of students made a difference for the Overall Achievement in English language of the Class XI students. Girls were performing better than boys with Analytics-based Feedback.
11. Socio-economic statuses of students did not affect BICS, CALP, and Overall Achievement in English language of the Class XI students.
12. Learning Styles of students did not affect BICS, CALP, and Overall Achievement in English language of the Class XI students.
13. Analytics-based Feedback was better in terms of Study Habits in English Language of Class XI students as compared to traditional method.
14. Analytics-based Feedback and Gender together did not affect Study Habits in English language of Class XI students.
15. Analytics-based Feedback was better in terms of Attitude towards English language of Class XI students compared to traditional method in the context of Gender.
16. Analytics-based Feedback and Gender together did not affect Attitude towards English language of Class XI students.
17. Analytics-based Feedback and Gender together did not affect Attitude towards English language of the Class XI students.
18. Analytics-based Feedback was better in terms of Motivation level of Class XI students as compared to traditional method in the context of Gender.
19. Analytics-based Feedback and Gender together did not affect Motivation level of the Class XI students.
20. Opinion of Teacher towards Analytics-based Feedback was positive.
21. Opinion of Principal towards Analytics-based Feedback was positive.
22. Opinion of Parents towards Analytics-based Feedback was positive.
23. Issues and challenges related to the study may be addressed that revolve around financial constraints, developing courses, course availability, data ethics and privacy, infrastructure, unawareness, stakeholders' preparedness, student-teacher ratio, syllabus completion and portfolio management.

Thus, the model of Analytics-based Feedback addresses problem areas using data captured and identifying pattern in the performance, making meaning out of it. Constant reminder and conscious efforts can provide needed support to improve and work upon those to improve learning.

Bibliography

Abidin, M. J. Z., Pour-Mohammadi, M., & Alzwari, H. (2012). EFL Students' Attitudes towards Learning English Language: The Case of Libyan Secondary School Students. *Asian Social Science, 8*(2), 119.

Abilasha, R., & Ilankumaran, M. (2018). English Language Teaching: Challenges and Strategies from the Indian Perspective. *International Journal of Engineering and Technology (IJET), 7*(3), 202–205.

Admiraal, W. & Bulterman-Bos, J.V.J. (2017). Learning Analytics in Secondary Education: Assessment for Learning in 7th Grade Language Teaching. *ECER.*

Agrawal, S., & Lalwani, A. (2020). Decoding the Performance in an Out-of-Context Problem during Blocked Practice. *In Proceedings of the Tenth International Conference on Learning Analytics & Knowledge* (pp. 118–123).

Aguiar, E., Ambrose, G. A. A., Chawla, N. V., Goodrich, V., & Brockman, J. (2014). Engagement vs Performance: Using Electronic Portfolios to Predict First Semester Engineering Student Persistence. *Journal of Learning Analytics*, *1*(3), 7–33.

Ahmed, S. (2015). Attitudes towards English Language Learning among EFL Learners at UMSKAL. *Journal of Education and Practice, 6*(18), 6–16.

Ali, L., Hatala, M., Gašević, D., & Winne, P. H. (2014). Leveraging MSLQ Data for Predicting Students Achievement Goal Orientations. *Journal of Learning Analytics*, *1*(3), 157–160.

Amanda Hilliard. (2019) Developing an English Learner Corpus for Materials Creation and Evaluation. *Companion Proceedings 9th International Conference on Learning Analytics & Knowledge (LAK19),* 44–49.

Anderson, J. M. (2005). Structuralism and Autonomy: from Saussure to Chomsky. Historiographia Linguistica, 32(1–2), 117–148.

Andergassen, M., Mödritscher, F., & Neumann, G. (2014). Practice and Repetition during Exam Preparation in Blended Learning Courses: Correlations with Learning Results. *Journal of Learning Analytics*, *1*(1), 48–74.

Ariani, M. G., & Ghafournia, N. (2016). The Relationship between Socio-Economic Status, General Language Learning Outcome, and Beliefs about Language Learning. *International Education Studies, 9*(2), 89–98.

Anjewierden, A. A. (2012). Explorations in Fine-grained Learning Analytics. *Universiteit Twente.*

Arkhipova, M. V., Belova, E. E., Gavrikova, Y. A., Lyulyaeva, N. A., & Shapiro, E. D. (2017, July). Blended learning in teaching EFL to different age groups. In International conference on Humans as an Object of Study by Modern Science (pp. 380–386). Springer.

Atapattu, T., & Falkner, K. (2018). Impact of Lecturer's Discourse for Student Video Interactions: Video Learning Analytics Case Study of MOOCs. *Journal of Learning Analytics, Volume 5*(3), 182–197.

Ayçiçek, B., & Yanpar Yelken, T. (2018). The Effect of Flipped Classroom Model on Students' Classroom Engagement in Teaching English. *International journal of instruction*, 11(2), 385–398.

Azizi, E., & Pachi, A. R. (2013). Self-Regulated Learning Strategies Among Bachelor Science Degree Students of Male and Female: A Comparative Study. *Acme International Journal of Multidisciplinary Research, I* (XII).

Azizi, E., & Yeshodhara, K. (2014). Relationship between Self-Regulated Learning Strategies and the Level of Internet Competency in Bachelor of Science Degree Students. *Research Journal of Recent Sciences*, *3*(8), 8–15.

Baepler, P., & Murdoch, C. J. (2010). Academic Analytics and Data Mining in Higher Education. *International Journal for the Scholarship of Teaching and Learning, 4*(2), 17.

Bailey, Phillip D. & Onwuegbuzie, Anthony J. (2002). The Role of Study Habits in Foreign Language Courses. *Assessment & Evaluation in Higher Education, 27*:5. DOI: 10.1080/0260293022000009339

Baker R. S. (2013). Learning, Schooling, and Data Analytics. *Handbook on Innovations in Learning,* 179–190.

Berland, M., Baker, R. S., & Blikstein, P. (2014). Educational Data Mining and Learning Analytics: Applications to Constructionist Research. *Technology, Knowledge and Learning*, *19*(1–2), 205–220.

Berthold, M., Ullrich, C. and Dhir, A. (2014). 'Self-Regulated Learning in Formal Education: Perceptions, Challenges and Opportunities', *International Journal of Technology Enhanced Learning*, *Vol. 6,* No. 2, pp.145–163.

Bhaskar, C. V., & Soundiraraj, S. (2013). A Study on Change in the Attitude of Students towards English Language Learning. *English Language Teaching, 6*(5), 111–116.

Bloom, B. S. (Ed.). (1956). *Taxonomy of Educational Objectives, Handbook 1: The Cognitive Domain*. New York: McKay.

Boelens, R., Voet, M., & De Wever, B. (2018). The design of blended learning in response to student diversity in higher education: Instructors' views and use of differentiated instruction in blended learning. *Computers & Education*, 120, 197–212.

Brooks, C., Thompson, C., & Greer, J. (2013). Visualizing Lecture Capture Usage: A Learning Analytics Case Study. *Proc. Work. Analytics on Video-based Learning (WAVe).*

Brown, M. (2011). Learning Analytics: The Coming Third Wave (EDUCAUSE Learning Initiative Brief). Retrieved from EDUCAUSE library https://net. educause. edu/ir/library/pdf/ELIB1101. pdf.

Buerck, J. P. (2014). A Resource-Constrained Approach to Implementing Analytics in an Institution of Higher Education: An Experience Report. *Journal of Learning Analytics*, *1*(1), 129–139.

Butler, D. L., Schnellert, L., & Cartier, S. C. (2013). Layers of Self-and Co-Regulation: Teachers Working Collaboratively to Support Adolescents' Self-Regulated Learning through Reading. *Education Research International, 2013.*

Campbell, J. P. (2007). Utilizing Student Data within the Course Management System to Determine Undergraduate Student Academic Success: An Exploratory Study. *ProQuest.*

Cavalcanti, A. P., Diego, A., Mello, R. F., Mangaroska, K., Nascimento, A., Freitas, F., & Gašević, D. (2020). How Good is My Feedback? A Content Analysis of Written Feedback. *In Proceedings of the Tenth International Conference on Learning Analytics & Knowledge* (pp. 428–437).

Cejnar, M. & Kao, C.H.T. (2018). Real Time Learning Analytics of Computer Use in K-12 Classrooms. *Companion Proceedings 8th International Conference on Learning Analytics & Knowledge (LAK18).*

Chalachew, A. A. & Hari Lakshmi V. (2013). Factors Influence Students Self-Regulation Learning Towards Their Academic Achievement in Undergraduate Programs in Ethiopia. *Abhinav Journals*, *Vol 2(7)*, 30–40.

Charleer, S., Klerkx, J., & Duval, E. (2014). Learning Dashboards. *Journal of Learning Analytics*, *1*(3), 199–202.

Chen, J., & Foung, D. (2020). A Motivational Story in Hong Kong: Generating Goals for Language Learners and Blended Learning Designers from a Mixed-Method Learning Analytics Approach in English for Academic Purposes. In *Technology and the Psychology of Second Language Learners and Users (pp. 491–516). Palgrave Macmillan, Cham.*

Chen, M. L. (2009). Influence of Grade Level on Perceptual Learning Style Preferences and Language Learning Strategies of Taiwanese English as a Foreign Language Learners. *Learning and Individual Differences, 19*(2), 304–308.

Chiu, M. M., & Fujita, N. (2014). Statistical Discourse Analysis: A Method for Modelling Online Discussion Processes. *Journal of Learning Analytics*, *1*(3), 61–83.

Cho, K., Lee, S., Joo, M. H., & Becker, B. (2018). The Effects of Using Mobile Devices on Student Achievement in Language Learning: A Meta-Analysis. *Education Sciences*, *8*(3), 105.

Chomsky, N. (2014). *Aspects of the Theory of Syntax* (Vol. 11). MIT press.

Chomsky, N. (1957). Syntactic Structures. The Hague: Mouton.

Colak, A. (2008). Attitudes, Motivation and Study Habits of English Language Learners: The Case of Başkent University Second Year Students. *Unpublished Master's Thesis, Middle East Technical University*.

Colaste, C.R. (2018). The Impact of Students' Attitude Towards the English Language on Academic *Achievement. International Journal of Trend in Scientific Research and Development, Vol. 3,* Issue 1.

Colthorpe, K., Zimbardi, K., Ainscough, L., & Anderson, S. (2015). Know thy Student! Combining Learning Analytics and Critical Reflections to Increase Understanding of Students' Self-Regulated Learning in an Authentic Setting. *Journal of Learning Analytics*, *2*(1), 134–155.

Cooper, A. (2012). A Brief History of Analytics. *Analytics Series*, *1*(9).

Cooper, A. (2012). What is Analytics? Definition and Essential Characteristics. *CETIS Analytics Series*, *1*(5), 1–10.

Corrin, L. & de Barba, P.G. (2017). Understanding Students' Views on Feedback to Inform the Development of Technology-supported Feedback Systems. *H. Partridge, K. Davis, & J. Thomas. (Eds.), Me, Us, IT! Proceedings ASCILITE2017: 34th International Conference on Innovation, Practice and Research in the Use of Educational Technologies in Tertiary Education* (pp. 47–51).

Council of Europe. Council for Cultural Co-operation. Education Committee. Modern Languages Division. (2001). Common European Framework of Reference for Languages: Learning, Teaching, Assessment. Cambridge University Press.

Crossley, S. A., Karumbaiah, S., Ocumpaugh, J., Labrum, M. J., & Baker, R. S. (2020). Predicting Math Identity Through Language and Click-Stream Patterns in a Blended Learning Mathematics Program for Elementary Students. *Journal of Learning Analytics, 7*(1), 19–37. https://doi.org/10.18608/jla.2020.71.3

Cummins, J. (1981). Empirical and Theoretical Underpinnings of Bilingual Education. *Journal of Education, 163*(1), 16–29.

Cummins, J. (2017). BICS and CALP: Empirical and Theoretical Status of the Distinction. *Literacies and Language Education*, 59–71.

Cutumisu, M., Blair, K. P., Chin, D. B., & Schwartz, D. L. (2015). Posterlet: A Game-Based Assessment of Children's Choices to Seek Feedback and to Revise. *Journal of Learning Analytics*, *2*(1), 49–71.

de Boer, H., Donker-Bergstra, A. S., Kostons, D. D. N. M., Korpershoek, H., & van der Werf, M. P. (2013). Effective Strategies for Self-regulated Learning: A Meta-Analysis. *GION/RUG.*

de Moraes, E. M., da Silva, M. T., & Souza, M. C. *Models to Implement Learning Analytics: A Literature Review.* Brazil.

Dimopoulos, I., Petropoulou, O., Boloudakis, M., & Retalis, S. (2013). Using Learning Analytics in Moodle for Assessing Students' Performance.

Divjak, B., & Vondra, P. (2016). Learning Analytics: Meeting the Needs of Students and Teachers in Pre-tertiary Education. In *Central European Conference on Information and Intelligent Systems.*

Dos Santos, H. (2017). Learning Style Preferences and Their Relationship to Second Language Acquisition in Students of English as a Second Language. PhD Dissertation, Auburn University, Alabama, USA.

Dowell, N. M. M., & Graesser, A. C. (2014). Modeling Learners' Cognitive, Affective, and Social Processes through Language and Discourse. *Journal of Learning Analytics*, *1*(3), 183–186.

Dowell, N. M., Graesser, A. C., & Cai, Z. (2016). Language and Discourse Analysis with Coh-Metrix: Applications from Educational Material to Learning Environments at Scale. *Journal of Learning Analytics, 3*(3), 72–95.

Dunbar, R. L., Dingel, M. J., & Prat-Resina, X. (2014). Connecting Analytics and Curriculum Design: Process and Outcomes of Building a Tool to Browse Data Relevant to Course Designers. *Journal of Learning Analytics*, *1*(3), 220–240.

Dvorak, T., & Jia, M. (2016). Online Work Habits and Academic Performance. *Journal of Learning Analytics, 3*(3), 318–330.

Ebner, M., & Schön, M. (2013). Why Learning Analytics in Primary Education Matters. *Bulletin of the Technical Committee on Learning Technology, 15*(2), 14–17.

Eccles, J. (1983). Expectancies, Values and Academic Behaviors. *In J. T. Spence (Ed.), Achievement and Achievement Motives.* San Francisco: Freeman. (pp. 75–46)

Effeney, G., Carroll, A., & Bahr, N. (2013). Self-regulated learning: Key strategies and their sources in a sample of adolescent males1. *Australian Journal of Educational and Developmental Psychology*, *13*, 58–74.

Elouazizi, N. (2014). Critical Factors in Data Governance for Learning Analytics. *Journal of Learning Analytics*, *1*(3), 211–219.

Epp, C. D. (2013, January). Mobile adaptive communication support for vocabulary acquisition. *Artificial Intelligence in Education*, Springer Berlin Heidelberg. (pp. 876–879).

Ferguson D. (2018). Mapping the Data Landscape in a Secondary School. *Companion Proceedings 8th International Conference on Learning Analytics & Knowledge (LAK18).*

Ferguson, R. (2012). Learning Analytics: Drivers, Developments and Challenges. *International Journal of Technology Enhanced Learning*, *4*(5–6), 304–317.

Ferguson, R. (2019). Ethical Challenges for Learning Analytics. *Journal of Learning Analytics, 6*(3), 25–30. https://doi.org/10.18608/jla.2019.63.5

Ferguson, R., & Shum, S. B. (2012). Social Learning Analytics: Five Approaches. *Proceedings of the 2nd International Conference on Learning Analytics and Knowledge* (pp. 23–33). ACM.

Ferguson, R., Brasher, A., Clow, D., Cooper, A., Hillaire, G., Mittelmeier, J., Rienties B., Ullmann T., & Vuorikari, R. (2016). Research Evidence on the Use of Learning Analytics: Implications for Education Policy.

Ferguson, R., Clow, D., Macfadyen, L., Essa, A., Dawson, S., & Alexander, S. (2014, March). Setting Learning Analytics in Context: Overcoming the Barriers to Large-scale Adoption. In *Proceedings of the Fourth International Conference on Learning Analytics and Knowledge* (pp. 251–253). ACM.

Fiel, J., Lawless, K. A., & Brown, S. W. (2018). Timing Matters: Approaches for Measuring and Visualizing Behaviours of Timing and Spacing of Work in Self-Paced Online Teacher Professional Development Courses. *Journal of Learning Analytics, 5*(1), 25–40.

Friedl, M., Ebner, M., & Ebner, M. (2020). Mobile Learning Applications for Android and iOS for German Language Acquisition based on Learning Analytics Measurements. *International Journal of Learning Analytics and Artificial Intelligence for Education (iJAI), 2*(1).

Gagné, R. M. (1965). The Conditions of Learning. New York: Holt, Rinehart and Winston.

Gasevic, D., & Pechenizkiy, M. (2016). Let's Grow Together: Tutorials on Learning Analytics Methods. *Journal of Learning Analytics, 3*(3), 5–8.

Gašević, D., Dawson, S., & Siemens, G. (2015). Let's Not Forget: Learning Analytics Are about Learning. *TechTrends*, *59*(1), 64–71.

Gayton, A. (2010). Socioeconomic Status and Language-learning Motivation: To What Extent Does the Former Influence the Latter. *Scottish Languages Review, 22*(1), 17–28.

Gilmore, D. M. (2014). Goffman's Front Stage and Backstage Behaviors in Online Education. *Journal of Learning Analytics, 1*(3), 187–190.

Gömleksiz, M. N. (2010). An Evaluation of Students' Attitudes toward English Language Learning in Terms of Several Variables. *Procedia-Social and Behavioral Sciences, 9*, 913–918.

Gray, G., McGuinness C., Owende P., & Carthy, A. (2014). A Review of Psychometric Data Analysis and Applications in Modelling of Academic Achievement in Tertiary Education. *Journal of Learning Analytics*, *1*(1), 75–106.

Gray, G., McGuinness, C., & Owende, P. (2016). Learning Analytics to Inform Teaching and Learning Approaches.

Griffiths, D. (2012). The Implication of Analytics for Teaching Practice in Higher Education. *CETIS Analytics Series*, *1*(10).

Gülbahar, Y., & Ilgaz, H. (2014). Premise of Learning Analytics for Educational Context: Through Concept to Practice. *International Journal of Informatics Technologies, 7*(3), 20.

Gunnarsson, B. L., & Alterman, R. (2014). Peer Promotions as a Method to Identify Quality Content. *Journal of Learning Analytics*, *1*(2), 126–150.

Gurung, A., Botelho, A. F., & Heffernan, N. T. (2021, April). Examining student effort on help through response time decomposition. In LAK21: 11th international learning analytics and knowledge conference (pp. 292-301).

Harrak, F., Bouchet, F., & Luengo, V. (2019). From Students' Questions to Students' Profiles in a Blended Learning Environment. *Journal of Learning Analytics, 6*(1), 54–84.

Harsono, Y. M. (2015). Developing Learning Materials for Specific Purposes. *Teflin Journal*, *18*(2), 169–179.

Harris, D. (1974). Testing English as a Second Language. New York: McGraw-Hill.

Harter, S. (1981). A New Self-report Scale of Intrinsic Versus Extrinsic Orientation in the Classroom: Motivational and Informational Components. *Developmental Psychology, 17,* 300–312.

Hashwani, M. S. (2008). Students' Attitudes, Motivation and Anxiety towards English Language Learning. *Journal of Research and Reflections in Education*, *2*(2).

Heath, J. (2014). Contemporary Privacy Theory Contributions to Learning Analytics. *Journal of Learning Analytics,1* (1), 140–149.

Hecking, T., Ziebarth, S., & Hoppe, H. U. (2014). Analysis of Dynamic Resource Access Patterns in Online Courses. *Journal of Learning Analytics*, *1*(3), 34–60.

Heritage, M., & Bailey, A. (2014). The Role of Language Learning Progressions in Formative Assessment for English Learners. Rotterdam, the Netherlands: Sense Publishers.

Holstein, K., McLaren, B. M., & Aleven, V. (2019). Co-Designing a Real-Time Classroom Orchestration Tool to Support Teacher–AI Complementarity. *Journal of Learning Analytics, 6*(2), 27–52. https://doi.org/10.18608/jla.2019.62.3

Howley, I. K., & Rose, C. P. (2016). Towards Careful Practices for Automated Linguistic Analysis of Group Learning. *Journal of Learning Analytics, 3*(3), 239–262.

Hrastinski, S. (2019). What do We Mean by Blended Learning?. TechTrends, 63(5), 564–569.

Iraj, H., Fudge, A., Faulkner, M., Pardo, A., & Kovanović, V. (2020). Understanding Students' Engagement with Personalised Feedback Messages. In *Proceedings of the Tenth International Conference on Learning Analytics & Knowledge* (pp. 438–447).

Islam, R. (2020). The Jigsaw Technique on Students' Reading Comprehension across Learning Styles. *Language-Edu, 9*(1).

Isemonger, I. (2008). Scores on a Japanese-language Version of the Learning Channel Preference Checklist: A Questionable Instrument within a Questionable Line of Instrumentation. *Journal of Psychoeducational Assessment, 26*(2), 148–155.

Ivančević, V. (2014). Constructing Programming Tests from an Item Pool: Pushing the Limits of Student Knowledge using Assessment and Learning Analytics. *Journal of Learning Analytics, 1*(3), 161–164.

Jahedi, S. (2012). A Study of Relationship between Motivational Beliefs and Self-regulated Strategies and Academic Achievement of School Students.

Jayaprakash, S. M., Moody, E. W., Lauría, E. J., Regan, J. R., & Baron, J. D. (2014). Early Alert of Academically At-risk Students: An Open Source Analytics Initiative. *Journal of Learning Analytics*, *1*(1), 6–47.

Jensen, E., L. Pugh, S., & K. D'Mello, S. (2021, April). A deep transfer learning approach to modeling teacher discourse in the classroom. In LAK21: 11th international learning analytics and knowledge conference (pp. 302-312).

Joksimovic, S., Gasevic, D., & Hatala, M. (2014). Learning analytics for Networked Learning Models. *Journal of Learning Analytics, 1*(3), 191–194.

Jørnø, R.L. & Gynther, K. (2018). What Constitutes an "Actionable Insight" in Learning Analytics? *Journal of Learning Analytics, Volume 5*(3), 198–221.

Kamatchi, P. (2017). Socio-Economic Factors in English Language Teaching. *Lang. Lit & Trans. Studies, Vol. 4.* Issue.2, 75–80.

Karthigeyan, K., & Nirmala, K. (2013). Learning Style Preference of English Language Learners. *Educationia Confab, 2*(1), 134–140.

Keshavamurthy, U., & Guruprasad, H. S. (2015). Learning Analytics: A Survey. *arXiv preprint arXiv:1501.06964*.

Khan, I. (2016). Positive Attitude and English Language Learning: Psycho-pedagogic Connections. *Arab World English Journal (AWEJ) Vol. 7*.

Khanlari, A., Zhu, G., & Scardamalia, M. (2019). Knowledge Building Analytics to Explore Crossing Disciplinary and Grade-Level Boundaries. *Journal of Learning Analytics, 6*(3), 60–75. https://doi.org/10.18608/jla.2019.63.9

Khansir, A. A., Jafarizadegan, N., & Karampoor, F. (2016). Relation between Socio-economic Status and Motivation of Learners in Learning English as a Foreign Language. *Theory and Practice in Language Studies, 6*(4), 742–750.

Khatib, M., & Taie, M. (2016). BICS and CALP: Implications for SLA. *Journal of Language Teaching and Research*, *7*(2), 382–388.

Kim, J. E., Park, H., Jang, M., & Nam, H. (2017). Exploring Flipped Classroom Effects on Second Language Learners' Cognitive Processing. Foreign Language Annals, 50(2), 260–284.

Kintu, M. J., Zhu, C., & Kagambe, E. (2017). Blended learning effectiveness: the relationship between student characteristics, design features and outcomes. *International Journal of Educational Technology in Higher Education*, 14(1), 7.

Kivinen, K. (2003). Assessing Motivation and the Use of Learning Strategies by Secondary Students in Three International Schools. *Tampere University Press.*

Knight, S., & Littleton, K. (2015). Discourse Centric Learning Analytics: Mapping the Terrain. *Journal of Learning Analytics*, *2*(1), 185–209.

Knight, S., Shum, S. B., & Littleton, K. (2014). Epistemology, Assessment, Pedagogy: Where Learning Meets Analytics in the Middle Space. *Journal of Learning Analytics*, *1*(2), 23–47.

Kobayashi, V. B., Mol, S., & Kismihok, G. (2014). Labour Market Driven Learning Analytics. *Journal of Learning Analytics*, *1*(3), 207–210.

Kormos, J., & Kiddle, T. (2013). The Role of Socio-economic Factors in Motivation to Learn English as a Foreign Language: The Case of Chile. *System, 41*(2), 399–412.

Kovanovic, V., Gasevic, D., & Hatala, M. (2014). Learning Analytics for Communities of Inquiry. *Journal of Learning Analytics*, *1*(3), 195–198.

Kovanović, V., Gašević, D., Dawson, S., Joksimović, S., Baker, R. S., & Hatala, M. (2015) Does Time-on-Task Estimation Matter? Implications on Validity of Learning Analytics Findings. *Journal of Learning Analytics*.

Kovanović, V., Gašević, D., Dawson, S., Joksimović, S., Baker, R. S., & Hatala, M. (2015, March). Penetrating the Black Box of Time-on-Task Estimation. In *Proceedings of the Fifth International Conference on Learning Analytics and Knowledge* (pp. 184–193). ACM.

Kruse, A. N. N. A., & Pongsajapan, R. (2012). Student-Centered Learning Analytics. *CNDLS Thought Papers,* 1–9.

Kukatlapalli, J., Doyle, S. & Bandyopadhyay, S. (2020). An Investigation into the English Language Experiences of Indian International Students Studying in New Zealand Universities. *Higher Education Research & Development, 39*:3, 485–499, DOI: 10.1080/07294360.2019.1685940

Kumar, V. S., Somasundaram, T. S., Boulanger, D., Seanosky, J., & Vilela, M. F. (2015). Big Data Learning Analytics: A New Perspective. In *Ubiquitous Learning Environments and Technologies* (pp. 139–158). Springer Berlin Heidelberg.

Kumari, V. S., & Chamundeswari, S. (2015). Achievement Motivation, Study Habits and Academic Achievement of Students at the Secondary Level. *International Journal of Emerging Research in Management and Technology*, *4*(10), 7–13.

Kvashnina, O. S., & Martynko, E. A. (2016). Analyzing the potential of flipped classroom in ESL teaching. *International Journal of Emerging Technologies in Learning (IJET)*, 11(03), 71–73.

Lang, C. (2014). An Adaptive Model of Student Performance Using Inverse Bayes. *Journal of Learning Analytics*, *1*(3), 154–156.

Lang, C., Siemens, G., Wise, A., & Gasevic, D. (Eds.). (2017). Handbook of Learning Analytics. *SOLAR, Society for Learning Analytics and Research.*

Lauría, E. J., Baron, J. D., Devireddy, M., Sundararaju, V., & Jayaprakash, S. M. (2012, April). Mining Academic Data to Improve College Student Retention: An Open Source Perspective. In *Proceedings of the 2nd International Conference on Learning Analytics and Knowledge* (pp. 139–142). ACM.

Lecailliez, L., Flanagan, B., Chen, M. R. A., & Ogata, H. (2020). Smart Dictionary for E-book Reading Analytics. In *Proceedings of the Tenth International Conference on Learning Analytics & Knowledge* (pp. 89–93).

Leelawong, K., & Biswas, G. (2008). Designing Learning by Teaching Agents: The Betty's Brain system. *IJ Artificial Intelligence in Education*, *18*(3), 181–208.

Leidinger, M., & Perels, F. (2012). Training Self-regulated Learning in the Classroom: Development and Evaluation of Learning Materials to Train Self-regulated Learning during Regular Mathematics Lessons at Primary School. *Education Research International*, *2012*.

Lewis, R., Anderson, T., & Carroll, F. (2020). Can School Enrolment and Performance be Improved by Maximizing Students' Sense of Choice in Elective Subjects?. *Journal of Learning Analytics*, *7*(1), 75–87. https://doi.org/10.18608/jla.2020.71.6

Lias, T. E., & Elias, T. (2011). Learning Analytics: The Definitions, the Processes, and the Potential.

Liebert, R., & Morris, L. (1967). Cognitive and Emotional Components of Test Anxiety: A Distinction and Some Initial Data. *Psychological Reports*, *29*, 975–978.

Lim, L., Bannert, M., van der Graaf, J., Singh, S., Fan, Y., Surendrannair, S., ... & Gašević, D. (2023). Effects of real-time analytics-based personalized scaffolds on students' self-regulated learning. Computers in Human Behavior, 139, 107547.

Liu, D. Y. T., Atif, A., Froissard, J. C., & Richards, D. (2019, January). An Enhanced Learning Analytics Plugin for Moodle: Student Engagement and Personalised Intervention. In *ASCILITE 2015–Australasian Society for Computers in Learning and Tertiary Education, Conference Proceedings.*

Liu, R., Stamper, J. C., & Davenport, J. (2018). A Novel Method for the In-Depth Multimodal Analysis of Student Learning Trajectories in Intelligent Tutoring Systems. *Journal of Learning Analytics*, *5*(1), 41–54.

Long, C., Ming, Z., & Chen, L. (2013). The Study of Student Motivation on English Learning in Junior Middle School - A Case Study of No. 5 Middle School in Gejiu. *English Language Teaching*, *6*(9), 136.

Lundsteen, S. W. (1979). Listening: Its Impact at All Levels on Reading and the Other Language Arts. *ERIC.*

Mahmoudi, E., Samad, A. & Razak, N. Z. B. A. (2012). Attitude and Students' Performance in Computer Assisted English Language Learning (CAELL) for Learning Vocabulary. *Procedia-Social and Behavioral Sciences*, *66*, 489–498.

McLoughlin, C., & Lee, M. J. (2010). Personalised and Self-regulated Learning in the Web 2.0 Era: International Exemplars of Innovative Pedagogy Using Social Software. *Australasian Journal of Educational Technology*, *26*(1).

Mehdipour, Y., & Balaramulu, D. (2013). The Influence of Teacher's Behavior on the Student's Self-Regulation. *IOSR Journal of Research & Method in Education*, *1*, 65–71.

Mendez, G., Ochoa, X., Chiluiza, K., & de Wever, B. (2014). Curricular Design Analysis: A Data-Driven Perspective. *Journal of Learning Analytics*, *1*(3), 84–119.

Mikroyannidis, A., Connolly, T., Law, E.L-C., Schmitz, H-C., Vieritz, H., Nussbaumer, A., Mirriahi, N., Dawson, S., Gasevic, D., & Long, P. D. (2015). Widening the Field and Sparks of the Future. *Journal of Learning Analytics*, *1*(3), 1–3.

Monroy, C., Rangel, V. S., & Whitaker, R. (2014). A Strategy for Incorporating Learning Analytics into the Design and Evaluation of a K-12 Science Curriculum. *Journal of Learning Analytics*, *1*(2), 94–125.

Moodle Logo Retrieved from https://commons.wikimedia.org/wiki/ File:Moodle-logo-large.jpg on April 20, 2021

Mori, Sakamoto and Mendori. (2019). Development of a Real Time Viewing Status Feedback System and Its Impact. *Companion Proceedings 9th International Conference on Learning Analytics & Knowledge (LAK19),* 174–175.

Mudasir, H. (2012). Study Habits and Academic Achievement - A Case Study of Higher Secondary School Students. *The Communications*, *10*(1), 146.

Murray, D. E. (2020). The World of English Language Teaching: Creating Equity or Inequity?. *Language Teaching Research, 24*(1), 60–70.

Nadeem, N. A., Puja, J. A., & Bhat, S. A. (2014). Study Habits and Academic Achievement of Kashmiri & Ladakhi Adolescent Girls: A Comparative Study. *Turkish Online Journal of Distance Education*, *15*(2), 91–97.

Nagy, R. P. (2016). Tracking and Visualising Student Effort: Evolution of a Practical Analytics Tool for Staff and Student Engagement. *Journal of Learning Analytics*, *3*(2), 164–192.

Naz, T. and Siddiqui, M.M. (2015). Self-Regulated Learning Strategies: A Survey Study of English Language Learners at the Undergraduate Level in Aligarh Muslim University. *International Journal of English Language, Literature and Humanities, 3(9).*

Nguyen, Q., Huptych, M., & Rienties, B. (2018). Using Temporal Analytics to Detect Inconsistencies between Learning Design and Student Behaviours. *Journal of Learning Analytics, 5*(3), 120–135.

Nicol, D. J., & Macfarlane-Dick, D. (2006). Formative Assessment and Self-regulated Learning: A Model and Seven Principles of Good Feedback Practice. *Studies in Higher Education*, *31*(2), 199–218.

Nilson, L. B. (2013). Creating Self-regulated Learners: Strategies to Strengthen Students' Self-awareness and Learning Skills. *Stylus Publishing, LLC.*

Nimmala, T., Nowbattula, P.K., Mylabattula, S., and Sodadasi, V.E. (2016). Socio-Economic Effects on English Language Learners in Andhra Pradesh. *International Journal of Science and Technology. Vol. No. 5,* Issue 8. 104–107

Nussbaumer, A., Hillemann, E. C., Gütl, C., & Albert, D. (2015). A Competence-based Service for Supporting Self-Regulated Learning in Virtual Environments. *Journal of Learning Analytics*, *2*(1), 101–133.

Nyamubi, G. J. (2016). Students' Attitudes and English Language Performance in Secondary Schools in Tanzania. *International Journal of Learning, Teaching and Educational Research*, *15*(2).

Nyamubi, G. J. (2019). Socio-Economic Status as Determinants of Students' Performance in English Language in Secondary Schools in Tanzania. *Education Journal, 8*(3), 110–119.

O'Brien, L. (1989). Learning styles: Make the Student Aware. *NASSP Bulletin, 73*(519), 85–89.

Ogata, H., Liu, S., & Mouri, K. (2014). Ubiquitous Learning Analytics Using Learning Logs. In *LAK Workshops*.

Oshima, J., Oshima, R., & Fujita, W. (2018). A Mixed-Methods Approach to Analyze Shared Epistemic Agency in Jigsaw Instruction at Multiple Scales of Temporality. *Journal of Learning Analytics, 5*(1), 10–24.

Pandey, A., & Singh, B. K. (2015). Educational Achievements of First and Subsequent Generation Learners in East Delhi/NCR Region in India-A Comparative Study. *Asian Development Policy Review*, *3*(2), 20–28.

Papamitsiou, Z., & Economides, A. A. (2014). Temporal Learning Analytics for Adaptive Assessment. *Journal of Learning Analytics*, *1*(3), 165–168.

Papantoniou, G., Moraitou, D., Kaldrimidou, M., Plakitsi, K., Filippidou, D., & Katsadima, E. (2012). Affect and Cognitive Interference: An Examination of Their Effect on Self-Regulated Learning. *Education Research International, 2012*.

Pardo, A., & Teasley, S. (2014). Learning Analytics Research, Theory and Practice: Widening the Discipline. *Journal of Learning Analytics*, *1*(3), 4–6.

Pardo, A., Aufflick, K.B., Shum, S.B., Dawson, Gao, J., Gašević, D., Leichtweis, S., Liu, D., Maldonado, R.M., Mirriahi, N., Moskal, A.C.M., Schulte, J., Siemens, G., & Vigentini L. (2018). OnTask: Delivering Data-Informed, Personalized Learning Support Actions. *Journal of Learning Analytics, Volume 5*(3), 235–249.

Pardos, Z. A., Baker, R. S., San Pedro, M., Gowda, S. M., & Gowda, S. M. (2014). Affective States and State Tests: Investigating How Affect and Engagement during the School Year Predict End-of-Year Learning Outcomes. *Journal of Learning Analytics*, *1*(1), 107–128.

Paris, S. G., & Paris, A. H. (2001). Classroom Applications of Research on Self-regulated Learning. *Educational psychologist*, *36*(2), 89–101.

Pawlak, M. (2020). The Effect of Proficiency, Gender, and Learning Style on the Occurrence of Negotiated Interaction in Communicative Task Performance. *Cross-theoretical Explorations of Interlocutors and their Individual Differences,* 53, 51.

Pechenizkiy, M., & Gasevic, D. (2015). Introduction into Sparks of the Learning Analytics Future. *Journal of Learning Analytics*, *1*(3), 145–149.

Peng, Y. (2017). Exploring Learning Analytics in College English Teaching and Learning in the Big Data Era. *Atlantis Press, Volume 99*, (501–512)

Pintrich, P. R., & De Groot, E. V. (1990). Motivational and Self-regulated Learning Components of Classroom Academic Performance. *Journal of Educational Psychology*, *82*(1), 33.

Porter, T., Catalán Molina, D., Blackwell, L., Roberts, S., Quirk, A., Lee Duckworth, A., & Trzesniewski, K. (2020). Measuring Mastery Behaviors at Scale: The Persistence, Effort, Resilience and Challenge-Seeking Task (PERC). *Journal of Learning Analytics, 7*(1), 5–18. https://doi.org/10.18608/jla.2020.71.2

Pozdniakov, S., Martinez-Maldonado, R., Tsai, Y. S., Cukurova, M., Bartindale, T., Chen, P., ... & Gasevic, D. (2022, March). The question-driven dashboard: how can we design analytics interfaces aligned to teachers' inquiry?. In LAK22: 12th international learning analytics and knowledge conference (pp. 175-185).

Rakovic, M., Fan, Y., Van Der Graaf, J., Singh, S., Kilgour, J., Lim, L., ... & Gasevic, D. (2022, March). Using learner trace data to understand metacognitive processes in writing from multiple sources. In LAK22: 12th International Learning Analytics and Knowledge Conference (pp. 130-141).

Rao, X. (2018). Learning Theories that Impact English Teaching and Learning. In University English for Academic Purposes in China (pp. 21–39). Springer, Singapore.

Rascón Moreno, D., & Bretones Callejas, C. M. (2018). Socioeconomic Status and Its Impact on Language and Content Attainment in CLIL Contexts.

Raval, D. K. (2014). Effectiveness of Self-Regulated Learning of Secondary School Students. *Education*, *3*(3).

Razi, H.R., Vahidian, Z., & Hashemi, S. (2015). Studying the Relationship Between Self-Regulation and High School Students' Academic Motivation of the Second Course in County of Larestan. *Indian Journal of Fundamental and Applied Life Sciences, Vol.5 (S1),* pp. 455–467.

Reinders, H. (2018). Learning Analytics for Language Learning and Teaching. *JALT CALL Journal, 14*(1), 77–86.

Rezaei, A. R., Keivanpanah, S., & Najibi, S. (2015). EFL Learners' Motivational Beliefs and Their Use of Learning Strategies. *Applied Research on English Language*, *4*(1), 1–17.

Rienties, B., Lewis, T., McFarlane, R., Nguyen, Q., & Toetenel, L. (2018). Analytics in Online and Offline Language Learning Environments: The Role of Learning Design to Understand Student Online Engagement. *Computer Assisted Language Learning, 31*(3), 273–293.

Rodríguez-Triana, M. J., Vozniuk, A., & Gillet, D. (2016). Using Learning Analytics at School: A Go-Lab Study.

Rotgans, J. I., & Schmidt, H. G. (2010). The Motivated Strategies for Learning Questionnaire: A Measure for Students' General Motivational Beliefs and Learning Strategies?. *Asia-Pacific Education Researcher (De La Salle University Manila)*, *19*(2).

Rubin, J. (1975). What the "Good Language Learner" Can Teach Us. TESOL Quarterly, 41–51.

Sa Liu, Min Liu, Zilong Pan, Wenting Zou and Chenglu Li. (2019). Examining Science Learning by At-Risk Middle School Students in a Multimedia-Enriched Problem-Based Learning Environment. *Companion Proceedings 9th International Conference on Learning Analytics & Knowledge (LAK19),* 237–239.

Sabbah, S. (2016). The Effect of Study Habits on English Language Achievement.

Saint. (2019). Analytics for the Measurement of Process Dimensions of Self-Regulated Learning and Feedback Impact. *Companion Proceedings 9th International Conference on Learning Analytics & Knowledge (LAK19),* 114–119.

Salameh, W. (2012). The Impact of Social and Economic Factors on Students' English Language Performance in EFL Classrooms in Dubai Public Secondary Schools (Doctoral dissertation, The British University in Dubai (BUiD)).

Saleem, S. M. (2018). Modified Kuppuswamy Scale Updated for Year 2018. *Indian J Res,* *7*(3), 6–7.

Scheffel, M., Drachsler, H., Stoyanov, S., & Specht, M. (2014). Quality Indicators for Learning Analytics. *Journal of Educational Technology & Society, 17*(4), 117.

Schunk, D. (1981). Modeling and Attributional Effects on Children's Achievement: A Self-efficacy Analysis. *Journal of Educational Psychology, 73*, 93–105.

Segedy, J. R., Kinnebrew, J. S., & Biswas, G. (2015). Using Coherence Analysis to Characterize Self-regulated Learning Behaviours in Open-ended Learning Environments. *Test*, *2*(1), 13–48.

Shum, S. B., & Ferguson, R. (2012). Social Learning Analytics. *Journal of Educational Technology & Society*, *15*(3), 3–26.

Shum, S. B., Sándor, Á., Goldsmith, R., Bass, R., & McWilliams, M. (2017). Towards Reflective Writing Analytics: Rationale, Methodology and Preliminary Results. *Journal of Learning Analytics, 4*(1), 58–84.

Siahi, E. A., & Maiyo, J. K. (2015). Study of the Relationship between Study Habits and Academic Achievement of Students: A Case of Spicer Higher Secondary School, India. *International Journal of Educational Administration and Policy Studies*, *7*(7), 134–141.

Siemens, G., & Baker, R. S. J. d. (2012). Learning Analytics and Educational Data Mining: Towards Communication and Collaboration. *Proceedings of the 2nd International Conference on Learning Analytics and Knowledge*, 252–254.

Siemens, G., & Long, P. (2011). Penetrating the Fog: Analytics in Learning and Education. *EDUCAUSE Review, 46*(5), 30.

Skinner, B. F. (1957). Verbal Behaviour. New York: Appleton-Century-Crofts.

Skinner, B. F. (1968). The Technology of Teaching. New York, NY: Appleton-Century-Crofts.

Solanki, V. (2017). Study Habit of School Going Students Rajkot District Area. *The International Journal of Indian Psychology.*

Sonnenberg, C., & Bannert, M. (2015). Discovering the Effects of Metacognitive Prompts on the Sequential Structure of SRL-Processes Using Process Mining Techniques. *Journal of Learning Analytics*, *2*(1), 72–100.

Suchithra, R., Vaidhehi, V., & Iyer, N. E. (2015). Survey of Learning Analytics based on Purpose and Techniques for Improving Student Performance. *International Journal of Computer Applications*, *111*(1).

Swalander, L., & Taube, K. (2007). Influences of Family-based Prerequisites, Reading Attitude, and Self-regulation on Reading Ability. *Contemporary Educational Psychology, 32*(2), 206–230.

Tan, J. P. L., Koh, E., Jonathan, C. R., & Yang, S. (2017). Learner Dashboards a Double-Edged Sword? Students' Sense-Making of a Collaborative Critical Reading and Learning Analytics Environment for Fostering 21st Century Literacies. *Journal of Learning Analytics, 4*(1), 117–140.

Thorndike, E. L. (1921). Elementary Principle of Education. New York: Macmillan.

Tomlinson, B., & Whittaker, C. (2013). Blended learning in English language teaching. London: British Council.

Tran, T. Q., & Duong, T. M. (2013). The Attitudes towards English Language Learning and Use of Self-Regulated Learning Strategies Among College Non-English Majors. *International Journal of Scientific and Research Publications*, 333.

Tsemrekal, T. M. (2013). The relationship between parenting style, self-regulated learning and academic achievement in selected primary schools in Ethiopia *(Doctoral dissertation).*

Turan, Z., & Akdag-Cimen, B. (2020). Flipped classroom in English language teaching: a systematic review. Computer Assisted Language Learning, 33(5–6), 590–606.

Van Barneveld, A., Arnold, K. E., & Campbell, J. P. (2012). Analytics in Higher Education: Establishing a Common Language. *EDUCAUSE Learning Initiative, 1*(1), 1–11.

van Harmelen, M., & Workman, D. (2012). Analytics for Learning and Teaching. *CETIS Analytics Series*, *1*(3).

Viberg, O., Hatakka, M., Bälter, O., & Mavroudi, A. (2018). The Current Landscape of Learning Analytics in Higher Education. *Computers in Human Behaviour, 89,* 98–110.

Vigentini, L., Liu, D., and Lim, L. (2019). 2nd Personalising Feedback at Scale Workshop: Focusing on Approaches and Students. *Companion Proceedings 9th International Conference on Learning Analytics & Knowledge (LAK19),* 806–810.

Vinker, E., & Rubinstein, A. (2022, March). Mining code submissions to elucidate disengagement in a computer science MOOC. In LAK22: 12th international learning analytics and knowledge conference (pp. 142-151).

Vitta, J. P., & Al-Hoorie, A. H. (2020). The flipped classroom in second language learning: A meta-analysis. Language Teaching Research, 1362168820981403.

Volk, H., Kellner, K., & Wohlhart, D. (2015). Learning Analytics for English Language Teaching. *J. UCS, 21*(1), 156–174.

Vyas, S., & Choudhary, G. (2016). Study Habits of Sr. Sec. School Adolescent Students in Relation to Their Socio-Economic Status. *IJAR*, *2*(6), 134–139.

Vygotsky, L. S. (1978). Mind in Society: The Development of Higher Psychological Processes. Cambridge, MA: Harvard University Press.

Vygotsky, L. S. (1981). The Genesis of Higher Mental Functions. In J. V. Wertsch (Ed.), The Concept of Activity in Soviet Psychology. M. E. Sharpe: Armonk, NY.

Wang, W., & Zhan, J. (2020). The Relationship between English Language Learner Characteristics and Online Self-Regulation: A Structural Equation Modelling Approach. *Sustainability, 12*(7), 3009.

Wang, X., & Eberhard, S. (2020). Using Existing LMS Technology and Learning Analytics Data to Support Student Learning. *Pacific Journal of Technology Enhanced Learning, 2*(1), 18–18.

Watson, J. (1925). Behaviourism. New York: The People's Institute Publishing Company.

Wei, J., Cutler, F., Macfadyen, L. P. & Shirazi, S. (2019). Implementing Learning Analytics: Instructor Perspectives. *Companion Proceedings 9th International Conference on Learning Analytics & Knowledge (LAK19),* 56–61.

Weinstein, C. E., Schulte, A., & Palmer, D. R. (1987). *The Learning and Study Strategies Inventory*. Clearwater, FL: H & H Publishing.

Wiliam, D. (2007). Content Then Process: Teacher Learning Communities in the Service of Formative Assessment. *In D.B. Reeves (Ed.), Ahead of the curve: the power of assessment to transform teaching and learning. Bloomington, IN: Solution Tree*

Wong, W. L. H. (2015). A Study of Language Learning Style and Teaching Style Preferences of Hong Kong Community College Students and Teachers in English for Academic Purposes (EAP) Contexts.

Worsley, M., & Blikstein, P. (2014). Analyzing Engineering Design through the Lens of Computation. *Journal of Learning Analytics*, *1*(2), 151–186.

Yang, B., Yao, Z., Lu, H., Zhou, Y., & Xu, J. (2020). In-classroom Learning Analytics Based on Student Behaviour, Topic and Teaching Characteristic Mining. *Pattern Recognition Letters, 129,* 224–231.

Yassin, B. M. (2012). The Academic Effects of Learning Styles on ESL (English as a Second Language) Students in Intensive English Language Centers.

Yazdani, K., & Sane Godbole, V. (2014). Studying the Role of Habits and Achievement Motivation in Improving Students' Academic Performance. *European Online Journal of Natural and Social Sciences*, *3*(4), pp.827.

Ye, C., & Biswas, G. (2014). Early Prediction of Student Dropout and Performance in MOOCs Using Higher Granularity Temporal Information. *Journal of Learning Analytics, 1*(3), 169–172.

Zaric, N., Roepke, R., & Schroeder, U. (2018). Concept for Linking Learning Analytics and Learning Styles in E-Learning Environments.

Zheng, G., Fancsali, S. E., Ritter, S., & Berman, S. (2019). Using Instruction-Embedded Formative Assessment to Predict State Summative Test Scores and Achievement Levels in Mathematics. *Journal of Learning Analytics, 6*(2), 153–174. https://doi.org/10.18608/1 0.18608/jla.2019.62.11

Zimmerman, B., & Pons, M. (1986). Development of a Structured Interview for Assessing Student Use of Self-regulated Learning Strategies. *American Educational Research Journal, 23,* 614–628.

Zimmerman, B. J., & Martinez-Pons, M. (1990). Student Differences in Self-regulated Learning: Relating Grade, Sex, and Giftedness to Self-Efficacy and Strategy Use. *Journal of Educational Psychology, 82*(1), 51.

Zimmerman, B. J., Bandura, A., & Martinez-Pons, M. (1992). Self-Motivation for Academic Attainment: The Role of Self-efficacy Beliefs and Personal Goal Setting. *American educational research journal, 29*(3), 663–676.

Zumbrunn, S., Tadlock, J., & Roberts, E. D. (2011). Encouraging Self-Regulated Learning in the Classroom: A Review of the Literature. *Metropolitan Educational Research Consortium (MERC).*

Zylich, B., & Lan, A. (2021, April). Linguistic skill modeling for second language acquisition. In LAK21: 11th International Learning Analytics and Knowledge Conference (pp. 141-150).